Sir John Gielgud 1904-

KING LEAR

KING LEAR

by William Shakespeare

THE FALCON

SHAKESPEARE

. . . and for his crest or cognizance a falcoun, his wings displayed argent, standing on a wreath of his colours, supporting a speare gould steeled as aforesaid. . . .

So in part reads the confirmation of the Grant of Arms made by the Heralds' office to John Shakespeare in 1599 as described by Garter King of Arms.

Edited by ERIC A. MCCANN

ACADEMIC PRESS CANADA

The photographs appearing on the end-papers are reproduced with the permission of the Shakespeare Memorial Theatre, Stratford-on-Avon; the Radio-Times Hulton Picture Library; The Mansell Collection; and the Mander and Mitchenson Collection.

ISBN 0-7747-1029-2

© 1964 BY ACADEMIC PRESS CANADA
55 BARBER GREENE ROAD, DON MILLS, ONTARIO   M3C 2A1
PRINTED AND BOUND IN CANADA
     12 13 BP 85

To Grace, David, and Stephen

Make no noise, make no noise; draw the curtains.

CONTENTS

DATE OF COMPOSITION AND PERFORMANCE

Shakespeare wrote *King Lear* between 1603 and 1606. From the evidence on the title page of the First Quarto and from the record of the Stationers' Register, in which *King Lear* is entered on November 26, 1607, we know that the play was first performed on December 26, 1606. Various editors who have attempted to date the play by means of Edmund's references to eclipses (I. ii. 102) have encountered difficulty because his words could refer to any of five different eclipses that occurred between 1601 and 1605. Since *Macbeth* was almost certainly written by the summer of 1606, *King Lear* was in all probability written before that date, unless we accept the idea that Shakespeare was working on both plays at the same time—a task that would have taxed even his creative energy. It may be said, therefore, without presenting more than a fraction of the circumstantial evidence, that *King Lear* was probably written during the winter of 1604 to 1605. Kenneth Muir[1] suggests an interesting comparison between Lear's divided Kingdom and James I's urging of parliament to unite England and Scotland, using the argument that many evils resulted from the political divisions in early Britain. Some critics, referring to these facts, have asserted that the theme of *King Lear* is political disunity.

SOURCES OF *KING LEAR*

The story of Lear was very familiar to English playgoers and readers in Elizabeth's day; in fact, it had been well-known for

[1]Kenneth Muir, *King Lear*, The Arden Shakespeare (London, Methuen & Co. Ltd., 1952), p. xxiv.

centuries. In 1605, a play entitled *The True Chronicle History of King Leir and his Three Daughters, Gonorill, Ragan and Cordella*, author unknown, was published. Probably composed in the sixteenth century, it was not well-written. A performance in April, 1594, in the Rose Theatre of a certain *King Lear* may have been of this very play. *The True Chronicle* bears very little similarity to Shakespeare's tragedy. Cordelia does not die; there is no Gloucester story, no storm, no insanity—and no Fool. Leir in *The True Chronicle* is a pitiful, tearful bore. Nonetheless, certain parallels in thought and expression indicate that Shakespeare was familiar with the play.

The story of Lear also appears in Holinshed's *Chronicles,* which were first printed in 1577, with a second edition in 1587 that Shakespeare, doubtless, read. Holinshed's story differs substantially from Shakespeare's. Lear, according to the chronicler, disappointed in Cordeilla's answers, marries the two older daughters to Cornwall and Albania, and promises them his Kingdom at his death. Cornwall and Albania, however, rebel against him, and he is saved from defeat by another son-in-law, Aganippus, Cordeilla's husband and one of the twelve kings of Gallia. At Lear's death, Cordeilla becomes Queen; but after five years, her nephews revolt against her and imprison her. In despair, Cordeilla commits suicide.

A Mirror for Magistrates, written by various authors, was published from 1559 on in successively enlarged editions. In poor verse, the tragic stories of twenty princes were recorded. One of these tales treated Lear, and it was written in 1574 by John Higgins. The narrator of the story is Cordell. In it, Gonorell reduces her father's guard, and her husband is Albany (not Albania, as in Holinshed). Gonorell is not, as in earlier versions, the wife of Cornwall.

The poet Edmund Spenser, who published *The Faerie Queene* in 1590, included half a dozen stanzas of incidental narrative on the Lear theme. He used the name "Cordelia" for the first time. In Spenser's version, Cordelia dies by hanging, although it is still an act of suicide.

All of these—*The True Chronicle,* Holinshed's *Chronicles, A Mirror for Magistrates,* and *The Faerie Queene*—appear to be the direct sources of the story that Shakespeare made into one of the greatest tragedies of all time. Other books, however, proved to be fruitful sources of ideas, despite their sometimes preposterous themes.

John Florio's translation of Montaigne's *Essais* was in all likelihood one of Shakespeare's favourite books. There is evidence in most Shakespearian plays of borrowing in both style and ideas from the *Essais,* and this is true of *King Lear.* A more direct dependence on Samuel Harsnett's *A Declaration of Egregious Popish Impostures* can be noted in *Lear.* Although the book is as quaint and absurd as its title suggests, it was a mine of suggestions for Shakespeare—for the mad talk, particularly that of Poor Tom, and for the names of the spirits supposedly affecting Tom. Many fascinating parallels in language, names, and ideas can be seen between this book and *King Lear.*[1] It has been established that Shakespeare read the story of the King of Paphlagonia and his two sons in Sidney's *Arcadia,* published in 1590, for it is here that he derives his ideas of "natural goodness" and "wretched ungratefulness". This story also provided the characterization of Edgar and Gloucester, the storm, and indeed the tragic implications of the play. It is possible, too, that the stratagem used by Edmund in deceiving Edgar came from another chapter of *Arcadia.*

Professor C. J. Sisson[2] has found records of contemporary events that may have suggested the theme of *King Lear* to Shakespeare. A certain Ralph Hansby of Yorkshire divided his estate among three daughters, two of whom were ungrateful and the third a Cordelia-type. Another Elizabethan, Sir William Allen, a wealthy, influential Londoner who became Lord Mayor and was knighted by Queen Elizabeth, desired as he approached

[1]Muir, *op. cit.,* pp. 253-6.
[2]C. J. Sisson, *Shakespeare's Tragic Justice* (Scarborough, W. J. Gage Limited, 1961), pp. 80-83.

the age of eighty to free himself from his responsibilities, since he was becoming forgetful. In order, as he thought, to enjoy his remaining time on earth, he divided his estate among his three daughters, one of whom was married to a Frenchman, and arranged to stay first with one and then another, seeing all from time to time and burdening none. Once the daughters had received their shares, they treated their aged parent badly, denying him service and comfort. The old gentleman died unhappy, leaving a curse on his ungrateful daughters. This story, fully documented in the Chancery Records of 1588-9, is most striking as a parallel to Shakespeare's play. It must have been well-known to Shakespeare, as it was the talk of London while it was before the courts and for a considerable time afterward.

One of the most poetic and profound books of the Old Testament is the Book of Job. Its theme is close to that of *King Lear*, and there are verbal parallels between the book and the play that indicate that Shakespeare read and admired it. Job has his Eliphaz, Bildad, and Zophar; and Lear has his Fool and Edgar. Like Job, Lear is driven to question the very justice of God. As Job is humbled by God's speaking out of the tempest, so Lear is humbled by exposure to the pelting of the pitiless storm. Job was a brother to dragons and a companion to owls; Lear chooses to become a comrade of the wolf and the owl. Job cries, "Naked came I out of my mother's womb, and naked shall I return thither." Lear observes,

> We come crying hither;
> Thou knowest, the first time that we smell the air
> We wawl and cry . . . .
> When we are born, we cry that we are come
> To this great stage of fools. (IV. vi. 194-9)

In the end, Job is restored to reason, having probed the mysteries of suffering. But for Lear—and here Shakespeare goes beyond Job's experience—there is no comfort and acceptance in the end, no mitigation of the desolating fact that Cordelia is dead. Shakespeare ruthlessly faced the problem that man can die purged and humbled, yet still suffering the unutterable pain of knowing that the one he loved most dearly is dead, and that he in the pride and folly of a moment was the cause of it.

Such then are the sources of *King Lear*. As always, Shakespeare added immeasurably to the theme as it developed in his mind, seeing beyond the mundane and the commonplace the tragic enigma of man's life, which Job acknowledged in his question, "What is man that thou art mindful of him?"

THE TEXT OF *KING LEAR*

The play was first printed in 1608. This edition is the famous First Quarto, Q1, or "Pied Bull Quarto", so named from its title page. Twelve copies are extant, each one somewhat different from the other, since proofreading, correction, and printing were carried on as the Quarto was being produced. To make matters worse, corrected sheets were bound in with uncorrected ones. In the twelve extant copies, there are 167 variations. The play is mainly punctuated in the First Quarto with commas.

The Second Quarto, Q2, of 1619 (misdated 1608 on the title page) was printed from a copy of the First Quarto that was partly in the original and partly in a corrected state. Such a casual attitude towards printing has led to considerable difficulties in establishing the text of *King Lear* for modern readers.

The third printing of *King Lear* was the First Folio in 1623. This text was printed from a different copy of the First Quarto to that used to print the Second Quarto. The Quarto on which the Folio was based was a much altered copy involving the deletion of about three hundred lines of the original Quarto text and

The Historie of King Lear.

Our deerest *Regan*, wife to *Cornwell*, speake?

Reg. Sir I am made of the selfe same mettall that my sister is,
And prize me at her worth in my true heart,
I find she names my very deed of loue, onely she came short,
That I professe my selfe an enemie to all other ioyes,
Which the most precious square of sence possesses,
And find I am alone felicitate, in your deere highnes loue.

Cord. Then poore *Cord.* & yet not so, since I am sure
My loues more richer then my tongue.

Lear. To thee and thine hereditarie euer
Remaine this ample third of our faire kingdome,
No lesse in space, validity, and pleasure,
Then that confirm'd on *Gonorill*, but now our ioy,
Although the last, not least in our deere loue,
What can you say to win a third, more opulent
Then your sisters.

Cord. Nothing my Lord.   (againe.

Lear. How, nothing can come of nothing, speake

Cord. Vnhappie that I am, I cannot heaue my heart into my
mouth, I loue your Maiestie according to my bond, nor more nor
lesse.

Lear. Goe to, goe to, mend your speech a little,
Least it may mar your fortunes.

Cord. Good my Lord,
You haue begot me, bred me, loued me,
I returne those duties backe as are right fit,
Obey you, loue you, and most honour you,
Why haue my sisters husbands if they say they loue you all,
Happely when I shall wed, that Lord whose hand
Must take my plight, shall cary halfe my loue with him,
Halfe my care and duty, sure I shall neuer
Mary like my sisters, to loue my father all.

Lear. But goes this with thy heart ?

Cord. I good my Lord.

Lear. So yong and so vntender.

Cord. So yong my Lord and true.

Lear. Well let it be so, thy truth then be thy dower,
For by the sacred radience of the Sunne,

B 2   The

[1]H. Granville-Barker and G. B. Harrison, *A Companion to Shakespeare Studies* (London, Sidgwick & Jackson Ltd.).

Our deerest *Regan*, wife of *Cornwall*?

   Reg. I am made of that selfe-mettle as my Sister,
And prize me at her worth. In my true heart,
I finde she names my very deede of loue:
Onely she comes too short, that I professe
My selfe an enemy to all other ioyes,
Which the most precious square of sense professes,
And finde I am alone felicitate
In your deere Highnesse loue.

   Cor. Then poore *Cordelia,*
And yet not so, since I am sure my Ioue's
More ponderous then my tongue.

   Lear. To thee, and thine hereditarie euer,
Remaine this ample third of our faire Kingdome,
No lesse in space, validitie, and pleasure
Then that conferr'd on *Generill.* Now our Ioy,
Although our last and least; to whose yong loue,
The Vines of France, and Milke of Burgundie,
Striue to be interest. What can you say, to draw
A third, more opilent then your Sisters? speake.

   Cor. Nothing my Lord.

   Lear. Nothing?

[*Verso.*]   *Cor.* Nothing.

   Lear. Nothing will come of nothing, speake againe.

   Cor. Vnhappie that I am, I cannot heaue
My heart into my mouth: I loue your Maiesty
According to my bond, no more nor lesse.

   Lear. How, how *Cordelia*? mend your speec ah little,
Least you may marre your Fortunes.

   Cor. Good my Lord,
You haue begot me, bred me, lou'd me.
I returne those duties backe as are right fit,
Obey you, Loue you, and most Honour you.
Why haue my Sisters Husbands, if they say
They loue you all? Happily when I shall wed,
That Lord, whose hand must take my plight, shall carry
Halfe my loue with him, halfe my Care, and Dutie,
Sure I shall neuer marry like my Sisters.

   Lear. But goes thy heart with this?

   Cor. I my good Lord.

   Lear. So young, and so vntender?

   Cor. So young my Lord, and true.

   Lear. Let it be so, thy truth then be thy dowre:
For by the sacred radience of the Sunne,

the inclusion of a hundred that had been missing from the Quarto copy. Numerous verbal alterations were also made in this Quarto, apparently in order to make the text agree with an original prompt book of Shakespeare's company. Whether a modern text is based on the Folio or on the Quarto text, the three hundred extra lines are always included.

Nowadays, there is fairly wide agreement that the Folio text is considerably nearer to what Shakespeare actually wrote than the text of the Quarto, and it is therefore generally the basis of modern editions. All modern versions of *King Lear* texts, however, are "conflations"; that is, fusings of variant readings of the texts of both the First Quarto and the First Folio into a composite text on the basis of the editor's trained judgement.

The text of this edition of the play is the conflation made by the Folger Library in Washington, D.C. Spelling and punctuation are modernized. In this Canadian edition, words such as "honor" and "favor" have been spelled "honour" and "favour".

THE STAGE HISTORY OF *KING LEAR*

We have no knowledge of how audiences in Shakespeare's day received a performance of *King Lear*. We know only that Richard Burbage is said to have undertaken the part successfully. Certainly, the popularity of stark tragedy in the theatre did not wane until well after Shakespeare's day. Whatever its initial fate may have been and despite the criticism implied in its transformation in the eighteenth century, *King Lear* has been at times a striking success on the modern stage. Though it has been performed much less often than *Othello, Macbeth,* or

Hamlet, and has suffered from even greater changes than those made in the Davenant version of *Macbeth, King Lear* has remained very much alive, and it is now performed more often than it once was.

All the eminent actors of our day have acted the part of Lear —Wolfit, Olivier, Gielgud, and Devlin. Famous actors of the past—Betterton, Garrick, Kean, Henry Irving, and Mantell— attempted the part with success or brilliance. The best performance, in the opinion of many critics, was that of Gielgud in 1950 at Stratford-on-Avon, even though the production was marred by mishandling of the storm. It was created realistically with the aid of sound effects, and a cloud cyclorama, instead of being unseen and heard only as a thunderous punctuation to Lear's lamentations.

Criticism of the play before the nineteenth century is as uncommon as its performance. Yet what there is, is not basically different from the critical opinion of our own day. It is true that Lamb's complaint that *King Lear* could not be acted because it was "beyond all art" has had more influence than Lamb intended. Nevertheless, this view has been balanced by Harley Granville-Barker's *Preface,* which has done much to reveal the strength of Shakespeare's dramatic technique in the play and to encourage producers to put the play on the stage. The very considerable amount of critical writing on this tragedy, though it cannot compare with the mass of criticism on *Hamlet,* indicates that modern scholars are engrossed by the implications that Shakespeare introduced into an otherwise commonplace and widely known story of his time. Undoubtedly, the extent of this criticism indicates that although the play is dramatically sound it is not as easy to produce as *Macbeth* or *Hamlet.*

A formidable difficulty that producers of *King Lear* have had to face is the common conception—not as common now as it once was—that the theme and outcome of the play are too distressing for the emotions of an audience. This view was first propounded by Lamb. Bradley's criticism was that the play is too huge for the stage. Other critics have confidently stated that

King Lear is not a good story, despite its impressive qualities. This sentiment must have commenced long before the writings of Lamb were published, since, in 1681, sixty-five years after Shakespeare's death, Nahum Tate, himself a popular and successful playwright, so completely modified *King Lear* that the Shakespearian play was virtually unrecognizable in its new version. Moreover, it was totally alien to Shakespeare's conception of the Lear-world as just emerging from the primitive to the enlightened. Tate introduced incredible changes in plot and text making the whole express the theme of Christian redemption and love, a theme that Bradley too saw in Shakespeare's play. Even more incredible is the fact that Tate's version held the stage for nearly 150 years, to the exclusion of Shakespeare's. Garrick, the famous actor, used the greater part of Tate's *King Lear* in his production of the play. Even Dr. Johnson, who confessed his inability to face the shock of Cordelia's death, and for this reason did not reread the play until he came to edit it, presumably would have preferred Tate's version. Tate omits the Fool, devises a love interest between Edgar and Cordelia, and ensures that virtue gains its reward. Hollywood in its most crassly successful heyday made no more drastic changes in a story than Tate did in *King Lear*. In 1823, Edmund Kean had the courage to restore the tragic ending, still making use, however, of the rest of Tate; and in 1838, W. C. Macready mercifully restored Shakespeare's play in its entirety to the stage.

Recently, we have seen works of both ancient and modern literature successfully turned into musical comedies. *Pygmalion* became *My Fair Lady*, the legends of King Arthur became *Camelot*, and *Oliver Twist* became *Oliver!* We have even seen *Romeo and Juliet* transformed successfully into *West Side Story*. None of these changes appears to have outraged the sensibilities of the audience, since the spirit of the original has been retained or at least not violated. With a work like *King Lear*, however, modification can only be described as perversion. The wonder is that Tate's version could have been so popular for so long. The argument that Tate was justified because he made a financial success of *King Lear*, as Garrick who used the Tate version did, is scarcely a valid one in judging Shakespeare's play. Despite this condemnation of Tate and his followers, it must be conceded that the impact on the reader's mind of Shakespeare's *King Lear*, especially the uncompromising agony of the final scene, is most intense, and in the less-sophisticated past may have produced a real fear that its pitiless implications could not be faced on the living stage. In a sense, this is the ultimate tribute to the success of Shakespeare's deepest tragedy.

THE IMPORTANCE OF EARLY EDITORS OF SHAKESPEARE

As we may surmise from the foregoing account of the textual jungle from which a satisfactory text must be rescued, the task of establishing what Shakespeare actually wrote is not easy and at times impossible, even today with all the resources available to modern scholars. Those who read Shakespeare and who enjoy his plays on the stage owe a debt of gratitude to the editors, from Shakespeare's day to ours, who have laboured over this problem. The following table indicates the kind and amount of work done in preserving the text and biography of Shakespeare, particularly by his early editors.

TABLE OF EARLY EDITORS OF SHAKESPEARE
SHOWING THEIR MAIN CONTRIBUTIONS TO
SHAKESPEARIAN STUDIES

Editor	Dates of Birth and Death	Main Contributions
NICHOLAS ROWE	1674-1718	Prefaced edition with a valuable biography of Shakespeare. Made many brilliant emendations, some coinciding accidentally with readings in the Folio, to which he had no access. Added *dramatis personae* to each play. Divided and numbered acts and scenes. Marked entrances and exits. Modernized grammar, spelling, and punctuation.
ALEXANDER POPE	1688-1744	Made some clever innovations. Improved on Rowe's division of plays into scenes. Indicated the *locale* of each new scene. Used Rowe's text, though he asserted that he made a thorough collation of texts.
LEWIS THEOBALD	1688-1744	Criticized Pope's edition. A competent textual editor. Brought out various editions, using the First Folio as his text.

More than 300 of his corrections or emendations are now part of the accepted text of Shakespeare.

SIR THOMAS HANMER 1677-1746 A country gentleman whose hobby was examining the text of Shakespeare's plays. Used texts of Pope and Theobald, since he had access to no others.

Certain of his emendations are accepted like those of Pope and Theobald; *e.g.*, *King Lear* III. vi. 70, he changed from "hym", which was meaningless, to "lym", meaning bloodhound, becoming the first editor to make sense of the line.

BISHOP WARBURTON 1698-1779 A borrower from Theobald and Hanmer on both of whom he poured scorn, only to find himself a much more vulnerable target for Thomas Edwards in *The Canons of Criticism*, 1748.

DR. SAMUEL JOHNSON 1709-1784 Brought out an eight-volume edition in 1765 and a second edition in 1768.

Though some of his comments are illuminating and witty, he was not a close student of the text, and did not advance textual knowledge.

His work was inadequate because he lacked knowledge of Elizabethan history and literature.

EDWARD CAPELL   1713-1781   A tireless collator of texts who conducted far more research than his predecessors.

His work was rendered less effective because of his own particularly wooden style.

He is said to have written out the entire text of Shakespeare ten times.

Brought out an edition of the plays in 1768.

His published notes, though quaint in style, show wide knowledge of Elizabethan literature, and aided later scholars greatly.

GEORGE STEEVENS   1736-1800   His greatest contributions were in the form of parallel quotations from writers contemporary to Shakespeare and in the clarification of obscure words and phrases. Towards the end of his career, he made unwarranted changes in the text, and composed obscene explanations of coarse words and phrases in the text, which he attributed to two innocent clergymen turned critics.

EDMUND MALONE   1741-1812   Sought out valuable biographical material.
Tried to establish the order of Shakespeare's plays.
Added considerably to our knowledge of the history of the stage.

Following the work of these early editors several variorum editions of Shakespeare were brought out. A variorum edition contains all the various readings of lines and passages from the text of Shakespeare, and is an essential part of the equipment of modern Shakespearian scholars. The most notable of these editions was that of Howard Furness of Philadelphia, the first volume of which appeared in 1871. Other editions followed.

The work of subsequent editors—those of the nineteenth century such as Dyce, Staunton, and Delius, and of the twentieth century such as Craig, Harrison, and Kittredge—is greatly dependent on the work of the first editors of Shakespeare. Without their work, modern Shakespearian scholarship would be much less advanced, and our enjoyment of Shakespeare on the stage would be considerably diminished.

REFERENCE TABLE

Shakespeare's Life and Work

Events Occurring in Shakespeare's Lifetime

(The dates of the various plays indicate the probable order of composition. The dates in parentheses after the titles indicate first publication, 1623 being the date of the First Folio.)

1564   Death of Michelangelo.
Birth of Christopher Marlowe.

April 23, 1564   Probable birth date of the poet. His father, John, was a trader in farm produce; later, a glover, and by tradition, also a butcher. He was a keen businessman and municipal politician. His mother, Mary, née Arden, was a woman of some means in her own right.

April 26, 1564   Baptism of William Shakespeare in the Church of the Holy Trinity, Stratford. William was the eldest living child; his younger brothers and sisters were Gilbert, Joan, Anna, Richard, and Edmund.

1567	*Ralph Roister Doister* by Nicholas Udall: the first English comedy.
1574	*A Mirror for Magistrates* (first edition 1559).
1575	*Gammer Gurton's Needle,* the second English comedy.
1576	The first permanent playhouse, The Theatre, opened in England.
1577	Holinshed's *Chronicles.* (See also 1586.)
1580	Drake's circumnavigation of the world.
	Montaigne's *Essais.*

| 1582 | There is no actual record of Shakespeare's marriage. A license was issued before November 28, 1582, according to references in other documents. Shakespeare was still a minor when married to Anne Hathaway, aged twenty-six. |

| May 26, 1583 | Susanna, daughter of William Shakespeare, was baptized. |

February 2,	1585	Baptism of the twin children of Shakespeare, Hamnet and Judith.		
	1586	Shakespeare, according to conjecture, was now working in London.	1586	Second edition of Holinshed's *Chronicles*.
			1588	Defeat of Spanish Armada. Sir William Allen's story in Chancery Records.
	1590	*Love's Labour's Lost* (1598)	1590	Marlowe's *Tamburlaine*. Spenser's *Faerie Queene, I, II, III*. (Lear story included.) Sidney's *Arcadia* (included story of the King of Paphlagonia).
	1591	*Comedy of Errors* (1623) *Henry VI, I and II* (1623)		
	1592	By this time Shakespeare had become a prominent playwright, who had aroused jealous sentiments in a rival dramatist, Robert Greene. *The Two Gentlemen of Verona* (1623) *Richard III* (1597)	1592	Death of Robert Greene.

	Henry VI, III (1623) *Romeo and Juliet* (1599)	
April 18, 1593	*Venus and Adonis* entered in the Stationers' Register; dedication signed by Shakespeare.	1593 Death of Marlowe.
1593	*King John* (1623) *Richard II* (1597) *Titus Andronicus* (1594)	
May 9, 1594	*The Rape of Lucrece* was entered in the Stationers' Register.	
Christmas, 1594	Shakespeare, the comic actor Will Kemp, and Richard Burbage, tragedian, were known to be members of the Lord Chamberlain's Company. *A Midsummer Night's Dream* (1600)	
1595	*All's Well That Ends Well* (1623) *The Taming of the Shrew* (1623)	
August 11, 1596	Hamnet, aged 11, was buried. John Shakespeare, probably urged	1596 Blackfriars Theatre adapted from a monastery by Burbage.

by his son, applied to the College of Heralds for a coat of arms. Request granted on October 20, 1596. The Shakespeare coat of arms appears on the cover of this edition.

Henry IV, I (1598)
Henry IV, II (1600)

May 4, 1597   Shakespeare bought New Place, the largest house in Stratford, for sixty pounds, and began acquiring additional property. From this time on, Shakespeare was clearly a man of considerable wealth.

The Merry Wives of Windsor (1623)
The Merchant of Venice (1600)

1598   *Much Ado About Nothing* (1600)

Henry V (1600)

1599   *As You Like It* (1623)

1597   Bacon's *Essays.*

1598   Jonson's *Every Man in His Humour.*

1599   Globe Theatre built. Shakespeare owned shares.
Birth of Oliver Cromwell.

Date	Shakespeare's Works & Life	Date	Historical & Literary Events
1600	*Twelfth Night* (1623)	1601	The Essex Plot.
1601	*Julius Caesar* (1623)		
1602	*Hamlet* (1603)		
May 19, 1603	The Lord Chamberlain's Company became The King's, and acted before the court more often than any other company.	1603	Death of Queen Elizabeth and accession of James I. John Florio's translation of Montaigne's *Essais*. Samuel Harnsnett's *A Declaration of Egregious Popish Impostures* entered in the Stationers' Register.
1603	*Troilus and Cressida* (1609)	1604	Marlowe's *Doctor Faustus*.
1604	*Measure for Measure* (1623) *Othello* (1622)	1605	The Gunpowder Plot. *The True Chronicle History of King Leir* published. Court performance of Shakespeare's *King Lear*.
1605	*Macbeth* (1623)		
1606	*King Lear* (1608)	1607	Settlement at Jamestown. *King Lear* entered in the Stationers' Register.
June 5, 1607	His daughter Susanna married John Hall, a Stratford physician. *Timon of Athens* (1623)		
September 9, 1608	Shakespeare's mother was buried.		

1608 *Pericles* (1609) *Anthony and Cleopatra* (1623)	1608 The First Quarto edition of *King Lear*. The Second Quarto, misdated 1608, was actually printed in 1619 from a copy of the First Quarto.
1609 *Coriolanus* (1623)	
1610 *Cymbeline* (1623)	
1611 *A Winter's Tale* (1623) *The Tempest* (1623)	1611 The King James Bible.
1613 *Henry VIII* (1623)	1613 The Globe Theatre burned. 1615 Harvey's lectures on the circulation of the blood.
January, 1616 Shakespeare's will drawn up.	
February 10, 1616 His daughter Judith married Thomas Quiney, a vintner and municipal politician.	
March 25, 1616 A draft of Shakespeare's will, much corrected, was signed and executed.	
April 25, 1616 Shakespeare was buried.	1619 The Second Quarto of *King Lear*. 1623 The First Folio, third printing, of *King Lear*.

THE IMAGERY OF *KING LEAR*

Numerous definitions of imagery have been made, none perhaps quite adequate. Thrall and Hibbard[1] define imagery as "the use of figurative language for poetic or rhetorical effect". Caroline Spurgeon[2] confines the term mainly to metaphor and simile, but makes interesting reference to the imagery implicit in verbs. Laurence Perrine[3] extends it to "the representation through language of sense experience". "Images," writes Alfred Harbage,[4] "operate, as one might deduce, in the realm of the imagination. They are the vehicle by which the poet's thoughts pass into the reader's mind as the reader's imagination responds to the poet's imagination."

Each play of Shakespeare yields its peculiar wealth of imagery. Since the images in *King Lear* are the means by which Shakespeare assists us to see as Lear saw and to feel as Lear felt, we are soon made to feel imaginatively through these images the disorder and unnaturalness that follow upon Lear's angry rejection of Cordelia and upon Gloucester's irresponsible act of fathering Edmund.

Throughout the play, there are frequent references to human beings and their unnatural similarity to animals. Lear cries, "Come not between the dragon and his wrath" (I. i. 130), and later laments,

---

[1] W. F. Thrall et al., *Handbook to Literature* (New York, Odyssey Press, Inc., 1936), pp. 205-6.

[2] Caroline Spurgeon, *Shakespeare's Imagery* (New York, Cambridge University Press, 1952), pp. 5, 339.

[3] Laurence Perrine, *Sound and Sense* (New York, Harcourt, Brace & World, Inc., 1956), p. 40.

[4] Alfred Harbage, *William Shakespeare, A Reader's Guide* (New York, Farrar, Strauss and Cudahy, Inc., 1963), p. 23.

> Allow not nature more than nature needs,
> Man's life's as cheap as beast's. (II. iv. 300-1)

Near the end of his wanderings on the heath, he learns that "unaccommodated man is no more but such a poor, bare, forked animal as thou art" (III. iv. 110-11). Goneril and Regan are "pelican daughters" (III. iv. 80) and "she-foxes" (III. vi. 22-23). Albany calls his faithless wife a "gilded serpent" (V. iii. 98). Edgar calls Edmund a "most toad-spotted traitor" (V. iii. 164). He calls man a "hog in sloth, fox in stealth, wolf in greediness, dog in madness, lion in prey" (III. iv. 97-98). The Fool tells Lear, "Truth's a dog must to kennel; he must be whipped out, when the Lady Brach may stand by the fire and stink" (I. iv. 109-11). When Lear curses Goneril, he calls her "detested kite" (I. iv. 263) and prays,

> that she may feel
> How sharper than a serpent's tooth it is
> To have a thankless child! (I. iv. 290-1)

Kent, about to be put into the stocks, protests to Regan,

> Why madam, if I were your father's dog,
> You should not use me so. (II. ii. 137-8)

Lear himself declares,

> O, Regan she hath tied
> Sharp-toothed unkindness, like a vulture, here!
> (II. iv. 146-7)

In his final agony, Lear's grief is expressed by the repetition of the word "howl" (V. iii. 306) and by the question,

> Why should a dog, a horse, a rat, have life,
> And thou no breath at all? (V. iii. 367-8)

Though not as frequently encountered as animal images, clothing images are common in *King Lear* and prepare the reader for an understanding of the disrobing of Lear (III. iv. 112). Each

clothing image expresses in a particular way the essential falsity
and duplicity of man, and affords Shakespeare the means of dis-
tinguishing sharply between the apparent and the real, between
blindness and insight. Edgar says,

> In nothing am I changed
> But in my garments. (IV. vi. 12-13)

On awakening, Lear is bewildered by his clothing:

> And all the skill I have
> Remembers not these garments. (IV. vii. 75-76)

Kent insults Oswald when he says, "a tailor made thee" (II. ii.
51-52). As Lear condemns the bitter justice in this world, he
cries,

> Through tattered clothes small vices do appear;
> Robes and furred gowns hide all. (IV. vi. 180-1)

and when he is at last purged of his bitterness and resentment, a
gentleman tells us, "We put fresh garments on him" (IV. vii.
26).

Miss Spurgeon points out the "floating image" that Shakespeare creates by the use of metaphors and verbs describing the
human body in torment—being tugged, wrenched, beaten,
pierced, stung, scourged, dislocated, flayed, gashed, scalded, tortured, and broken. Lear tells Cordelia that he is bound

> Upon a wheel of fire, that mine own tears
> Do scald like molten lead. (IV. vii. 53-54)

and at the end, Kent pleads,

> O, let him pass! He hates him
> That would upon the rack of this tough world
> Stretch him out longer. (V. iii. 377-9)

Images of sexual lust and sickness of the body also form an
important part of the imaginative impact of this play. Edmund

deceives himself into believing that he has more vigour than other men because he was conceived "in the lusty stealth of nature" (I. ii. 11), and asserts that man has a "goatish disposition" (I. ii. 125). Lear's daughters are the result of "three undivulged crimes" (III. ii. 53). Edgar as Poor Tom advises Lear to "Keep thy foot out of brothels, thy hand out of plackets" (III. iv. 100-1). Lear, demented, expresses his lack of humanity in several complex images (IV. vi. 128-43) and fiercely condemns the injustice of the world in a sexual reference to the "rascal beadle" (IV. vi. 175-8). Lear warns himself, "Take physic, pomp" (III. iv. 39) to purge himself of pride so that he may feel what wretches feel, and he realizes at length that he is not "ague-proof" (IV. vi. 120). Cordelia prays for her father's well-being with the words:

> restoration hang
> Thy medicine on my lips. (IV. vii. 31-32)

and Lear curses Goneril with disease:

> Into her womb convey sterility;
> Dry up in her the organs of increase. (I. iv. 280-1)

When rejected by Regan as well as Goneril, Lear exclaims,

> Thou art a boil,
> A plague sore or embossed carbuncle,
> In my corrupted blood. (II. iv. 250-2)

Images to be properly appreciated and understood must be read sensitively and discerningly. Only if we accept certain devices used by the poet can we enjoy poetry in general, or the particularly rich combination of poetry and drama of Shakespeare. With the images of Shakespeare—and indeed those of any other poet—we must be willing to accept the image for what it is, a powerful appeal to the imagination, and not an attempt to express a scientific statement. We must be willing to imagine and to interpret according to the spirit of the image, to keep the image in its exact context, and to dismiss from the mind any irrelevant and absurd ideas that may suggest themselves. If Lear's daughters are described as "dog-hearted" (IV. iii. 53), we must be receptive to this poetic statement, disregarding its biological inaccuracy and literal absurdity.

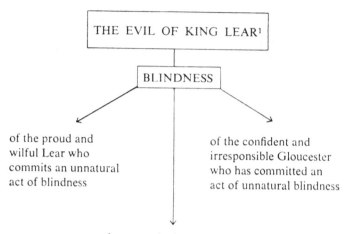

THE EVIL OF KING LEAR[1]

BLINDNESS

of the proud and wilful Lear who commits an unnatural act of blindness

of the confident and irresponsible Gloucester who has committed an act of unnatural blindness

becomes the instrument of fate producing tragic events as the eyes of these two men are opened:

↓

rejection of Lear   destruction of Regan and Goneril
betrayal of Edgar   death of Edmund
death of Cornwall   banishment and death of Cordelia
death of Gloucester   death of Lear

↓

survivors of the unnatural course of events are Albany, Kent, and Edgar.

[1]Suggested by John Masefield's "Introduction to *King Lear*" from *Five Great Tragedies*, William Aldis Wright, ed. (New York, Pocket Books Inc., 1942), pp. 326-9.

THE MAIN ACTION OF *King Lear*

(The excerpts referred to are in Critics' Comments p. li.)

	I	II	III	IV	V
Order Stability	Order imperilled (Excerpts 1, 4, 12, 13)		The storm (Excerpts 5, 6)	(Excerpt 15)	Humility, love, and understanding (Excerpts 9, 10)
					Devastation (Excerpts 6, 7, 8, 11)
	Pride and vanity blind Lear, causing him to divide his Kingdom and reject Cordelia (I. i.).		Lear disrobes and strips himself of the arrogance and egocentricity of the past (III. iv. 112).		Cordelia hanged (V. iii. 283) Lear's unbearable grief. The agony of eternal separation. Death of Lear (V. iii. 372)
				EXPERIENCE	
		LEAR'S	SPIRITUAL		
		THE STORM			
	Rejection by Goneril, followed by Lear's curse (I. iv.).	Rejection by Regan. Sounds of approaching storm (II. iv.).	He begins to question and philosophize (III. iv. 157-85). He sleeps (III. vi. 84).	Lear, mad raves against lust (IV. vi. 173-81). Lear is in the care of Cordelia (IV. vii).	Lear and Cordelia are prisoners but happy (V. iii. 9-27). Albany becomes ruler.

Stripping of Lear.

Blind pride and vanity.

Reclothing of Lear.

Opening of Lear's eyes.

Lear's agony.

Disorder Chaos

	I	II
Peaceful family life.	Mirthful reference to Edmund's illegitimate birth (I. i. 8-10).	
A.	Edmund's rise to power.	
B.	Decline of Gloucester's fortunes.	
		Linking of main and secondary plots
A.	Edmund's letter builds distrust of Edgar in Gloucester. Edmund warns Edgar of their father's wrath (I. ii.).	Cornwall's arrival aids Edmund's plot. Edmund warns Edgar to flee, and the main and secondary plots are linked (II. i.). Edgar becomes Poor Tom (II. iii.).
B.	Gloucester jokes with Kent about Edmund's birth (I. i.).	Gloucester disinherits Edgar in favour of Edmund, after hearing Edmund's story (II. i.).

III	IV	V
		Gloucester's blindness is paid for.
Dissension in Kingdom Incrimination of Gloucester		
		Family peace destroyed.
Edmund learns of the strained relations between the Dukes from Gloucester (III. iii.). Edmund tells Cornwall of the letter that is to right Lear's wrongs, implicating Gloucester as a traitor. Edmund is virtually Earl of Gloucester (III. v.).	Edmund has Goneril's love (IV. ii.).	Edmund has Regan's love and denies his love for Goneril. He hopes Goneril will kill Albany, and that he may destroy Lear, Goneril, and Cordelia himself; then he will have both Regan and the rule of Britain (V. i.). He commissions a captain to kill Cordelia and she dies. Edgar kills Edmund (V. iii.).
Gloucester defies Cornwall to help Lear (III. iii.). Cornwall is determined to apprehend Gloucester (III. v.). Gloucester is captured and blinded; Cornwall fatally wounded (III. vii.).	Gloucester's self-knowledge is complete, and he is ready to die. He is led by Poor Tom (Edgar) towards Dover (IV. ii.). Edgar saves his father by deceiving him at the cliff. Lear and Gloucester meet, and Lear talks of justice (IV. vi.).	Gloucester dies.

SOME NOTES ON THE CHARACTERS

Lear

Lear is not a complex, enigmatic character like Hamlet. It is what happens to him in the last days of his life rather than what he is that makes us wonder at the dark inscrutability of man's fate in this world. He has no fund of wit, no easy familiarity with those around him, no darting brilliance of mind, like the Prince of Denmark. Lear is proud, serious, arbitrary, impatient, peremptory, humorless, and capricious, and his position in life has allowed him to indulge all these traits to the full. Nothing, no one, has ever dared to stand in his way during his reign. Supreme over all these characteristics is one other, which Kent calls authority. Fortunately, Lear can inspire as well as command loyalty and obedience. The few of "his hundred knights" whom we see are as quick to obey him when his power is gone as they were when it was at its height. Kent is the embodiment of allegiance to the King when there is nothing to be gained but humiliation, danger, and sorrow. Lear's fatal flaw, however, is his inability to accept the slightest check to his plans. When his favourite daughter Cordelia gives him an honest, if unexpected, answer, he dismisses every consideration, banishes her, and turns savagely on Kent when he attempts to stay the royal hand. The rest of the story we know: Lear from this moment on begins to pay for his self-indulgence until, at the end, we question how much a man is required to pay for the sin of pride and whether there is any justice in this world.

We are fascinated by Lear because we know that although he is not a man of intellectual brilliance he is a "great soul", with the capacity for feeling deeply the sorrow of rejection and abandonment by his own. The vehemence of his banishment of Cordelia, of his curse on Goneril, and of his rage during the storm are frightening exhibitions of his fierce, primitive emotions. Even in his madness, Lear seems larger than life itself, a titan who cannot die. Nothing in English dramatic literature excites us to pity more than the contrast between the Lear we first meet—proud, passionate, confident, dictatorial, and regal—and the Lear we see restored to Cordelia at the end of the play —gentle, penitent, affectionate, humble, and still a king.

The Duke of Cornwall

Although the Duke inspires distaste, he is nonetheless a successful ruler in the society in which he was born, a society just emerging from the primitive and still searching for standards of morality and decency. He is successful because he is not hampered by nice considerations of the methods by which his will is imposed. Like his wife Regan, he is actuated by the instincts of a predatory animal for ruthless mastery of his domain. Nothing can stand in his way: when the aging Lear surrenders all real power, but insists on keeping a few of the trappings, he becomes, to Cornwall, an irritant that must be destroyed; when Gloucester shows humane feelings for the distressed Lear and disobeys orders to leave him to perish on the heath, and when he is in touch with the French on Lear's behalf, the Duke feels that his execution is not sufficient revenge; instead, Gloucester should suffer a living death after mutilation.

The fiery Duke's most restrained and judicial moment comes when Kent is provoking a quarrel with Oswald. The Duke listens to both sides, but Kent's truculence and insolence are too much for his temper, and he claps Kent unceremoniously in the stocks, prompting Gloucester's observation that his "disposition . . . will not be rubbed nor stopped" (II. ii. 157-8). Nor does the Duke lack courage. He is willing to face Lear's wrath, and he is completely calm as he realizes that the sword-thrust of the servant is a fatal one (III. vii. 114-15). A practitioner of violence himself, he accepts it as the natural instrument by which an objective may be gained.

The Duke of Albany

The Duke of Albany provides a striking contrast to the ruthless, fiery Duke of Cornwall. In the primitive, cruel world of Lear, Albany is a misplaced idealist, as blind in his way to evil as Gloucester and Lear are in theirs. He has married Goneril, evidently for love, and is slow to understand what his wife has actually done to her father. There is no doubt about who the dominant partner in their marriage is. At the ceremonial dividing of the lands, he seems unaware of any hypocrisy in Goneril; at any rate, he stands silently by, protesting only in conventional fashion with Cornwall at Lear's verbal assault on Kent (I. i. 175). As he begs Lear to be calm (I. iv. 262, 274-5) after Goneril has rejected her father, he seems unaware that Goneril could have caused such fury. His first protest to Goneril—and it is a bland one—comes after Lear has flung himself out of their presence (I. iv. 316-17). It takes some time for the scales to fall from his eyes, but when they do he is fortunately equal to his role as virtual ruler of the country.

At no time is Albany associated with violence or cruelty. He is in no way a party to Cornwall's blinding of Gloucester (IV. ii. 89-92). He kills no one, and escapes death himself only because fate takes Goneril before her plans are completed. As a military leader, Albany lacks the initiative, cunning, and daring of Edmund, and Edmund therefore wins. Albany's position is difficult especially for an idealist: he wants to fight the French army as an invading force, but he also wants to aid Cordelia, the leader of this force, in her rescue of Lear. He is therefore a man to double business bound. When Edmund, Regan, and Goneril are dead, Albany surrenders his power to Lear for the remainder of the King's life, not knowing that Lear is about to die a moment later. Whatever we may think of Albany's blindness and mildness, his firmness and courage at the end arouse our sympathy, and his selfless devotion to the right claims our admiration.

The Earl of Gloucester

Gloucester is not an appealing character at first. Where Lear towers like a titan, Gloucester appears insignificant—a white-haired old man. He is rather proud of himself as the father of the illegitimate Edmund, and inclined to joke about the escapade that produced this son. The astuteness so evident in Edmund must have been inherited from his mother, whoever she was, because Gloucester possesses none. The ease with which he is deceived by Edmund makes us pity his simplicity, and we find ourselves in partial sympathy at least with Edmund's contempt of his father's superstitious faith in astrology. But it is Gloucester who shows deep concern for Lear when Goneril openly turns against him, who finds shelter for him, and who refuses to beg for mercy when Cornwall gouges out his eyes.

Like Lear, Gloucester is blind to the real qualities of his children. Through suffering he learns the truth, and sees it most clearly after he has been blinded. In contrast to Lear, who dies in the full knowledge that Cordelia is dead through his own fault, Gloucester dies joyfully, knowing that his son Edgar loves him, and that the son produced by his sinfulness betrayed him.

The Earl of Kent

Cornwall is cruel, Albany is mild, and Kent is rough. The Earl of Kent appears in the first scene as an affable but cautious partner in conversation with the boastful Gloucester, and in the last as a faithful, broken-hearted follower of the dead King. He has more man than wit about him, as he is quick to point out. We see Kent at his worst when he abuses Oswald for Oswald's treatment of Lear—and the worst is in reality only a hot temper combined with a rough tongue, weaknesses of the flesh forgivable in one devoted so completely to Lear, even though Lear cursed and banished him from the realm. Unless aroused, Kent speaks little and relies on actions to speak more loudly than words (III. iv.), and we gain the impression that he is a man of infinite tenderness behind the rough exterior—which is throughout the play a disguise covering the real man. Bradley[1] tells us, "The king is not to him old, wayward, unreasonable, piteous: he is terrible, grand, the king of men. Through his eyes we see the Lear of Lear's prime, whom Cordelia never saw." As he sits alone in the stocks, we see a cheerful realist, who makes the best of every situation in which he finds himself, and who can take the blows of chance like a man. He tells Lear he is forty-eight, but the epithets hurled at him by Cornwall indicate that he is an older man and therefore has the most to sacrifice in his allegiance to Lear.

Edgar

"A credulous father! and a brother noble" (I. ii. 173) are the words used by Edmund to describe his father and his half-brother. These terms might well be applied to both men, since both are easy marks for Edmund's deception, and Gloucester is truly noble when he allows no plea for mercy to cross his lips as Cornwall blinds him. During the period of hiding, when his life is at stake, Edgar proves to have the same unselfish devotion to his father as Kent has towards Lear. Like Kent, he is cheerful in adversity and never gives up hope. It is characteristic that he should take as his disguise the appearance of the lowest of human creatures—a Bedlam beggar—and yet never despair. Unlike Kent, who believes that man hangs precariously on the wheel of fortune or blind chance, Edgar has a religious view, believing that "the gods are just" and that man has the right to believe in the future. At the end of the play, when there is every reason for despair, Edgar, who has through bitter experience learned to be a worthy champion of the just and the right, has the last word:

> The weight of this sad time we must obey,
> Speak what we feel, not what we ought to say. (V. iii. 388-9)

---

[1] A. C. Bradley, *Shakespearean Tragedy* (London, Macmillan & Co., Ltd., 1904), p. 256.

Obedience to the just gods and the acceptance of their dictates
are his beliefs. From Poor Tom to champion in the lists represents a profound spiritual growth in Edgar.

Edmund

Characters like Edmund in *King Lear*, Iago in *Othello*, and
the King in *Richard III* arose out of an Elizabethan misunder-
standing of machiavellianism. The idea of Machiavelli's prince
haunted the minds of the restless, adventurous Elizabethans, particularly the quality of *virtù*: audacity, clear-sightedness, decisive-
ness, and resolution. What they missed was Machiavelli's theory
that these qualities were to be devoted to noble goals, even if the
means of achieving these ends were evil. In the dramatic literature of this period, these qualities were invariably devoted to
ruthless self-advancement in a villain whose body is twisted at
birth like Richard III's or whose mind is obsessed, like Edmund's, with his bastardy. To Shakespeare, Edmund is a blem-
ished soul—a human being gone fundamentally wrong and incapable of any but evil purposes.

For Edmund, the code of honour that moves Edgar, Kent, and
Cordelia is impossible. He makes Nature—the selfish, greedy,
ruthless nature of man, which ignores moral obligations—his
goddess, and proceeds to gain his ends with the vigour and
cynicism of any *arriviste*. Persons and lies, he looks upon as instruments of advancement. He deceives father and brother with
bravura; he fascinates both Goneril and Regan and seems in-
different as to which shall be his mate. He receives his title as
Earl of Gloucester from Cornwall because he informed Cornwall promptly of the letter Gloucester received. He lies with
easy grace. To Goneril he ironically swears, "Yours in the ranks
of death!" (IV. ii. 28). Nowhere, except in the final moments
of life, does he show the slightest indication of fine feelings:

> Some good I mean to do,
> Despite mine own nature. (V. iii. 290-1)

He asks that Lear and Cordelia be saved, but only when all is lost—power, Goneril, Regan, life itself, and we accept this as a deathbed repentance forced out of him by the realization of the complete failure of his life.

Oswald

Shakespeare must have studied servants with a critical eye, for each one that he portrays, however slightly, has a realistic personality of his own, whether it is Sampson or Gregory in *Romeo and Juliet*, Lucius in *Julius Caesar*, Osric in *Hamlet*, or Seyton in *Macbeth*. Of these, Seyton is the one who most resembles Oswald. Oswald has nothing to recommend him except his faithfulness to Goneril, and we see this only in evil circumstances. He finds malicious pleasure in taunting Lear. He grimaces with fear at the thought that Kent is about to duel with him, and he makes a disgracefully noisy exhibition of cowardice when Kent, an old man, beats him with the flat of his sword. He is eager to kill the blind and helpless Gloucester and makes a brave speech upon apprehending him (IV. vi. 249-53). He is only too willing to sweep from his path the peasant (Edgar in disguise) who opposes him. In fairness, it must be added that he tries to arrange to have his last duty for Goneril completed by Kent (IV. vi. 271-5). Edgar sums him up as

> A serviceable villain,
> As duteous to the vices of thy mistress
> As badness would desire. (IV. vi. 276-8)

He shares the savagery of Cornwall, Regan, and Goneril, without having acquired any of their nerveless resolution.

Goneril and Regan

Two sisters could be scarcely more like each other. The Fool observes of Regan in comparing her to Goneril, "she's as like this as a crab's like an apple" and that "she'll taste as like this as a crab does to a crab" (I. v. 14-17). Nor could they be more unlike Cordelia. From the beginning, we know them as hypo-

crites and deceivers intent upon gaining for themselves the greatest possible amount of territory and power from their father by
means of the most elaborate protestations of love. They are
jubilant when Cordelia refuses to play their game and loses her
portion of the old King's domain, and they are in immediate
agreement that Lear must have even the shadow of his authority
removed. "If our father," says Goneril, "carry authority with
such disposition as he bears, this last surrender of his will but
offend us" (I. i. 332-4). The cool contempt with which they
look on the father who gave them all (II. iv. 280) is appalling,
and as we observe them tearing from him the last shreds of his
dignity we understand why Lear is driven to calling Goneril a
"degenerate bastard" (I. iv. 252) and a "detested kite" (I. iv.
263), and to cursing her with unparalleled vehemence (I. iv.
277-91).

As is Goneril, so is Regan. When Lear arrives at Gloucester's
palace after being turned away by Goneril, Regan and her
husband are "not at home" to him, and he is incredulous. Regan
is as harsh with Lear as Goneril is, and he leaves them both,
calling them "unnatural hags" (II. iv. 312) and "pelican
daughters" (III. iv. 80).

Both Goneril and Regan are animated by the same spirit that
moves Edmund, after whom they both lust—wealth and power.
Nor are they more fastidious about the means they use to
achieve their ends than he is. Machiavellianism is as great in
these two women as it is in Edmund, and in them it lacks the
baffling charm that Edmund possesses, not only for them as
women, but for us as readers of the play. As evil as Lady Macbeth, they have greater strength in the end, but entirely lack
the devotion that she gave in full measure to her husband.

Cordelia

The devotion and service that Cordelia gives her father, if set
against the bestial savagery of her sisters, needs no other emphasis. With her love goes a shining honesty of which her father

in his eagerness to manage the court procedure exactly as he has planned it is totally and tragically unaware. A moment's consideration in his headlong course would have saved him, but Lear plunges furiously on. He has been balked, embarrassed, crossed, and Cordelia, who is his favourite daughter and yet the cause of his anger, must pay for her presumption. But it is Lear who really pays, for in this moment of pique he sets the course of his own last days.

Cordelia appears very little upon the stage during the play. We see her for a moment at the beginning, standing her ground firmly as every eye in the court is upon her. We see her in the tenderest moment of the play, as she holds her father in her arms. At the end, we see her lovely young body limp in Lear's arms. She speaks little more than a hundred lines. But her pure and noble nature, and her resolution, which matches that of her sisters, compel our admiration; and the fact that she is completely innocent and deeply wronged wins our sympathy and affection. She receives few of the joys rightly expected in a young girl's life and too many misfortunes—rejection by her father, anxiety during the short days of her married life, and cruel murder as her end. In Cordelia, we see most clearly and most pitiably the tragedy of waste.

The Fool

The role of the Fool is one of the triumphs of Shakespeare's dramatic art. Unquestionably, the Fool is slightly unbalanced, but not so much that his words carry no meaning—quite the opposite. His words are like a chorus to the actions and outbursts of Lear, and they help us to understand the turmoil and agony of Lear's mind.

In his way, the Fool is as loyal as Kent and as faithful as Edgar. But where these two are tender and affectionate, the Fool is bitter and cynical. "A pestilent gall to me!" (I. iv. 112) is Lear's exclamation when the Fool's barbed comments sting him too sharply. Perhaps, this attitude of the Fool's is in part his revenge for having been separated from Cordelia, for whom he pines when she is in France. He stands, an appalled, fearful, and silent little figure in the great quarrels of Lear with his two daughters, and he has already suffered too much when Kent drags him from the shelter to follow Lear (III. vi. 103-5). After this, the Fool disappears, and we hear no more of him. While he is with Lear, we are aware of the devotion that Lear can inspire in followers as unlike as the rough and ready Kent and this nervous, frightened, and disturbed child-man.

DRAMATIC DEVICES IN *KING LEAR*

A STRUCTURAL DEVICES

1. *Establishment of the main plot and subplots:* apparent in Act I and in the skilful interweaving of these plots throughout the play.

2. *Conflict:* the clash of opposing forces without which there is no drama:
   a) man vs. man: Edgar vs. Edmund.
   b) man vs. himself: Lear's inner struggle.
   c) man vs. nature: Lear against the tempest.

3. *Crisis:* the turning point in the play. (In a Shakespearian play, it usually occurs in the third act.) In *King Lear*, most critics consider that Lear's disrobing is the turning point.

4. *Catastrophe:* the destruction (or failure) of the leading character (the protagonist). Lear's death is the catastrophe, whereas the *climax* would be the defeat of Edmund. The *outcome* is that Albany and Edgar remain to

rule the state, while Kent, his duty done, goes to his death.

B DEVICES THAT ADD INTEREST

1. *Suspense:* a state of anxious uncertainty. In *King Lear*, suspense pervades the whole play from the moment that Lear is rejected. What will happen to Lear? Will Cordelia be able to help him? How successful will Edmund be? Can Lear and Cordelia be saved at the end by Edmund's dying words? All these questions are raised as the action proceeds.

2. *Surprise:* the occurrence of the unexpected; *e.g.*, Edgar's donning of a beggar's disguise; the frightening of the Fool by Poor Tom in the hovel; the sudden quarrel between Kent and Oswald.

3. *Coincidence:* the occurrence of events without apparent causal connection; *e.g.*, the meeting of Lear and Poor Tom on the heath; the arrival of Cornwall and Regan at Gloucester's palace, and the arrival, at almost the same time, of Lear; the meeting of blind Gloucester and Edgar on the heath.

4. *Contrast:* the juxtaposition of opposites; *e.g.*, within Lear himself; between characters; *e.g.*, Edmund and Edgar, and Albany and Cornwall; in atmosphere; *e.g.*, between Act III, Scene 2 and Act III, Scene 4.

5. *Parallelism:* here, the fact that two characters find themselves in similar situations; *e.g.*, Gloucester and Lear, and Edgar and Cordelia.

6. *Nemesis:* the principle of retributive justice; *e.g.*, the deaths of Cornwall, Regan, Goneril, and Edmund.

7. *Foreshadowing of events:* a premonitory warning of what may happen; *e.g.*, Lear says, "O, let me not be mad, not mad, sweet heaven!"

8. *Irony:* the juxtaposition of incongruous elements; *e.g.*,

Lear regally dressed at the beginning and in "fantastic garlands" in his madness.

9. *Dramatic irony:* the effect produced when a speech or situation has one meaning for the actor and an inner or opposite one for the audience. In the first scene, Lear hopes to end his days "unburdened", and later says tartly to Cordelia, "Nothing will come of nothing".

10. *Pathos:* that which excites pity; *e.g.*, the plight of Edgar, the sufferings of Gloucester and Lear, and the sight of the dead Cordelia.

11. *Humour:* a) word play; *e.g.*, the Fool's use of the word "crown" (I. iv. 154-62).

    b) nimble repartee; *e.g.*, the exchanges between Kent and Oswald in Act II, Scene 2.

    c) satire (the use of irony or ridicule to expose or discourage vice or folly); *e.g.*, The character of Oswald seems a satire on undesirable qualities in a servant. In a special sense, the Fool provides a running satire of Lear's folly.

CRITICS' COMMENTS

I   THE OPENING MOVEMENT OF *King Lear*

1. The First Scene of *King Lear*

The scene in which Lear divides his kingdom is a magnificent statement of a magnificent theme. It has a proper formality, and there is a certain megalithic grandeur about it, Lear dominating it, that we associate with Greek tragedy. Its probabilities are neither here nor there. A dramatist may postulate any situation he has the means to interpret, if he will abide by the logic of it after. The producer should observe and even see stressed the scene's characteristics; Lear's two or three passages of such an eloquence as we rather expect at a play's climax than its opening, the strength of such single lines as

The bow is bent and drawn, make from the shaft. (I. i. 145)

with its hammering monosyllables; and the hard-bitten

Nothing. I have sworn, I am firm. (I. i. 248)

together with the loosening of the tension in changes to rhymed couplets, and the final drop into prose by that businesslike couple, Goneril and Regan. Then follows, with a lift into lively verse for a start, as a contrast and as the right medium for Edmund's sanguine conceit, the development of the Gloucester theme. Shakespeare does this at his ease, allows himself diversion and time. He has now both the plot of the ungrateful daughters and the subplot of the treacherous son under way.[1]

2. Lear's Passion as a Disruptive Force

Both aspects of Lear's position, the personal and the social, contribute to the unity of a tragedy whose various stages correspond, in the external action, to a closely knit development. The first stage in this development, occupying roughly the first two acts, is concerned with the entry of uncontrolled passion as a disruptive force into Lear's mind and with the consequent overthrow of ordered balance in himself, in his family, and in the state of whose unity he has been hitherto the royal guardian. In the second stage, which covers the central part of the play, personal disorder finds in the tempest to which the protagonists are exposed a symbol which at once reflects and transcends it; the elements at war, besides corresponding to the conflict in

[1]H. Granville-Barker, *Prefaces to Shakespeare* (Cambridge, Cambridge University Press, 1946).

Lear's distraught person, act through the intense suffering which they impose upon him with the force of a self-revelation to become the necessary prelude to rebirth. That rebirth, however, although achieved in the personal order during the third and final stage, cannot affect Lear's external fortunes. His reconciliation with Cordelia is followed almost immediately by their final defeat and death against a background of almost unrelieved disaster; the personal and social themes, hitherto so closely united, now separate to produce the concluding catastrophe, and the tragedy, after touching unprecedented heights in its treatment of the personal theme, is rounded off in a mood of Stoic acceptance.

The first stage in an understanding of *King Lear* is a proper interpretation of the opening scene. When Cordelia, in answer to her father's implied request for flattery, follows up her uncompromising "Nothing" with the equally direct assertion:

> I love your majesty
> According to my bond; nor more nor less,

she introduces the central conception of the whole play. The "bond" to which she refers is, of course, far more than a legal obligation. Lear's fatherhood bears a "symbolic" value similar to that of Duncan's kingship in *Macbeth*. The family, like the Scottish state, is a "symbol" of ordered living. The authority of the father is balanced by the love of his children, and their devotion aspires normally to the grace of his benediction, just as Macbeth's loyalty in the early stages of his career is rewarded by Duncan's bounty.[1]

3. The Unleashing of Lear's Violent Passion After Cordelia's Action

Lear's pilgrimage commences true to a pattern now familiar. A man is wounded to the quick—not an ordinary man, but for

[1] D. A. Traversi, *An Approach to Shakespeare* (London, Sands & Company Ltd., 1956), pp. 182-3.

his age and time "the first of men." His estimate of himself, of his position in the state, in society, in his family, his view of man and the universe, are suddenly called in question. Gloucester's dire thoughts are in part Lear's also, as in Cordelia's action and later in Goneril's and Regan's, he sees his universe tottering. His response is not despair but violence—characteristic, as Goneril and Regan assure each other, of the rashness of old age and of a temperament never stable; but characteristic also, as the developing action of the play shows, of the initial response of the hero. His new and shattering knowledge of the irrational and the demonic forces in himself and in the world around him drives him to the edge of madness. He has moments of fearful nihilism. His curses against his daughters and his railings in the storm recall the dark and destructive mood of Job's opening curse or the frenzy of violence in which Oedipus struck out his eyes. But, like Job and Oedipus, he does not stay long in such a mood, which, even at its worst, is ennobled by his appeal to justice beyond and above the world of man. And in his time of stress new and saving qualities appear—not only his remorse but his increasing efforts toward restraint and patience (hard won from his knowledge of the disastrous effects of his own impatience) and his enlarged sympathies for the humble and the oppressed.

As the Chorus said about Oedipus, Lear is "twice-tormented," in body and mind, and his mental suffering is in itself twofold. As he sees the large consequences of his moment of rashness, he feels guilty and innocent at the same time. He is plunged into the middle of Job's problem: effect is out of all proportion to cause; justice has lost its meaning. "I am more sinned against than sinning." Like Job's, his universe has gone awry, and a recurrent theme of the scenes of his madness, or near-madness, is his longing, like Job's, for instruction. He wants to know the reason of things. "Teach me, and I will hold my peace," Job said to the Counselors. Lear in his confusion takes Edgar for a scholar, a "learned Theban," an "Athenian," one who can give him instruction:

First let me talk with this philosopher.
What is the cause of thunder?

"What is man that thou art mindful of him?" Job had asked, and Lear's questions are of the same kind, the basic and (as here) often explicit question of all tragedy, "Is man no more than this?" "Is there any cause in nature that makes these hard hearts?" Finding no answer, he would, in his fantasy, himself bring reason and justice to the world, as in his mad "arraignment" of Goneril and "anatomizing" of Regan.[1]

II   DESTRUCTION OF ORDER IN *King Lear*

4. The Importance of Order—the "Great Chain of Being"

Recent scholarship has sufficiently demonstrated the main outlines of the Elizabethan world-view which, inherited from the teachings of the medieval theologians, the tragic dramatists now ventured to put to the full test of action. For all the centrifugal, disruptive forces at work in the Renaissance, what remained deep in the imagination of western man was the sense that, in spite of appearances, there was order in the universe which should find its counterpart (and did, when society was in a healthy state) in the ordered life of man on earth. The terrestrial hierarchy was an emblem of the celestial, with king, priest, father (of the family), and master (of servants) exercising each in his area of influence a divinely sanctioned authority. In man the individual, reason was king and the passions were its subjects. Thus the father was God and King in the family, and his children were bound to him by more than filial ties of love and devotion. Below man was the world of animals and below animals the world of inanimate things. This "great chain of being" was, moreover, a sensitive affair. Disorder in any of the parts might affect the whole; weakness in any link might cause

[1] R. B. Sewall, *Vision of Tragedy* (New Haven, Yale University Press, 1962), pp. 74-75.

a vital break, even to cutting man off from God and the hope
of salvation.[1]

III ACT III OF *King Lear*

5. The Third Act of *King Lear*

The Third Act of *King Lear*, which covers the storm and its
counterpart in human behaviour, is a marvellous example of
poetic elaboration for dramatic ends. At the centre of it, at once
the main protagonist and symbol of the spiritual state of a
humanity exposed to fundamental disorder, wrenched out of its
"fixed place" in the "frame of nature," stands the figure of the
aged king. The intimate dovetailing of personal conflict with
external convulsions has often been noted, and is indeed an
essential part of the conception. The storm which has broken
out in Lear's mind, the result of his treatment at the hands of
his children, is admirably fused with the description of the
warring elements mainly entrusted to his lips; the external storm,
while exercising upon his aged physique the intolerable strain
under which it finally breaks, is itself a projection of his inner
state, beng fused with it as a single poetic reality. Thus related
to the action of the elements Lear clearly assumes a stature that
is more than purely personal, becomes man, the microcosm of
the universe, exposed to a suffering to which the frame of things
itself contributes, but which finds its acutest symbol in the intimate disunion which the earlier action has introduced into the
family bond.

The whole act is beautifully contrived around this central
situation. If Lear has himself become "unaccommodated man,"
it is clearly felt that he is unable to bear alone the whole weight
of the situation for which the tragic conception has destined
him. He is, therefore, by a superb piece of artistic tact, surrounded during his exposure to the elements by a number of
characters who serve, as it were, as the external buttresses of a

[1]Sewall, *op. cit.*, p. 69.

great architectural construction to take from him some of the strain to which he would otherwise, as a dramatic conception, be subjected. It is the presence of these buttresses in *Lear* that are the best measure of the play's success, speaking in terms of artistic conception, when compared with a play which suggests a certain partial coincidence of mood, *Timon of Athens*. Timon is too isolated in his suffering, and his denunciation of the human environment is too extensive, too generalized, to carry complete conviction. The situation of Lear is different. Although he bears throughout the storm the main weight of suffering, and although his situation is, as I have suggested, a concentration of that of man in general, he is surrounded by beings who, in varying degrees, suffer with him, and who are further used, each in his appropriate way, to illuminate some aspect of his central situation. The Fool, Kent, and Edgar bear some fraction of Lear's tragic burden, show an insight into some part of its significance; and before the act ends, he is further joined by Gloucester, whose fortunes have been from the first evidently parallel to his own. The result is an intricate and progressive dovetailing of characters and situations which leads us, step by step, further and further into an understanding of the full depth and meaning of the universal tragedy embodied in Lear's outraged fatherhood and shattered royalty.[1]

IV THE CLOSING MOVEMENT OF *King Lear*

6. The Agony of Lear

But what are we to say of the . . . conclusion of the tragedy, the "unhappy ending," as it is called, though the word "unhappy" sounds almost ironical in its weakness? Is this too a blot upon *King Lear* as a stage-play? The question is not so easily answered as might appear. Doubtless we are right when we turn with disgust from Tate's sentimental alterations, from his marriage of Edgar and Cordelia, and from that cheap moral which

[1]Traversi, *op. cit.*, pp. 191-2.

every one of Shakespeare's tragedies contradicts, "that Truth and Virtue shall at last succeed." But are we so sure that we are right when we unreservedly condemn the feeling which prompted these alterations, or at all events the feeling which beyond question comes naturally to many readers of *King Lear* who would like Tate as little as we? What they wish, though they have not always the courage to confess it even to themselves, is that the deaths of Edmund, Goneril, Regan and Gloster should be followed by the escape of Lear and Cordelia from death, and that we should be allowed to imagine the poor old King passing quietly in the home of his beloved child to the end which cannot be far off. Now, I do not dream of saying that we ought to wish this, so long as we regard *King Lear* simply as a work of poetic imagination. But if *King Lear* is to be considered strictly as a drama, or simply as we consider *Othello* it is not clear that the wish is unjustified . . . . I find that my feelings call for this "happy ending". . . .

Of course this is a heresy and all the best authority is against it. But then the best authority, it seems to me, is either influenced unconsciously by disgust at Tate's sentimentalism or unconsciously takes that wider point of view. When Lamb—there is no higher authority—writes, "A happy ending!—as if the living martyrdom that Lear had gone through, the flaying of his feelings alive, did not make a fair dismissal from the stage of life the only decorous thing for him," I answer, first, that it is precisely this *fair* dismissal which we desire for him instead of renewed anguish; and, secondly, that what we desire for him during the brief remainder of his days is not "the childish pleasure of getting his gilt robes and sceptre again," not what Tate gives him, but what Shakespeare himself might have given him—peace and happiness by Cordelia's fireside. And if I am told that he has suffered too much for this, how can I possibly believe it with these words ringing in my ears:

> Come, let's away to prison.
> We two alone will sing like birds i' the cage.

> When thou dost ask me blessing, I'll kneel down
> And ask of thee forgiveness. So we'll live,
> And pray, and sing, and tell old tales, and laugh
> At gilded butterflies, . . .

And again when Schlegel declares that, if Lear were saved, "the whole" would "lose its significance," because it would no longer show us that the belief in Providence "requires a wider range than the dark pilgrimage on earth to be established in its whole extent," I answer that, if the drama does show us that, it takes us beyond the strictly tragic point of view.[1]

7. The Final Scene of *Lear*

If to the reader, as to the bystanders, that scene brings one unbroken pain, it is not so with Lear himself. His shattered mind passes from the first transports of hope and despair, as he bends over Cordelia's body and holds the feather to her lips, into an absolute forgetfulness of the cause of these transports. This continues so long as he can converse with Kent; becomes an almost complete vacancy; and is disturbed only to yield, as his eyes suddenly fall again on his child's corpse, to an agony which at once breaks his heart. And, finally, though he is killed by an agony of pain, the agony in which he actually dies is one not of pain but of ecstasy. Suddenly, with a cry represented in the oldest text by a four-times repeated 'O', he exclaims:

> Do you see this? Look on her, look, her lips,
> Look there, look there!

These are the last words of Lear. He is sure, at last, that she *lives*: and what had he said when he was still in doubt?

> She lives! if it be so,
> It is a chance which does redeem all sorrows
> That ever I have felt!

[1]A. C. Bradley, *Shakespearean Tragedy* (New York, St. Martin's Press, Inc.; Toronto, The Macmillan Company of Canada Ltd.; London, Macmillan & Co. Ltd., 1958), pp. 205-8.

To us, perhaps, the knowledge that he is deceived may bring a culmination of pain: but, if it brings *only* that, I believe we are false to Shakespeare, and it seems almost beyond question that any actor is false to the text who does not attempt to express, in Lear's last accents and gestures and look, an unbearable *joy*.

To dwell on the pathos of Lear's last speech would be an impertinence, but I may add a remark on the speech from the literary point of view. In the simplicity of its language, which consists almost wholly of monosyllables of native origin, composed in very brief sentences of the plainest structure, it presents an extraordinary contrast to the dying speech of Hamlet and the last words of Othello to the bystanders. The fact that Lear speaks in passion is one cause of the difference, but not the sole cause. The language is more than simple, it is familiar. And this familiarity is characteristic of Lear (except at certain moments, already referred to) from the time of his madness onwards, and is the source of the peculiarly poignant effect of some of his sentences (such as 'The little dogs and all . . .'). We feel in them the loss of power to sustain his royal dignity; we feel also that everything external has become nothingness to him, and that what remains is 'the thing itself', the soul in its bare greatness. Hence also it is that two lines in this last speech show, better perhaps than any other passage of poetry, one of the qualities we have in mind when we distinguish poetry as 'romantic'. Nothing like Hamlet's mysterious sigh 'The rest is silence', nothing like Othello's memories of his life of marvel and achievement, was possible to Lear. Those last thoughts are romantic in their strangeness: Lear's five-times repeated 'Never', in which the simplest and most unanswerable cry of anguish rises note by note till the heart breaks, is romantic in its naturalism; and to make a verse out of this one word required the boldness as well as the inspiration which came infallibly to Shakespeare at the greatest moments. But the familiarity, boldness and inspiration are surpassed (if that can be) by the next line, which shows the bodily oppression asking for bodily relief. The imagination that produced Lear's curse or his defiance of the storm may be paralleled in its kind, but where else are we to seek the imagination that could venture to follow that cry of 'Never' with such a phrase as 'undo this button', and yet could leave us on the topmost peaks of poetry?[1]

8. No Mitigation in the Final Scene of *Lear*

But it was fated that Lear learn too late. Fatefully free, Lear was free to choose his own fate. He became by that action freely fated, and fate must run its course. The peace and harmony of the reconciliation were real but momentary. Nothing saves him —not his own hard-won self-knowledge and humility or Cordelia's richer humanity and more expressive love or Gloucester's regeneration or Edgar's bravery or even Edmund's last-minute repentance. The repeated mischances of the last act seem, like Job's misfortunes, systematic. Edmund repented too late. His message revoking Cordelia's execution arrived too late. Lear slew her executioner, but too late to save her life. There is nothing Christian in Lear's response to this awful fact, and the heaven he invokes as he carries her in is deaf indeed:

> Howl, howl, howl, howl! O, you are men of stones!
> Had I your tongues and eyes, I'd use them so
> That heaven's vault should crack. She's gone for ever.
> I know when one is dead, and when one lives.
> She's dead as earth.

No wonder Edgar sees in the scene a world where time and chance happeneth to all, deserving and undeserving alike.

Although some have pointed to the redeeming fact that Lear seems to die in an ecstasy of love and hope in his moment of fancy that Cordelia is still alive, the final scene hardly affords such comfort. Nor does the scene say anything about a reunion of father and daughter in a Christian heaven. It says much about loss, decay, suffering, and endurance. "The wonder is," says

[1]Bradley, *op. cit.,* pp. 241-3.

Kent, "he hath endur'd so long." "The oldest," concludes Edgar,

> . . . hath borne most; we that are young
> Shall never see so much, nor live so long.

It says nothing about salvation, only a wan restoration, after great loss, of a kind of order. The kingdom has, in a sense, been purged—even, indirectly, by Lear, whose defiance of his daughters precipitated the crisis, brought Cordelia back, kept the dialectic of action going and the future still open to possibility. It is not that the "forces for good" triumph over the "forces for evil." Practically speaking, no one triumphs. Lear, Gloucester, and Cordelia die, and they are as dead as Goneril, Regan, and Edmund. Kent sees his own death near. The monstrous and the bestial, the petty and the weak in man have taken a fearful toll, and with these qualities a perverse fate has worked in seeming conspiracy. The play suggests no adequate compensation; there is no discharge in that war, except in death, which, as Edgar pleads for Lear, means only a cessation of pain.[1]

9. Tragedy Arises from Human Actions

A Shakespearean tragedy . . . may be called a story of exceptional calamity leading to the death of a man in high estate. But it is clearly much more than this, and we have now to regard it from another side. No amount of calamity which merely befell a man, descending from the clouds like lightning, or stealing from the darkness like pestilence, could alone provide the substance of its story. Job was the greatest of all the children of the east, and his afflictions were well-nigh more than he could bear; but even if we imagined them wearing him to death, that would not make his story tragic. Nor yet would it become so, in the Shakespearean sense, if the fire, and the great wind from the wilderness, and the torments of his flesh were conceived as sent by a supernatural power, whether just or malignant. The

[1]Sewall, *op. cit.*, pp. 77-78.

calamities of tragedy do not simply happen, nor are they sent; they proceed mainly from actions, and those the actions of men.

We see a number of human beings placed in certain circumstances; and we see, arising from the co-operation of their characters in these circumstances, certain actions. These actions beget others, and these others beget others again, until this series of inter-connected deeds leads by an apparently inevitable sequence to a catastrophe. The effect of such a series on imagination is to make us regard the sufferings which accompany it, and the catastrophe in which it ends, not only or chiefly as something which happens to the persons concerned, but equally as something which is caused by them. This at least may be said of the principal persons, and, among them, of the hero, who always contributes in some measure to the disaster in which he perishes.

This second aspect of tragedy evidently differs greatly from the first. Men, from this point of view, appear to us primarily as agents, 'themselves the authors of their proper woe'; and our fear and pity, though they will not cease or diminish, will be modified accordingly. We are now to consider this second aspect, remembering that it too is only one aspect, and additional to the first, not a substitute for it.

The 'story' or 'action' of a Shakespearean tragedy does not consist, of course, solely of human actions or deeds; but the deeds are the predominant factor. And these deeds are, for the most part, actions in the full sense of the word; not things done ' 'tween asleep and wake', but acts or omissions thoroughly expressive of the doer,—characteristic deeds. The centre of the tragedy, therefore, may be said with equal truth to lie in action issuing from character, or in character issuing in action.

Shakespeare's main interest lay here. To say that it lay in *mere* character, or was a psychological interest, would be a great mistake, for he was dramatic to the tips of his fingers. It is possible to find places where he has given a certain indulgence to his love of poetry, and even to his turn for general reflections; but it would be very difficult, and in his later tragedies perhaps impossible, to detect passages where he has allowed such freedom to the interest in character apart from action. But for the opposite extreme, for the abstraction of mere 'plot' (which is a very different thing from the tragic 'action'), for the kind of interest which predominates in a novel like *The Woman in White*, it is clear that he cared even less. I do not mean that this interest is absent from his dramas; but it is subordinate to others, and is so interwoven with them that we are rarely conscious of it apart, and rarely feel in any great strength the half-intellectual, half-nervous excitement of following an ingenious complication. What we do feel strongly, as a tragedy advances to its close, is that the calamities and catastrophe follow inevitably from the deeds of men, and that the main source of these deeds is character.[1]

10. The Character of Lear as a Tragic Hero

Lear himself is a complex of primitive and civilized elements: he is a selfish, high-tempered, autocratic old man. He is wrong-headed without being vicious. He deceives himself. He swerves from sentiment to cruelty: neither are real. He has in fact "ever but slenderly known himself" (I. i. 296-7). Then comes his purgatory, in the shape of a return to nature, a knowledge of his animal kinship, a wide and sweeping sympathy, a tempestuous mental torment on the tempest-riven heath. In madness thoughts deep-buried come to the surface: though at first he acts his futile desire for revenge in his mock-trial, later a finer lunatic apprehension glimpses profound human truths. His thoughts fix on the sex-inhibitions of civilized man, delving into the truth of man's civilized ascent. He finds sex to be a pivot-force in human affairs, sugared though it be by convention. All human civilization and justice are a mockery. He is all the time working deep into that which is real, in him or others, facing truth, though it be hideous. He has been forced from a deceiving consciousness

[1]Bradley, *op. cit.*, pp. 6-7.

built of self-deception, sentiment, the tinsel of kingship and authority, to the knowledge of his own and others' nature. His courtiers lied to him, since he is not ague-proof (IV. vi. 106-7). He wins his purgatorial reward in finding that which is most real to him, his love for Cordelia. For the first time he compasses his own reality, and its signs are humility and love. He falls back on the simplicity of love: next of death. His purgatory then closes. This is the movement from civilization, through a return to nature and a revulsion from civilized man to death, which is later massively reconstructed in *Timon of Athens*.[1]

11. Tragedy in *Lear* Springs From Human Relationships

In *King Lear* the wheel comes full circle. The world of it is shorn of all its acquired circumstance and most of its cultural trappings. The tragic situation, though it enmeshes a king, is not the outcome of a social order even so far developed as to have organised a simple monarchical system. The tragedy of it springs from the simplest and the primary social entity, the family, and from the human relationship which is the absolute beginning of all and every human society, parenthood, the relation of father to child and of child to father. Like the setting and the circumstance, the people of *King Lear* mark the backward reaches of symbolic human time. Man is near indeed to the animal, sometimes in sheer simplicity of innocence, but more often in worse than animal bestiality, his intellectual sense serving only as craft to add a finer edge to his cruelty. With such people as its persons, and parentage as its sole plot, *King Lear* bares the tragedy of human life to absolute simplicity and to almost absolute universality.[2]

[1]G. Wilson Knight, *The Wheel of Fire* (London, Methuen & Co. Ltd., 1960), pp. 200-1.

[2]H. B. Charlton, *Shakespearean Tragedy* (Cambridge, Cambridge University Press, 1948), p. 14.

V THE PRIMITIVE WORLD OF *King Lear*

12. The Simplicity of the Theme of *Lear*

As the heavens and the earth of it, as its men and its women, so is the theme of *King Lear*. It is resolved into elemental simplicity. Its plot is a simple domestic circumstance; and of all such circumstances, the most intimately personal, the breaking of the bond between parent and child. Such an episode is within the imaginative capacity of all mankind; and the emotions which it will excite are within the range of common experience. The particular plot grows easily into a more general theme of equal simplicity: life assaulted by the impact of sheer evil. So by its very simplification, *King Lear* universalises the tragedy which it represents. It involves all humanity in the tragic conflict of life. It achieves this largely by the prevailing primitiveness of its realm and the inhabitants of it. It maintains as its persistent impression a sense of the nearness of man and beast. In one family and of one blood, man and beast are born; Cordelia is own sister to Goneril; Edmund is half-brother to Edgar. But the nearness is even more intimate; in the single state of man, beast and human dwell intermittently together. That is, of course, a mere truism. Shakespeare gives it vital and urgent reality. In his scenes, human nature is palpably a part of nature. The line dividing man from beast is a tenuous thread, and common to both in these elemental conditions are all the impulses of appetite and all passions of the blood. The thin dividing line, however, is the consciousness within man of his human nature. This sense in him of human kindness, recognisable in divergent urgings towards gratifications refining on or transcending the mere satisfaction of appetite, is beginning to flower as a sentiment of human kindliness, and so it is establishing a simple moral ideal of 'man-ness' or virtue. But even as he is growing to this self-consciousness of his human kindness, man does not discard his natural attributes: they lurk within him, ready to break through whenever the constraint of his human kindliness relaxes. Hence the fragility of man; the beast is strong within him, more

violent, more thrustful than the frail and faint promptings of
his humanity. But at least the beast is becoming clearly recog-
nised as the beast. What *King Lear* throws into such impressive
prominence is the ever-present sense of the universality of evil
and of its power; of its dwelling amongst men and within man;
of the plight of poor naked mortals under its onslaught; of the
vast and expensive ravages which it makes on life; of the hard-
ness of the conflict to repel it, the pain and the suffering entailed,
and the apparent uncertainty of victory. In no other play is evil
made so human; in no other play are there humans so evil.[1]

13. The Primitive World of *King Lear*

King Lear's is a church-less and a priest-less world. Its political
organisation is a simple scheme of monarchy wherein the
king's authority is uncontrolled and unlimited in its absoluteness.
A robed man of justice may appear sporadically, but he is a
mere appendage of the regal household and an interpreter of
the royal will. The few geographical and historical references
would help the Elizabethans to thrust Lear's world backwards
into the remote past. It belongs to the age of the barbarous
Scythians and of others who made their generation messes to
gorge their appetite. Its accredited wise men are Thebans; its
more gorgeously dressed are apers of Persian fashions in their
attire. It lived its life in days long before the mythical Merlin
prophesied, and at a time when Albion was not a literary
archaism for England but its regular everyday name. Its material
furniture is of the sparsest, a bare minimum for the maintenance
of life and government. Its people are courtiers, warriors,
farmers and fishermen; and its instruments and arts are as
primitive as its needs. Government has its prisons, its halters,
its whips, its stocks and, more widely, its arms. Its subject, man,
has his house or his hovel, his clothes and his food. There are
tailors and stone-masons; there are sheep-cotes, mills and pin-

[1]Charlton, *op. cit.*, pp. 226-7.

folds, pins and pricks and red-burning spits,—and of all of it one remembers a mere button better than anything else. In such a primitive society, even houses are but solid tents wherein to eat, to sleep and to take shelter from wind and cold and rain, to seek cover from the pelting of the pitiless storm. A larger house may pile itself into a steeple, and thereby have a means of throwing up a weathercock, for with this as a kind of radar prognostication, man may know and counter the powers which are the real stuff and furniture of his universe, the wind, the cold, the rain and the storm. The least enviable of mortals is he with houseless head and unfed sides.[1]

14. Good and Evil in *King Lear*

For the truth is, or so it seems to me, that in this play Shakespeare is little enough concerned with strict dramatic plot or with character in the ordinary sense. He is, above all, concerned to exhibit certain moral ideas or states, imaginatively apprehended indeed, yet still ideas of evil and of good. His imagination sifts out these essences. To Evil he gives the initiative, the force, the driving power of the plot. Over against it he sets Good; but he forbids it, so far as he may, to interfere with and control the action and consequences of Evil; it is made silent and patient; it is suffering love; it has little influence upon the executive ordering of the world; it merely *is* and suffers; it is not what it does but what it is, as it is shown in a Cordelia and an Edgar, that we contemplate. Evil drives on, dynamic and masterful, but to its own destruction; Good is still, patient, and enduring, but is also destroyed; no limit, not even that of death, is put to what it must endure.[2]

15. Lear's Preoccupation With Justice

This question of human justice is, indeed, part of the wider

[1]Charlton, *op. cit.*, pp. 218-19.
[2]D. G. James, *The Dream of Learning* (Oxford, The Clarendon Press, 1951).

question: that of universal justice. In the *Lear* universe we see humanity working at cross-purposes, judging, condemning, pitying, helping each other. They are crude justicers: Lear, unjust himself, first cries for human justice, then curses it. But he also cries for heavenly justice: so, too, others here cry out for heavenly justice. Their own rough ideas of equity force them to impose on the universal scheme a similar judicial mode. We, who watch, who view their own childish attempts, are not surprised that "the gods" show little sign of a corresponding sense. According to human standards things happen here unjustly. The heavens do not send down to take Lear's part; his curses on Goneril and Regan have no effect. The winds will not peace at his bidding. Common servants demanded that Heaven shall assert its powers:

SEC. SERVANT. I'll never care what wickedness I do . . .
Women will all turn monsters. (III. vii. 116-17)

So, too, Albany cries that if "the heavens" do not quickly "send down their visible spirits" to avenge the offences of man humanity will prey on itself like sea-monsters (IV. ii. 56). And when he hears of the servant's direct requital of Gloucester's wrong by the slaying of Cornwall, he takes it as proof of divine justice:

This shows you are above,
You justicers, that these our nether crimes
So speedily can venge.   (IV. ii. 89-91)

And again:

This judgment of the Heavens, that makes us tremble,
Touches us not with pity.   (V. iii. 276-7)

But there is no apparent justification of the thought: men here are good or bad in and by themselves. Goodness and cruelty flower naturally, spontaneously. A common servant instinctively lays down his life for an ideal, because goodness is part of his nature; in another, his nature may prompt him to wrong—so the captain promises to obey Edmund's dastardly command with these words:

> I cannot draw a cart, nor eat dried oats.
> If it be man's work, I'll do't.   (V. iii. 43)

His nature as a man, his station in life as a soldier, both seem to point him to obedience: again the emphasis is on nature and there is again the suggestion, percurrent in *King Lear*, of animals and country life. The story of the play indeed suggests that wrongful action first starts the spreading poison of evil; and that sin brings inevitable retribution.[1]

16. Emotional Effect Through Repetition and Echoing

The tragedy lies in the opposition between paternal love and filial ingratitude, and in the contrast between the old King's thoughts of the two whom he has cherished and of the one whom he has cast off. His casting her off and his yearning for her are not psychologically reconciled, as by vanity and anger they might have been, turning baffled love to hate. That would have greatly alienated the spectators' sympathy; as would a predisposition to jealousy in Othello, or a deranged or enfeebled spirit in Hamlet, or mere ambition in Macbeth. And his love and the memory of the injury she has done him (or he has done her), having, like Othello's love and jealous hatred for Desdemona, *not* sprung from one root, as in a veritable human bosom, or in Racine or Ibsen, they would have, do not contend or struggle but are simply opposed. So they keep to the end; where, save in the Venetian tragedy, is presented the extremest case of irony in Shakespeare. There, however, it is better realized—

> Cold, cold, my girl,
> Even like thy chastity!

[1] Knight, *op. cit.*, pp. 193-4.

Moreover, the dramatist's concern for emotional effect again asserts itself, though at the expense of character; and is heightened by the aid of the artifices of music. The violence and variety of the passions call for a greater violence and variety of expression; and the orchestration that Mr. Granville-Barker analyses is particularly fine and imposing. The device of repetition and echoing that we have found in the other great plays here takes a different form. The King's ravings, the Fool's babblings, and Gloster's murmurings offer continual opportunities to recall the errors and griefs of the past, one's own and others', new and old. In his feigned madness Edgar, as he whines,

> Through the sharp hawthorn blows the cold wind.
> (III. iv. 47)

and, after an interval,

> Still through the hawthorn blows the cold wind.
> (III. iv. 102)

is far better than any possible stage wind and tree. And instead of the spaced recurrence of a *leitmotiv*, as here, and in *Othello* and *Macbeth*, there is frequently also, in Lear's outcries, an immediate, hammering reiteration; as in

> Oh, let me not be mad, not mad, sweet Heaven!
> Keep me in temper. I would not be mad! (I. v. 50-51)

> Hear, Nature, hear! dear goddess, hear! (I. iv. 297)

> Howl, howl, howl, howl! Oh, you are men of stones.
> (V. iii. 257)

> Thou'lt come no more,
> Never, never, never, never, never!   (V. iii. 307-8)

And that is in keeping with the Titanic vehemence and impulsiveness of the play. Now though in this there is not necessarily any damage to character, certainly in the King's volcanic curses, apostrophes, and ravings the representative or mimetic function of dramatic art falls into abeyance; and at similar cost, but still greater profit, emotional effect is attained in the dénouement. There, indeed, the musical method is less apparent than in the *finale* of *Othello* or *Macbeth*. Lear and Cordelia have entered as captives and been sent to prison—to death, as the Queen (like the audience) expects, but, as the broken King imagines, only to the henceforth uninterrupted happiness of her company. At this point, if ever, in the fitness and the fullness of his speeches—

No, no, no, no! Come, let's away to prison. (V. iii. 8)
and

Upon such sacrifices, my Cordelia, . . . (V. iii. 20)

drama and lyric meet and merge. Speeches to be spoken, they are all but to be sung.[1]

17. Reinforcement of the Action of *King Lear*

But, in *Lear*, in addition to such minor figures as Curan, two or three Gentlemen and Cornwall's servants, we have Kent, the Fool, Edgar and Albany—all of whom, in various ways, comment on the action and both reinforce and expand its implications. Even Lear himself in his madness—and at this point Shakespeare uses to the fullest possible extent the resources of the Elizabethan stage convention of presenting mad scenes—even Lear himself acts as a chorus to his own situation, and in the fourth act, his madness giving him an extra personality, he comments with desperate irony on the general evil and injustice which for the moment are more universal than the particular evil and injustice that have driven him insane.

Every cruelty in the action is re-inforced. There is not one evil daughter, there are two; in the scene of the blinding of Gloucester, Regan invariably presses her husband's violence as far as possible by adding to it—it is she, for example, who, immediately after one of Gloucester's eyes is put out, eagerly urges

[1]E. E. Stoll, *Art and Artifice in Shakespeare* (Cambridge, Cambridge University Press, 1962), pp. 140-2.

Cornwall to put out the other. In what is, as far as tragic terror is concerned, the climactic scene of the play, the scene in which the blind Gloucester meets the crazed Lear, Lear *rubs in* (there are no other words for it) his mad, cruel mockery of Gloucester's blindness:

> GLO.:   Dost thou know me? . . .
> LEAR: I remember thine eyes well enough. Dost thou squiny at me? No, do thy worst, blind cupid, I'll not love. Read thou this challenge, mark by the penning on't.
> GLO.: Were all the letters suns, I could not see one.
>   (IV. vi. 151-5)

No wonder that the feelings of the audience have to be relieved by Edgar's aside:

> I would not take this from report. It is,
> And my heart breaks at it.

And there is the final overwhelming re-inforcement of cruelty in the death of Cordelia; when all the villains are destroyed, and everything seems to be settled, Lear suddenly enters "with Cordelia dead in his arms."

"If my sensations could add anything to the general suffrage," said Dr. Johnson, "I might relate, that I was many years ago so shocked by Cordelia's death, that I know not whether I ever endured to read again the last scenes of the play till I undertook to revise them as an editor."[1]

---

[1]T. Spencer, *Shakespeare and the Nature of Man* (New York, The Macmillan Co., 1938).

KING LEAR

DRAMATIS PERSONAE

LEAR, *King of Britain.*
KING OF FRANCE.
DUKE OF BURGUNDY.
DUKE OF CORNWALL, *Regan's husband.*
DUKE OF ALBANY, *Goneril's husband.*
EARL OF KENT.
EARL OF GLOUCESTER.
EDGAR, *Gloucester's son.*
EDMUND, *Gloucester's bastard son.*
CURAN, *a courtier.*
OLD MAN, *Gloucester's tenant.*
DOCTOR.
THE FOOL.
OSWALD, *Goneril's steward.*
A Captain in Edmund's employ.
GENTLEMEN.
A HERALD.
Servants of Cornwall.
GONERIL,
REGAN,   } *Lear's daughters.*
CORDELIA,

Knights in Lear's service, Officers, Messengers, Soldiers, Attendants.

SCENE: *Britain.*

1   **affected:** favoured.
2   **Albany:** an old name for Scotland.
5-6   **qualities:** F1 reading; Q1 reads *equalities*. The mental and moral qualities of the Dukes are so evenly balanced, one against the other, that no difference can be observed between their shares of the Kingdom; **curiosity:** careful scrutiny; **moiety:** share; cf. *moitié* (Fr.).
8   **His breeding . . . charge:** I am responsible for his birth. Edmund does not hear this conversation. Why?
9   **acknowledge him:** recognize him as my son, though he is illegitimate.
10   **brazed:** hardened, accustomed; literally, plated with brass. Consider our modern slang term *brassy*, or the word *brazen*.
11   **conceive:** understand; a slightly indelicate pun.
15   **smell:** detect.
16   **issue:** offspring, child, son.
17   **proper:** handsome.
18-19   **by order of law:** legitimate; **some year elder:** about a year older (than Edmund).
20   **knave:** boy. Here, the word has the connotation of *fellow*, and is playfully affectionate; **something:** somewhat, rather; **saucily:** boldly.
21   **fair:** beautiful.
22   **whoreson:** literally, son of a whore; rascal.
27   **My services . . . lordship:** equivalent to: I am at your service, sir.
28   **sue:** beg, desire greatly.

ACT I

Scene 1

INSIDE LEAR'S PALACE.

Enter Kent, Gloucester, and Edmund, in rear.

Kent. I thought the King had more affected the Duke of Albany than Cornwall.

Gloucester. It did always seem so to us; but now, in the division of the kingdom, it appears not which of the Dukes he values most, for qualities are so weighed that curi- 5 osity in neither can make choice of either's moiety.

Kent. Is not this your son, my lord?

Gloucester. His breeding, sir, hath been at my charge. I have so often blushed to acknowledge him that now I am brazed to it. 10

Kent. I cannot conceive you.

Gloucester. Sir, this young fellow's mother could, where-upon she grew round-wombed, and had indeed, sir, a son for her cradle ere she had a husband for her bed. Do you smell a fault? 15

Kent. I cannot wish the fault undone, the issue of it being so proper.

Gloucester. But I have a son, sir, by order of law, some year elder than this, who yet is no dearer in my account. Though this knave came something saucily to the world before 20 he was sent for, yet was his mother fair, there was good sport at his making, and the whoreson must be acknowl-edged.—Do you know this noble gentleman, Edmund?

Edmund (advancing). No, my lord.

Gloucester. My Lord of Kent: remember him hereafter as 25 my honourable friend.

Edmund. My services to your lordship.

Kent. I must love you, and sue to know you better.

29 **I shall study deserving:** I shall make every effort to be worthy of your interest in me.

30 **out:** away, abroad, probably in military service.

31 S.D. **sennet:** trumpet call, probably of seven notes, used to announce the coming of a group of important persons. This is Lear's household call. It differs from a *flourish* in being less decorative. See S.D., line 204.

32 S.D. **coronet:** small crown, used to designate rank lower than that of a king, intended to be given to Cordelia as the sign of her authority. See line 147.

33 **attend:** wait upon, be of assistance to; a royal command.

35 **shall:** Modern English requires *will*. The use of "shall" in this line suggests only futurity, since the servant dedicated to service cannot have any will in matters of obedience; he must obey willy-nilly.

36 **we:** the "royal" plural. Lear speaks officially as King; **darker purpose:** obscurer, more secret intention; the intention that, up to this point, is not clearly explained.

37 **know:** be informed that; take notice that; observe that.

38 **fast intent:** fixed purpose, firm intention.

41 **crawl:** move slowly, a reference to the slowness of age rather than to weakness or feebleness; **son:** son-in-law.

43 **constant will:** See "fast intent", line 38; **publish:** make public, make known to all.

44 **several dowers:** separate endowments, gifts, bequests; separate portions of the Kingdom.

45 **prevented:** forestalled, stopped before it (strife) starts.

47 **rivals:** contestants.

48 **amorous sojourn:** time spent in Lear's Kingdom for the purpose of finding a wife; *i.e.*, Cordelia.

53 **largest bounty:** greatest reward, dower.

54 **where nature . . . challenge:** to the daughter whose merit may, in addition to my natural affection (nature), claim (make challenge for) the greatest share of my Kingdom.

56-57 **than word . . . matter:** than words can possibly express.

58 **space:** freedom to move about at will; **liberty:** personal freedom, freedom to think and speak as one would desire.

59 **what:** whatever, anything that.

60 **grace:** favour with other persons, popularity.

61 **found:** *i.e.*, in a child.

Edmund. Sir, I shall study deserving.

Gloucester. He hath been out nine years, and away he shall 30
again. *Sound a sennet.*
The King is coming.
> *Enter one bearing a coronet, King Lear, Cornwall,*
> *Albany, Goneril, Regan, Cordelia, and Attendants.*

Lear. Attend the lords of France and Burgundy,
Gloucester.

Gloucester. I shall, my lord. 35
> *Exeunt Gloucester and Edmund.*

Lear. Meantime we shall express our darker purpose.
Give me the map there. Know that we have divided
In three our kingdom, and 'tis our fast intent
To shake all cares and business from our age,
Conferring them on younger strengths while we 40
Unburdened crawl toward death. Our son of Cornwall,
And you, our no less loving son of Albany,
We have this hour a constant will to publish
Our daughters' several dowers, that future strife
May be prevented now. The princes, France and Bur- 45
gundy,
Great rivals in our youngest daughter's love,
Long in our court have made their amorous sojourn,
And here are to be answered. Tell me, my daughters
(Since now we will divest us both of rule, 50
Interest of territory, cares of state),
Which of you shall we say doth love us most?
That we our largest bounty may extend
Where nature doth with merit challenge. Goneril,
Our eldest-born, speak first. 55

Goneril. Sir, I love you more than word can wield the
matter;
Dearer than eyesight, space, and liberty;
Beyond what can be valued, rich or rare;
No less than life, with grace, health, beauty, honour; 60
As much as child e'er loved, or father found;

62   **a love . . . unable:** a love that takes all of one's breath to express, and is beyond speech or expression.

63   **Beyond all . . . you:** I love you past any kind of comparison that may be made.

66   **of all . . . this:** Lear points to areas on a map. Evidently, these areas have been decided on beforehand, and Lear's actions are mere ceremony. To whom does he intend to give the largest part of his Kingdom?

67   **champaigns riched:** fertile fields.

68   **wide-skirted meads:** abundant pastures.

69   **to thine . . . issues:** to children from your marriage to Albany.

70   **perpetual:** in absolute possession forever.

73   **self metal:** same material, stuff, substance.

74   **and prize . . . worth:** value myself the same as my sister.

75   **my very . . . love:** my love exactly. My love is exactly the same as hers.

76-78   **Only she . . . possesses:** These lines may be paraphrased as follows: But she falls short of its proper expression, in that she has not stated what I must assert (profess) that there are no other joys that the most sensitive judgement can recognize to compare with the joy of loving you.

79   **felicitate:** *felix* (Lat.), happy; here, *made happy*.

80   **in your . . . love:** in the love I have for your Majesty.

83   **more ponderous . . . tongue:** My love is heavier than my words. Kittredge insists on *more richer than my tongue* (though F1 reads "ponderous") because of "poor", line 81. The double comparative was common in Elizabethan English.

86   **validity:** value, worth; **pleasure:** ability to give pleasure.

88   **least:** smallest in stature.

89   **vines . . . milk:** references to the main industries of the two regions.

90   **interested:** interested, closely concerned.

91   **more opulent:** richer, more valuable.

95   **Nothing will . . . nothing:** Latin proverb, *Ex nihilo nihil fit.*

96-97   **I am . . . mouth:** I cannot give mere lip-service to love; *i.e.*, I cannot pretend to love you more than I do.

A love that makes breath poor, and speech unable.
Beyond all manner of so much I love you.
Cordelia (*aside*). What shall Cordelia speak? Love, and 65
    be silent.
Lear. Of all these bounds, even from this line to this,
    With shadowy forests and with champaigns riched,
    With plenteous rivers and wide-skirted meads,
    We make thee lady. To thine and Albany's issues
    Be this perpetual.—What says our second daughter, 70
    Our dearest Regan, wife of Cornwall? Speak.
Regan. I am made
    Of that self metal as my sister,
    And prize me at her worth. In my true heart
    I find she names my very deed of love, 75
    Only she comes too short, that I profess
    Myself an enemy to all other joys
    Which the most precious square of sense possesses,
    And find I am alone felicitate
    In your dear Highness' love. 80
Cordelia (*aside*).   Then poor Cordelia!
    And yet not so, since I am sure my love's
    More ponderous than my tongue.
Lear.   To thee and thine hereditary ever
    Remain this ample third of our fair kingdom, 85
    No less in space, validity, and pleasure
    Than that conferred on Goneril.—Now, our joy,
    Although our last and least; to whose young love
    The vines of France and milk of Burgundy
    Strive to be interessed; what can you say to draw 90
    A third more opulent than your sisters? Speak.
Cordelia. Nothing, my lord.
Lear. Nothing?
Cordelia. Nothing.
Lear. Nothing will come of nothing. Speak again. 95
Cordelia. Unhappy that I am, I cannot heave
    My heart into my mouth. I love your Majesty

98 **according to my bond:** according to the duty of a daughter towards her father. The importance in the play of broken bonds
is obvious.

103 **right fit:** properly due, properly owing to (you).

110 **to love . . . all:** to love my father only. Cordelia suggests that
love is divisible and that since her sisters have declared that all
of their love has gone to Lear, no other love is possible for
them.

115 **dower:** See line 44.

117 **Hecate:** queen of witches, a pagan goddess.

118 **orbs:** stars.

120 **disclaim:** renounce, give up.

121 **propinquity:** nearness of relationship; *i.e.*, father to daughter;
property of blood: blood relationship, quality of your blood
from being related to me (Lear). This and the phrase above
have almost the same meaning. The point is that Lear renounces all connection with Cordelia.

123 **Scythian:** one of an ancient tribe of southern Russia, noted for
roughness and brutality.

124 **makes his generation messes:** eats his own children.

128 **Good my liege:** a common inversion of words: My good sire, or
lord.

130 **dragon:** Lear, angry, uses his own heraldic device to refer to
himself.

131-2 **to set . . . nursery:** to risk everything on the strength of re-
ceiving tender and loving care from Cordelia. "To set my rest"
was a phrase used in the card game *primero*; **avoid:** remain
out of, keep out of.

    According to my bond, no more nor less.
Lear.   How, how, Cordelia? Mend your speech a little,
    Lest you may mar your fortunes.   100
Cordelia.   Good my lord,
    You have begot me, bred me, loved me; I
    Return those duties back as are right fit,
    Obey you, love you, and most honour you.
    Why have my sisters husbands, if they say   105
    They love you all? Happily, when I shall wed,
    That lord whose hand must take my plight shall carry
    Half my love with him, half my care and duty.
    Sure I shall never marry like my sisters,
    To love my father all.   110
Lear.   But goes thy heart with this?
Cordelia.   Ay, good my lord.
Lear.   So young, and so untender?
Cordelia.   So young, my lord, and true.
Lear.   Let it be so! thy truth then be thy dower!   115
    For, by the sacred radiance of the sun,
    The mysteries of Hecate and the night;
    By all the operation of the orbs
    From whom we do exist and cease to be;
    Here I disclaim all my paternal care,   120
    Propinquity and property of blood,
    And as a stranger to my heart and me
    Hold thee from this for ever. The barbarous Scythian,
    Or he that makes his generation messes
    To gorge his appetite, shall to my bosom   125
    Be as well neighboured, pitied, and relieved,
    As thou my sometime daughter.
Kent.   Good my liege—
Lear.   Peace, Kent!
  Come not between the dragon and his wrath.   130
    I loved her most, and thought to set my rest
    On her kind nursery.—Hence and avoid my sight!—
    So be my grave my peace as here I give

134 **Call France! Who stirs:** Call the King and do it quickly. Lear is most impatient.

136 **digest:** combine, incorporate, add.

137 **Let pride . . . her:** Let her own pride, which she calls candour or plain speech, be her dowry to attract a husband.

138 **invest . . . with:** bestow upon.

139 **preëminence:** authority; **large effects:** the fine outward evidences or signs.

140 **troop:** go along with.

141 **reservation:** *i.e.,* knights especially designated or reserved for Lear.

143 **by due turn:** Each of the daughters would have Lear as a guest in proper turns.

144 **additions:** honours, titles, prerogatives; **sway:** power.

145 **revenue:** income. Accent the second syllable; **execution of the rest:** the carrying out of the remaining royal duties and responsibilities.

147 **part:** divide.

152 **make from the shaft:** Avoid the arrow. Explain the use made of the metaphor of the bow and arrow.

153 **fork:** double-pointed arrow-head, which doubtless inflicted a more painful wound than an ordinary point.

154-5 **Be Kent . . . mad:** May Kent be unmannerly when you behave like a madman. "Be" is in the subjunctive mood expressing a strong wish or prayer; **old man:** What does this term of address, directed at Lear, who is still King, indicate about Kent's temper?

156-8 **duty, power, flattery, plainness, honour's, majesty:** Each of the six words exemplifies the rhetorical device called *metonymy.* The speech means: Do you think that my sense of loyalty to you will make me afraid to speak out when you relinquish your royal power to those who flatter you? My honour compels me to speak plainly when a king begins to act foolishly.

160 **Answer my . . . judgement:** I stake my life on my judgement (that).

163 **reverb:** re-echo; **hollowness:** contains the double meaning of *insincerity* and *loudness.* ("Empty barrels make the most noise.") The fact that Cordelia said little does not mean that she is devoid of love (empty-hearted).

165 **pawn:** in chess, the least important chess-man, which can advance a player's game considerably but which is not a serious loss when removed by an opponent. The "pawn" may be used to protect the most important piece, the king, protection of the king being a prime consideration of the game.

Her father's heart from her! Call France! Who stirs?
Call Burgundy! Cornwall and Albany,   135
With my two daughters' dowers digest the third;
Let pride, which she calls plainness, marry her.
I do invest you jointly with my power,
Preëminence, and all the large effects
That troop with majesty. Ourself, by monthly course,   140
With reservation of an hundred knights
By you to be sustained, shall our abode
Make with you by due turn. Only we shall retain
The name, and all th' additions to a king. The sway,
Revenue, execution of the rest,   145
Beloved sons, be yours; which to confirm,
This coronet part between you.
Kent.   Royal Lear,
Whom I have ever honoured as my king,
Loved as my father, as my master followed,   150
As my great patron thought on in my prayers—
Lear.   The bow is bent and drawn, make from the shaft.
Kent.   Let it fall rather, though the fork invade
The region of my heart! Be Kent unmannerly
When Lear is mad. What wouldst thou do, old man?   155
Thinkest thou that duty shall have dread to speak
When power to flattery bows? To plainness honour's bound
When majesty falls to folly. Reserve thy state
And in thy best consideration check
This hideous rashness. Answer my life my judgement,   160
Thy youngest daughter does not love thee least,
Nor are those empty-hearted whose low sounds
Reverb no hollowness.
Lear.   Kent, on thy life, no more!
Kent.   My life I never held but as a pawn   165
To wage against thine enemies, nor fear to lose it,
Thy safety being motive.
Lear.   Out of my sight!
Kent.   See better, Lear, and let me still remain

170 **blank:** white spot in the centre of the target. Kent implies: Use your eyes, Lear, to see your object with absolute clarity (or, Listen to your wisest adviser).

171 **Apollo:** a Greek god, used here by an early British king who is a pagan, though not a worshipper of Hellenic deities. An unimportant historical error.

174 **miscreant:** literally, unbeliever; *i.e.,* in the god Apollo, whose name Kent takes from Lear's mouth.

175 **forbear:** Be merciful, or understanding.

176-7 **Kill thy . . . disease:** Who is the physician, and what is the disease?

180 **recreant:** traitor.

182 **that:** since, seeing that, inasmuch as.

183 **durst:** past tense of *dare*; **strained:** excessive, overstrained (referring to Kent).

184 **sentence:** decree, decision.

185 **nor . . . nor:** neither . . . nor (Elizabethan); **nature:** temperament; **place:** royal position, status as King.

186 **potency:** royal power. The phrase is an absolute construction; **reward:** punishment (ironical).

188 **disasters:** misfortunes, accidents; Q1 has *diseases*.

191 **trunk:** contemptuous expression meaning *body*, or more freely, *person*.

192 **Jupiter:** See note on Apollo, line 171.

194 **since thus:** Q1 reads *in the role of tyrant*.

196 **Freedom lives . . . here:** To keep my freedom, I must leave Britain. Since banishment means the loss of my freedom, my true banishment is here in Britain where there is no freedom.

200 **large:** noble-sounding.

201 **approve:** confirm.

204 **shape:** pursue, carry on; **his old course:** What is his course?

194-204 **Fare thee . . . new:** What reasons can you suggest for concluding this part of the scene with three rhyming couplets? For a king who is in the very act of giving up his royal authority, Lear provides in his treatment of Kent an example of how unjustly he can wield these powers. Even Albany and Cornwall, who stand to gain from Lear's decision, protest against the violence of his temper (line 175).

The true blank of thine eye.   170
Lear.   Now by Apollo—
Kent.   Now by Apollo, King,
   Thou swearest thy gods in vain.
Lear.   O vassal! miscreant!
         Reaches for his sword.
Albany, Cornwall.   Dear sir, forbear!   175
Kent.   Kill thy physician and thy fee bestow
   Upon the foul disease. Revoke thy gift,
   Or, whilst I can vent clamour from my throat,
   I'll tell thee thou dost evil.
Lear.   Hear me, recreant!   180
   On thine allegiance, hear me!
   That thou hast sought to make us break our vows,
   Which we durst never yet, and with strained pride
   To come betwixt our sentence and our power,
   Which nor our nature nor our place can bear,   185
   Our potency made good, take thy reward.
   Five days we do allot thee for provision
   To shield thee from disasters of the world,
   And on the sixth to turn thy hated back
   Upon our kingdom. If, on the tenth day following, 190
   Thy banished trunk be found in our dominions,
   The moment is thy death. Away! By Jupiter,
   This shall not be revoked.
Kent.   Fare thee well, King. Since thus thou wilt ap-
      pear,   195
   Freedom lives hence, and banishment is here.
   (*To Cordelia*).   The gods to their dear shelter take thee,
      maid,
   That justly thinkest and hast most rightly said!
   (*To Regan and Goneril*).   And your large speeches may 200
      your deeds approve,
   That good effects may spring from words of love.
   Thus Kent, O princes, bids you all adieu;
   He'll shape his old course in a country new.
                                        Exit.

204 **S.D. Flourish:** fanfare, or elaborate sounding of trumpets, to mark and honour the entry of eminent persons—in this case, an earl, a duke, and a king—into Lear's court. The fanfare is sounded by Lear's musicians. A *sennet*, on the other hand, is a warning call made on a trumpet or trumpets to precede the entry or exit of a group or procession. See line 1 and line 31.

208 **rivalled:** contended or competed for Cordelia's hand in marriage.

209 **require:** ask, request; **present:** immediate; **dower:** See line 44.

212-13 **I crave . . . less:** What has Lear already offered? **tender:** offer.

215 **dear:** with the double meaning *beloved* and *valuable*; **hold:** consider, regard, esteem.

217 **aught:** anything; **that little seeming substance:** that little creature who seems so genuine, or real, but is so false.

218 **pieced:** added.

219 **fitly like:** be to your complete liking.

221 **I know no answer:** Why is Burgundy unable to reply?

222 **infirmities:** weaknesses, defects; **owes:** has, possesses, suffers from.

223 **unfriended:** without a friend; **adopted to our hate:** accepted only as an object of my hatred.

224 **dowered with our curse:** with only my curse on her as her dowry now; **strangered:** made a stranger (to her father) by oath, or disowned by my oath. See lines 115-27.

227 **Election makes . . . conditions:** No one can choose under such unfavourable conditions. Burgundy, now understanding Lear, desires to withdraw his offer of marriage.

228-9 **by the . . . me:** I swear by whatever god made me.

230 **for:** as for; **King:** the King of France.

231 **I would . . . stray:** I would not stray so far from your friendship.

232 **to:** as to; **match you . . . hate:** to have you married to one I hate; **beseech:** I beg.

233 **to avert . . . way:** to turn your affection to some other woman. Another double comparative is used in this line.

234 **wretch:** Cordelia is now an outcast; **nature:** a recurring word in the play; here, it means the essential quality of mankind. Lear expresses a harsh sentiment in this line.

237 **whom:** F1 reading; Q1 reads *that*; F2, *who*. By modern standards, Shakespeare is occasionally ungrammatical, but his usage is correct for his time; **best object:** the object of your love.

238 **argument:** theme, constant subject; **balm:** comfort.

*Flourish. Enter Gloucester, with France and
Burgundy; Attendants.*

Gloucester.   Here's France and Burgundy, my noble lord.   205
Lear.   My Lord of Burgundy,
   We first address toward you, who with this king
   Hath rivalled for our daughter. What in the least
   Will you require in present dower with her,
   Or cease your quest of love?   210
Burgundy.   Most royal Majesty,
   I crave no more than hath your Highness offered,
   Nor will you tender less.
Lear.   Right noble Burgundy,
   When she was dear to us, we did hold her so,   215
   But now her price is fallen. Sir, there she stands.
   If aught within that little seeming substance,
   Or all of it, with our displeasure pieced,
   And nothing more, may fitly like your Grace,
   She's there, and she is yours.   220
Burgundy.   I know no answer.
Lear.   Will you, with those infirmities she owes,
   Unfriended, new adopted to our hate,
   Dowered with our curse, and strangered with our oath,
   Take her, or leave her?   225
Burgundy.   Pardon me, royal sir.
   Election makes not up in such conditions.
Lear.   Then leave her, sir; for by the power that made
      me,
   I tell you all her wealth. (*To France*). For you, great King, 230
   I would not from your love make such a stray
   To match you where I hate; therefore beseech you
   To avert your liking a more worthier way
   Than on a wretch whom nature is ashamed
   Almost to acknowledge hers.   235
France.   This is most strange,
   That she whom even but now was your best object,
   The argument of your praise, balm of your age,

239 **trice:** moment.
240-1 **dismantle so . . . favour:** strip away affection as if taking down a curtain of many folds, or as if pulling out the many folds of a garment; **sure:** certain, it is certain that.
242 **unnatural:** See line 234 above.
243 **monsters it:** makes it a monster, or something ugly and abnormal; **fore-vouched:** previously asserted or declared.
244-6 **fall into taint:** become bad, corrupted, contaminated, or spoiled; **which to . . . me:** which goes so much against reason that only a miracle could make me believe it.
248 **glib and oily art:** the art of using words easily and smoothly without meaning what is said.
251-2 **blot, murder . . . step:** the worst offences Cordelia can think of.
250-7 **that you . . . liking:** Cordelia's argument runs thus: I beg you to make quite clear to the King of France that you have not deprived me of your affection because of some monstrous crime, but that you have deprived me of my birthright because (a) I lack the cunning to seek favours constantly—for which I am the richer, actually, and (b) because I lack a flattering tongue, which I am glad I do not possess, though I am bound to add that the lack of it has cost me your love.
260 **a tardiness in nature:** natural reluctance or slowness.
261 **unspoke:** unspoken.
264-5 **mingled with . . . point:** mixed with other motives (the dowry), not connected with the main object, love.
266 **dowry:** gift.
268 **but:** just, merely, only; **that portion . . . proposed:** the original grant to be made to Cordelia.
271 **Nothing! I . . . firm:** Nothing! She shall have nothing!
274 **Peace be with Burgundy:** a formal dismissal or farewell.

The best, the dearest, should in this trice of time
Commit a thing so monstrous to dismantle   240
So many folds of favour. Sure her offense
Must be of such unnatural degree
That monsters it, or your fore-vouched affection
Fall into taint; which to believe of her
Must be a faith that reason without miracle   245
Should never plant in me.

Cordelia.   I yet beseech your Majesty
(If for I want that glib and oily art
To speak and purpose not, since what I well intend,
I'll do it before I speak), that you make known   250
It is no vicious blot, murder, or foulness,
No unchaste action or dishonoured step,
That hath deprived me of your grace and favour;
But even for want of that for which I am richer,
A still-soliciting eye, and such a tongue   255
As I am glad I have not, though not to have it
Hath lost me in your liking.

Lear.   Better thou
Hadst not been born than not to have pleased me better.

France.   Is it but this—a tardiness in nature   260
Which often leaves the history unspoke
That it intends to do? My Lord of Burgundy,
What say you to the lady? Love's not love
When it is mingled with regards that stand
Aloof from th' entire point. Will you have her?   265
She is herself a dowry.

Burgundy.   Royal King,
Give but that portion which yourself proposed,
And here I take Cordelia by the hand,
Duchess of Burgundy.   270

Lear.   Nothing! I have sworn; I am firm.

Burgundy.   I am sorry then you have so lost a father
That you must lose a husband.

Cordelia.   Peace be with Burgundy!

275 **respect and fortunes:** cold calculation and mercenary considerations. Q1 reads *respects of fortune.*

279 **most choice . . . despised:** After "choice" and "loved", add
when.

281 **be:** may it be—a petitionary assertion in the subjunctive mood.
See line 154.

283 **inflamed:** passionate; **respect:** a word used in a different sense
by Cordelia in the previous speech; here, it means *affection.*

284 **dowerless:** still another reference to Cordelia's inheritance, now
lost.

286 **waterish:** two meanings, *having many rivers* and *weak.*

287 **unprized precious:** (antithetical), unappreciated by Lear and
Burgundy, but precious to me; **of:** from.

288 **though unkind:** though they (Lear and Burgundy) are unkind.
France is generous.

289 **here . . . where:** Johnson thought that these words were nouns.
Certainly, "where" is a noun: a better place or station in life.

293 **grace:** favour; **benison:** blessing (pronounced *ben-i-zon,* to rhyme
with *gone*).

281-94 **Be it . . . Burgundy:** These lines are in couplets, each
couplet in France's speech being a statement in itself. Lear's
lines are not end-stopped. Why are these lines written in this
way?

296 **jewels:** ironical reference to Goneril and Regan as the precious
possessions of Lear; **washed:** used with double force to mean
tearful and *clear-sighted,* or *discerning.*

298 **loath:** unwilling, reluctant.

300 **professed:** which have professed (love). Accent the first syllable.

301 **stood I:** if I stood; **grace:** favour, blessing.

302 **prefer:** recommend.

304 **prescribe not us:** do not set down for us; do not dictate to us.

305 **study:** purpose, intention, endeavour.

307 **at fortune's alms:** a sarcastic and insulting phrase meaning:
when fortune (chance) was giving out charity (or, as an act of
charity from fortune); **You have obedience scanted:** You have
neglected obedience (to your father). Goneril could scarcely be
more inaccurate or more hypocritical.

308 **and well . . . wanted:** and well deserve the lack of affection
from your husband that you have shown your father.

Since that respect and fortunes are his love,   275
  I shall not be his wife.
France. Fairest Cordelia, that art most rich, being
    poor;
  Most choice, forsaken; and most loved, despised!
  Thee and thy virtues here I seize upon.   280
  Be it lawful I take up what's cast away.
  Gods, gods! 'tis strange that from their coldest neglect
  My love should kindle to inflamed respect.
  Thy dowerless daughter, King, thrown to my chance,
  Is queen of us, of ours, and our fair France.   285
  Not all the dukes of waterish Burgundy
  Can buy this unprized precious maid of me.
  Bid them farewell, Cordelia, though unkind.
  Thou losest here, a better where to find.
Lear. Thou hast her, France; let her be thine; for we   290
  Have no such daughter, nor shall ever see
  That face of hers again. Therefore be gone
  Without our grace, our love, our benison.
  Come, noble Burgundy.
          Flourish. Exeunt Lear, Burgundy, Cornwall,
          Albany, Gloucester, and Attendants.
France. Bid farewell to your sisters.   295
Cordelia. The jewels of our father, with washed eyes
  Cordelia leaves you. I know you what you are;
  And, like a sister, am most loath to call
  Your faults as they are named. Love well our father.
  To your professed bosoms I commit him;   300
  But yet, alas, stood I within his grace,
  I would prefer him to a better place!
  So farewell to you both.
Goneril. Prescribe not us our duty.
Regan.   Let your study   305
  Be to content your lord, who hath received you
  At fortune's alms. You have obedience scanted,
  And well are worth the want that you have wanted.

309 **unfold:** reveal, discover; **plighted cunning:** cunning that has been concealed by pledges of love.

313 **not little:** much, a great deal.

314 **appertains to:** concerns; **will hence:** (verb ellipsis) will leave this place. Why is Goneril made to speak in prose?

318 **changes:** whims, vagaries, notions, quirks.

319 **hath not been little:** has been extensive. See line 313 above.

320-1 **with what . . . grossly:** a surprising but true observation made by Goneril; **grossly:** plainly, clearly. What is Goneril confessing to Regan?

322-3 **he hath . . . himself:** He has been impulsive throughout his life; *i.e.*, he has seldom known his own mind. Goneril expands on this in her reply to Regan.

326 **imperfections of . . . condition:** faults arising from long habit. "Engraffed" is a form of *grafted*, a term used when a small branch of a tree is inserted under the bark of another, so that the two eventually grow together and become one.

327 **therewithal:** together with them (imperfections); **infirm:** senile.

328 **choleric:** irritable.

329 **unconstant starts:** sudden impulses, like those of a skittish horse. Kent is Lear's most devoted follower.

331 **compliment:** formal courtesy.

332 **hit together:** agree (upon how we shall conduct ourselves towards Lear).

333 **carry authority:** wield power. "Carry" is in the subjunctive mood, expressing a condition; **disposition:** attitude of mind.

334 **last surrender:** recent renunciation, or giving up, of the throne and domain; **but:** only; **offend:** be a nuisance to. Goneril's comment is cynical.

336 **i' the heat:** immediately. The word "do" here is in direct contrast to Regan's "think". Goneril intends to lose no time in putting into effect the new power and wealth conferred on her and her husband, Albany. She has clearly decided to see that her father will retain no vestige of authority. The last line of this scene, therefore, foreshadows the development of the main plot.

See also p. 221.

Cordelia.   Time shall unfold what plighted cunning hides,
Who covers faults, at last with shame derides.   310
Well may you prosper!
France.   Come, my fair Cordelia.
                          Exeunt France and Cordelia.
Goneril.   Sister, it is not little I have to say of what most
nearly appertains to us both. I think our father will hence
tonight.   315
Regan.   That's most certain, and with you; next month
with us.
Goneril.   You see how full of changes his age is. The observation we have made of it hath not been little. He
always loved our sister most, and with what poor judge-   320
ment he hath now cast her off appears too grossly.
Regan.   'Tis the infirmity of his age; yet he hath ever but
slenderly known himself.
Goneril.   The best and soundest of his time hath been but
rash; then must we look from his age to receive, not 325
alone the imperfections of long-engraffed condition,
but therewithal the unruly waywardness that infirm and
choleric years bring with them.
Regan.   Such unconstant starts are we like to have from
him as this of Kent's banishment.   330
Goneril.   There is further compliment of leave-taking between France and him. Pray you let's hit together. If our
father carry authority with such disposition as he bears,
this last surrender of his will but offend us.
Regan.   We shall further think of it.   335
Goneril.   We must do something, and i' the heat.
                                        Exeunt.

2-6 **Wherefore should . . . brother:** Why should I allow myself to suffer the disadvantages that custom inflicts, and permit the petty distinctions that nations make to deprive me of my right to be an heir, because I am a year, or fourteen months, younger than my legitimate brother? Edmund could not, as the younger son, inherit from his father, even if he had been legitimate. This is the strange custom that Edmund complains of; **Why bastard? wherefore base:** Why is the term "bastard" attached to me? I had nothing to do with my birth. Why am I regarded as low and vile (base) simply because I am illegitimate?

7 **dimensions:** proportions; **compact:** made.

8 **generous:** noble; **shape:** figure; **as true:** as true a resemblance to my father.

9 **honest:** virtuous, pure; presumably, with the secondary sense of *married*; **madam's:** woman's; **issue:** child, son.

10 **base . . . bastardy:** Although Elizabethans evidently thought that *bastard* derived from "base", there is no relationship between the two words.

11 **who:** a relative pronoun whose antecedent is "us".

15 **got:** begotten, fathered, bred.

9-15 **Why brand . . . wake:** Why do they brand with baseness and bastardy those of us who on occasions of stealthy lust require more fierce energy in our conception than goes into the procreation in the passionless marriage bed of a whole tribe of (legitimate) fools? Edmund uses this peculiar argument in trying to prove the essential superiority of his own illegitimate birth.

15-16 **Well then . . . land:** Edmund feels that he has justified a claim to what Edgar, Gloucester's legitimate son, will inherit.

17-18 **Our father's . . . legitimate:** Our father's love of us is the same; **fine word:** but, after all, only a word.

19 **speed:** (subjunctive mood) should succeed, bring about the expected results.

1-22 **Thou, Nature . . . bastards:** The key to Edmund's soliloquy is in the word "Nature", who is to be his goddess. Here, Nature stands for the belief that every man acts for himself alone. Edmund thus renounces law, morality, and religion in planning his own future. The deepest grievance of his life is that he is illegitimate.

25 **prescribed:** limited, restricted. Q1 reads *subscribed*: signed away.

26 **Confined to exhibition:** Limited to an allowance of money (from Goneril and Regan)?

27 **gad:** literally, *goad*; **upon the gad:** on the spur of the moment.

Scene 2

INSIDE GLOUCESTER'S CASTLE.

Enter Edmund the Bastard, a letter in his hand.

Edmund.   Thou, Nature, art my goddess; to thy law
My services are bound. Wherefore should I
Stand in the plague of custom and permit
The curiosity of nations to deprive me,
For that I am some twelve or fourteen moonshines   5
Lag of a brother? Why bastard? wherefore base?
When my dimensions are as well compact,
My mind as generous, and my shape as true,
As honest madam's issue? Why brand they us
With base? with baseness? bastardy? base, base?   10
Who, in the lusty stealth of nature, take
More composition and fierce quality
Than doth, within a dull, stale, tired bed,
Go to the creating a whole tribe of fops
Got 'tween asleep and wake? Well then,   15
Legitimate Edgar, I must have your land.
Our father's love is to the bastard Edmund
As to the legitimate. Fine word, "legitimate"!
Well, my legitimate, if this letter speed
And my invention thrive, Edmund the base   20
Shall top the legitimate; I grow; I prosper.
Now, gods, stand up for bastards!
        Enter Gloucester.
Gloucester.   Kent banished thus? and France in choler
        parted?
And the King gone tonight? prescribed his power?   25
Confined to exhibition? All this done
Upon the gad? Edmund, how now? What news?
Edmund.   So please your lordship, none.
        Puts away the letter.

33 **terrible dispatch:** desperate haste.
35 **Come:** Gloucester expects to be given the letter. The parental authority exercised in Elizabethan times seems to us most arbitrary and oppressive.
36 **spectacles:** Elizabethan gentlemen, but not those of Lear's time, wore spectacles, or what we commonly call *glasses*. A quaint and unimportant anachronism, one among many in the play.
38 **o'er-read:** read over.
39 **o'erlooking:** looking over.
41-42 **The contents . . . blame:** The matter in the letter is responsible for the fact that whether I show it to you or not, I shall do wrong.
45 **essay or taste:** synonymous terms for *test*.
46-48 **this policy . . . age:** the clever scheming (of Gloucester), hidden to us by the respect that is given to older people; **makes the . . . times:** makes life uncomfortable for us when we should be able to enjoy it most, or makes life unpleasant in our best years; **fortunes:** what we are entitled to in life; **oldness:** age; **relish:** appreciate.
49 **idle and fond:** useless and foolish; **bondage:** oppression.
50-51 **aged tyranny:** tyranny of an older person (Gloucester); **sways:** rules; **not as . . . suffered:** not because he has power so much as because we allow it.
52 **If our . . . him:** a thinly veiled suggestion of *murder*.
53 **revenue:** estate, wealth. Accent the second syllable.
56-57 **Had he . . . this:** Could he possibly have written this?
60 **casement:** window that opens like a door on side hinges, a French window.
61 **closet:** room.
62 **character:** handwriting.
63 **matter:** content of the letter, what the letter contains (Edmund uses the form "contents", line 42); **durst:** would dare.

Gloucester.   Why so earnestly seek you to put up that letter?
Edmund.   I know no news, my lord.   30
Gloucester.   What paper were you reading?
Edmund.   Nothing, my lord.
Gloucester.   No? What needed then that terrible dispatch of
   it into your pocket? The quality of nothing hath not such
   need to hide itself. Let's see. Come, if it be nothing, I   35
   shall not need spectacles.
Edmund.   I beseech you, sir, pardon me. It is a letter from
   my brother that I have not all o'er-read; and for so much
   as I have perused, I find it not fit for your o'erlooking.
Gloucester.   Give me the letter, sir.   40
Edmund.   I shall offend, either to detain or give it. The
   contents, as in part I understand them, are to blame.
Gloucester.   Let's see, let's see!
Edmund.   I hope, for my brother's justification, he wrote
   this but as an essay or taste of my virtue.   45
Gloucester (reads).   "This policy and reverence of age makes
   the world bitter to the best of our times; keeps our fortunes from us till our oldness cannot relish them. I begin
   to find an idle and fond bondage in the oppression of
   aged tyranny, who sways, not as it hath power, but as it   50
   is suffered. Come to me, that of this I may speak more.
   If our father would sleep till I waked him, you should
   enjoy half his revenue for ever, and live the beloved of
   your brother."
                                                          EDGAR.
   Hum! Conspiracy? "Sleep till I waked him, you should   55
   enjoy half his revenue." My son Edgar! Had he a hand
   to write this? a heart and brain to breed it in? When
   came you to this? Who brought it?
Edmund.   It was not brought me, my lord; there's the
   cunning of it. I found it thrown in at the casement of my 60
   closet.
Gloucester.   You know the character to be your brother's?
Edmund.   If the matter were good, my lord, I durst swear

64 **fain:** gladly.
69 **sounded:** *sounded you out,* tested your feelings. *Sounding* is done at sea to test the depth of water. The metaphor is therefore nautical.
72-73 **at perfect age:** when fully mature; **declined:** past their best years; **ward:** a person under guardianship.
75 **his very opinion:** the very thing he stated in his letter.
76 **brutish:** animal-like (adj.).
77 **sirrah:** usually addressed to a servant in the sense of *fellow.* A mark of impatience in Gloucester; **apprehend:** arrest.
78 **abominable:** hated, unnatural, unfit for the society of men.
80 **suspend your indignation:** control your anger.
82 **you should . . . course:** You would be following a calculated plan of action; **where:** whereas.
84 **gap:** breach, infraction; perhaps best understood in the sense of *a stain upon your own honour,* though this is not the literal meaning of "gap"; **shake in pieces:** destroy.
85 **heart:** spirit; **obedience:** filial obedience, duty as a son; **pawn:** stake, wager.
86 **writ:** written; **feel:** test.
87 **pretense of danger:** dangerous purpose.
89 **judge it meet:** (subjunctive) think it fit.
90-91 **auricular assurance:** assurance of your own hearing.
96-99 **wind me into him:** Worm your way into his confidence for me (Kittredge); **frame the . . . wisdom:** Carry out the plan according to your own common sense; **unstate:** disinherit, give up my estate; **in a due resolution:** in a state of having a proper solution (to this business of Edgar).

it were his; but in respect of that, I would fain think it
were not.   65
Gloucester.   It is his.
Edmund.   It is his hand, my lord, but I hope his heart is
not in the contents.
Gloucester.   Hath he never before sounded you in this busi-
ness?   70
Edmund.   Never, my lord. But I have heard him oft main-
tain it to be fit that, sons at perfect age, and fathers declined, the father should be as ward to the son, and the
son manage his revenue.
Gloucester.   O villain, villain! His very opinion in the letter!   75
Abhorred villain! Unnatural, detested, brutish villain!
worse than brutish! Go, sirrah, seek him. I'll apprehend
him. Abominable villain! Where is he?
Edmund.   I do not well know, my lord. If it shall please
you to suspend your indignation against my brother till   80
you can derive from him better testimony of his intent,
you should run a certain course; where, if you violently
proceed against him, mistaking his purpose, it would
make a great gap in your own honour and shake in pieces
the heart of his obedience. I dare pawn down my life for   85
him that he hath writ this to feel my affection to your
honour, and to no other pretense of danger.
Gloucester.   Think you so?
Edmund.   If your honour judge it meet, I will place you
where you shall hear us confer of this and by an auricular   90
assurance have your satisfaction, and that without any
further delay than this very evening.
Gloucester.   He cannot be such a monster.
Edmund.   Nor is not, sure.
Gloucester.   To his father, that so tenderly and entirely loves   95
him. Heaven and earth! Edmund, seek him out; wind
me into him, I pray you; frame the business after your
own wisdom. I would unstate myself to be in a due resolution.

102 **late:** recent; **these late . . . moon:** An eclipse of the sun occurred in October 1605, and an eclipse of the moon in September. Scholars use this information in dating the play.

103 **wisdom of nature:** man's reasoning powers; **reason:** explain.

104 **nature:** world of man; **scourged:** punished, afflicted.

105 **sequent effects:** results that follow.

107 **bond:** obligation of son to father and father to son. "Bond" is the key word in Cordelia's reply to her father (I. i. 98) and the most important single word in the play.

105-8 **Love cools . . . father:** These are Gloucester's "sequent effects"; **This villain . . . prediction:** Edgar's actions come under the prediction afforded by the "late eclipses".

109-10 **the King . . . nature:** The King (Lear) departs from his own natural tendencies—the love of his child, Cordelia. "Bias" is the term used to mean the natural curve followed by a bowling ball; **there's father against child:** There's a case of father against child for you.

111 **best of our time:** best example of our times; **hollowness:** deceit, duplicity.

113-14 **it shall . . . nothing:** You have nothing to lose (since all predictions are of ruin anyhow). Perhaps a half-promise of reward.

116 **foppery:** foolishness, stupidity.

118-19 **make guilty . . . stars:** make the sun, moon, and stars guilty of our misfortunes; **villains on necessity:** through sheer inability to prevent its happening.

121 **spherical predominance:** power of the planets.

123-4 **divine thrusting on:** supernatural influence; **whoremaster:** a term of contempt suggesting man's coarse nature, similar to "goatish" in line 125.

125 **goatish:** lustful; **charge:** responsibility, liability.

126 **compounded with my mother:** united with my mother (to produce me); **under the Dragon's Tail:** in reference to the position of the moon and the constellation *Draco*, the Dragon.

129 **that:** what; **maidenliest:** most innocent, benign; **firmament:** starry heavens.

131 **Pat:** On the dot, exactly as needed; **catastrophe:** awkwardly contrived incident completing the plot of a play.

132-3 **Tom o' Bedlam:** name given to those who had been in Bethlehem Hospital in London, an institution for the mentally deranged. An obvious anachronism; **My cue . . . o' Bedlam:** I am prompted to act as if I were profoundly sad, and to sigh like a Bedlam beggar; **portend:** See I. ii. 102; **divisions:** between brother and brother.

Edmund. I will seek him, sir, presently, convey the busi- 100
ness as I shall find means, and acquaint you withal.
Gloucester. These late eclipses in the sun and moon portend
no good to us. Though the wisdom of nature can reason
it thus and thus, yet nature finds itself scourged by the
sequent effects. Love cools, friendship falls off, brothers 105
divide. In cities, mutinies; in countries, discord; in
palaces, treason; and the bond cracked 'twixt son and
father. This villain of mine comes under the prediction;
there's son against father: the King falls from bias of
nature; there's father against child. We have seen the 110
best of our time. Machinations, hollowness, treachery,
and all ruinous disorders follow us disquietly to our
graves. Find out this villain, Edmund; it shall lose thee
nothing; do it carefully. And the noble and true-hearted
Kent banished! his offense, honesty! 'Tis strange.   115

Exit.

Edmund. This is the excellent foppery of the world, that,
when we are sick in fortune, often the surfeits of our
own behaviour, we make guilty of our disasters the sun,
the moon, and stars; as if we were villains on necessity;
fools by heavenly compulsion; knaves, thieves, and treach- 120
ers by spherical predominance; drunkards, liars, and
adulterers by an enforced obedience of planetary influence; and all that we are evil in, by a divine thrusting
on. An admirable evasion of whoremaster man, to lay his
goatish disposition to the charge of a star! My father 125
compounded with my mother under the Dragon's Tail,
and my nativity was under Ursa Major, so that it follows
I am rough and lecherous. Fut! I should have been
that I am, had the maidenliest star in the firmament
twinkled on my bastardizing.   130

Enter Edgar.

Pat! he comes, like the catastrophe of the old comedy.
My cue is villainous melancholy, with a sigh like Tom
o' Bedlam. O, these eclipses do portend these divisions!

134 **Fa, sol, la, mi:** notes of the singing scale. Edgar hums idly to himself to appear unaware of his brother's presence.

137-9 **I am . . . that:** Edgar marvels that Edmund should develop a sudden interest in astrology. Edmund is merely repeating what his father had spoken in all seriousness.

140 **he:** no antecedent. Edmund is thinking of the author of the predictions he mentions.

141 **unnaturalness:** cessation of reciprocal affection between parent and child.

142 **dearth:** shortage, famine; **dissolutions of ancient amities:** breaking up of old friendships.

143 **divisions in state:** differences of opinion within the country; **menaces:** threats.

144 **diffidences:** instances of mistrust; **banishment of friends:** Kent, probably.

145 **dissipation of cohorts:** disbanding of soldiers; **nuptial breaches:** breaking up of marriages.

147 **a sectary astronomical:** a follower of astrology.

148 **When saw . . . last:** Edmund answers Edgar's question, but not in a way that Edgar can understand.

155 **Bethink yourself:** Ponder, consider.

156 **at my entreaty:** with my strong urging; **forbear his presence:** give up seeing him.

157 **qualified the . . . displeasure:** has softened his anger.

158-9 **with the . . . allay:** that his anger would scarcely be satisfied, even with physical harm done to you.

161-2 **That's my fear:** the glib reply of an easy liar; **continent forbearance:** controlled restraint.

164 **fitly:** at a suitable time.

167 **to the best:** *i.e.,* of my ability and knowledge.

168 **meaning:** intention.

169 **faintly:** inadequately.

Fa, sol, la, mi.

Edgar. How now, brother Edmund? What serious con- 135
templation are you in?

Edmund. I am thinking, brother, of a prediction I read
this other day, what should follow these eclipses.

Edgar. Do you busy yourself with that?

Edmund. I promise you, the effects he writes of succeed 140
unhappily: as of unnaturalness between the child and
the parent; death, dearth, dissolutions of ancient amities;
divisions in state, menaces and maledictions against king
and nobles; needless diffidences, banishment of friends,
dissipation of cohorts, nuptial breaches, and I know not 145
what.

Edgar. How long have you been a sectary astronomical?

Edmund. When saw you my father last?

Edgar. The night gone by.

Edmund. Spake you with him? 150

Edgar. Ay, two hours together.

Edmund. Parted you in good terms? Found you no displeasure in him by word nor countenance?

Edgar. None at all.

Edmund. Bethink yourself wherein you may have of- 155
fended him; and at my entreaty forbear his presence until
some little time hath qualified the heat of his displeasure,
which at this instant so rageth in him that with the mischief of your person it would scarcely allay.

Edgar. Some villain hath done me wrong. 160

Edmund. That's my fear. I pray you have a continent forbearance till the speed of his rage goes slower; and, as I
say, retire with me to my lodging, from whence I will
fitly bring you to hear my lord speak. Pray ye, go! There's
my key. If you do stir abroad, go armed. 165

Edgar. Armed, brother?

Edmund. Brother, I advise you to the best. I am no honest
man if there be any good meaning toward you. I have
told you what I have seen and heard; but faintly, nothing

170 **the image and horror:** the horrible reality of. An example of one of Shakespeare's favourite syntactical devices, *hendiadys*, which is the use of two words joined by a conjunction, though one logically modifies the other. The phrase ordinarily would be *the horrible image.*

171 **anon:** soon, in due time.

173 **noble:** too honourable himself to suspect others.

176 **practices:** intrigues; **ride easy:** go easily (as the rider fits the horse's back); **I see the business:** I see the way I must go (to achieve my objectives).

178 **All's with . . . fit:** Everything that I can use to achieve my ends is suitable for me; **fashion fit:** make fitting.

See also p. 222.

4 **by day and night:** constantly.

5 **flashes into . . . other:** has outbreaks of impulsive behaviour that is deeply offensive. The word "crime" has become specialized in meaning since Shakespeare's day.

7 **riotous:** boisterous and unrestrained. Probably a lie uttered by Goneril for her own purposes. Kittredge points out the deference of the knights in I. iv; **upbraids:** reproaches.

10 **if you . . . services:** if you serve (Lear) with less attention than before.

11 **the fault . . . answer:** I will take the responsibility for your actions; S.D. **horns:** The calls sounded on hunting horns were important in keeping the hunt properly organized. Horns are used extensively in Germany today for this purpose. Here, the horns are used by Lear to announce formally his return. He evidently expects to be received royally. Lear, though eighty years of age, is still vigorous enough to hunt.

13 **Put on:** Pretend; **what:** whatever; **weary negligence:** neglect (of Lear) because of fatigue.

14 **I'd have . . . question:** I want it (this neglect) to be discussed.

15 **distaste:** dislike (subjunctive).

16 **whose mine . . . one:** whose views are exactly the same as mine in this matter.

like the image and horror of it. Pray you, away!   170
Edgar. Shall I hear from you anon?
Edmund. I do serve you in this business.

                          Exit Edgar.

A credulous father! and a brother noble,   HIS PLAN
Whose nature is so far from doing harms
That he suspects none; on whose foolish honesty   175
My practices ride easy! I see the business.
Let me, if not by birth, have lands by wit;
All with me's meet that I can fashion fit.   *Exit.*

Scene 3

INSIDE THE DUKE OF ALBANY'S PALACE.

Enter Goneril and Oswald, her Steward.

Goneril. Did my father strike my gentleman for chiding of
   his fool?
Oswald. Ay, madam.
Goneril. By day and night, he wrongs me! Every hour
   He flashes into one gross crime or other   5
   That sets us all at odds. I'll not endure it.
   His knights grow riotous, and himself upbraids us
   On every trifle. When he returns from hunting,
   I will not speak with him. Say I am sick.
   If you come slack of former services,   10
   You shall do well; the fault of it I'll answer.

                       Horns within.

Oswald. He's coming, madam; I hear him.
Goneril. Put on what weary negligence you please,
   You and your fellows. I'd have it come to question.
   If he distaste it, let him to my sister,   15
   Whose mind and mine I know in that are one,

17 **not to be overruled:** not to be changed by any authority that Lear may attempt to wield.

20-21 **Old fools . . . flatteries:** Lear, Goneril says, is in his second childhood and must be disciplined with restraints that seem flattering to him; **are seen:** appear to be.

25 **grows:** comes as a result.

26 **I would . . . occasions:** I want to create opportunities (for complaint against Lear) from these grievances (of the knights) contrived by Goneril.

28 **my very course:** the same course as I.

See also p. 223.

2 **diffuse:** disguise, cause (my speech) to be indistinct or broad (Theobald's emendation). Q1 and F1 read *defuse*; the sense is the same. Rowe, Pope, and Johnson preferred *disuse*.

3 **that full issue:** that main objection (aiding Lear).

4 **razed:** got rid of; literally, the word means *shaved*. Cf. *raser* (Fr.). Kent may, in fact, have shaved off his beard.

7 **full of labours:** ready to do any work (for Lear) that needs doing.

8 **jot:** instant; **Let me . . . ready:** Lear *is* indeed peremptory; he wants instant service. He is so accustomed to absolute power that he continues the habit of a lifetime quite unselfconsciously. There is no doubt that Lear creates a serious domestic problem, since he has divested himself of power, but wants to wield the same authority, at least in personal matters, as before.

Not to be overruled. Idle old man,
That still would manage those authorities
That he hath given away! Now, by my life,
Old fools are babes again, and must be used   20
With checks as flatteries, when they are seen abused.
Remember what I have said.

Oswald.   Very well, madam.

Goneril.   And let his knights have colder looks among you.
What grows of it, no matter. Advise your fellows so.   25
I would breed from hence occasions, and I shall,
That I may speak. I'll write straight to my sister
To hold my very course. Prepare for dinner.

Exeunt.

Scene 4

INSIDE THE DUKE OF
ALBANY'S PALACE.

Enter Kent, disguised.

Kent.   If but as well I other accents borrow,
That can my speech diffuse, my good intent
May carry through itself to that full issue
For which I razed my likeness. Now, banished Kent,
If thou canst serve where thou dost stand condemned,   5
So may it come, thy master, whom thou lovest,
Shall find thee full of labours.

Horns within. Enter Lear, Knights, and Attendants.

Lear.   Let me not stay a jot for dinner; go get it ready.
(*Exit an Attendant*). How now? What art thou?

Kent.   A man, sir.   10

Lear.   What dost thou profess? What wouldst thou
with us?

Kent.   I do profess to be no less than I seem, to serve

16-17 **to eat no fish:** to ignore fast days. An anachronistic pleasantry indicating that Kent is not a Roman Catholic.

27 **countenance:** bearing, demeanour.

28 **fain:** willingly.

30 **authority:** the attitude of a true ruler. This is not flattery on Kent's part.

32-33 **keep honest counsel:** hold my tongue when necessary; **mar a . . . it:** botch an elaborate story in telling it (by not using fancy words); *i.e.*, I'm a blunt sort of fellow.

37-38 **Not so . . . anything:** Kent answers indirectly and indelicately that since he is young enough to have sex-interest, he is therefore not old enough to be foolishly affectionate for other reasons. His answer evidently pleases Lear, who engages him on the spot.

45 **So please you:** Oswald, in compliance with Goneril's instructions, ignores Lear's question.

46 **clotpoll:** blockhead, nitwit. Observe that a knight instantly does Lear's bidding. Surely, such obedience indicates the falsity of Goneril's assertion that Lear's knights were becoming riotous.

him truly that will put me in trust, to love him that is
honest, to converse with him that is wise and says little, 15
to fear judgement, to fight when I cannot choose, and to
eat no fish.

Lear. What art thou?

Kent. A very honest-hearted fellow, and as poor as the
King. 20

Lear. If thou be'st as poor for a subject as he is for a
king, thou art poor enough. What wouldst thou?

Kent. Service.

Lear. Who wouldst thou serve?

Kent. You. 25

Lear. Dost thou know me, fellow?

Kent. No, sir, but you have that in your countenance
which I would fain call master.

Lear. What's that?

Kent. Authority. 30

Lear. What services canst thou do?

Kent. I can keep honest counsel, ride, run, mar a
curious tale in telling it, and deliver a plain message
bluntly. That which ordinary men are fit for, I am qualified in, and the best of me is diligence. 35

Lear. How old art thou?

Kent. Not so young, sir, to love a woman for singing,
nor so old to dote on her for anything. I have years on
my back forty-eight.

Lear. Follow me; thou shalt serve me. If I like thee no 40
worse after dinner, I will not part from thee yet. Dinner,
ho, dinner! Where's my knave? my fool? Go you and call
my fool hither.

Exit an Attendant.

Enter Oswald the Steward.

You, you, sirrah, where's my daughter?

Oswald. So please you— *Exit.* 45

Lear. What says the fellow there? Call the clotpoll
back. (*Exit a Knight*). Where's my fool, ho? I think the

47-48 **Where's my . . . asleep:** Lear is impatient. This is the second time he has called for his fool, and there is no response. Probably, a part of Goneril's tactics.

49 **mongrel:** Oswald.

53 **roundest:** bluntest, surliest.

57-58 **your Highness . . . wont:** You are not treated with love shown through formal ceremony as you used to be.

59-60 **abatement:** lessening, decrease; **general dependants:** most of the servants.

64-65 **for my . . . wronged:** Because of my loyalty to you, I cannot be silent in the face of the wrong done to you.

66 **rememberest:** *Remember* meant *remind* as well as *recall.*

67 **faint neglect:** either *hardly noticeable neglect* or the *weary negligence* suggested by Goneril.

68-69 **mine own jealous curiosity:** my own watchful suspicion; **pretense:** deliberate showing.

77 **Who am I, sir:** What reply did Lear expect?

79-80 **My lord's knave:** *i.e.,* Albany's villain. Lear does not refer to Goneril until she enters (line 185); **whoreson:** This word was used both as a noun and an adjective, often in the rather generalized sense of *base* or *low*. There is no doubt that Lear is explosively angry and means to be grossly insulting.

world's asleep.

Enter Knight.

How now? Where's that mongrel?

Knight. He says, my lord, your daughter is not well.   50

Lear. Why came not the slave back to me when I called him?

Knight. Sir, he answered me in the roundest manner, he would not.

Lear. He would not?   55

Knight. My lord, I know not what the matter is, but to my judgement your Highness is not entertained with that ceremonious affection as you were wont. There's a great abatement of kindness appears as well in the general dependants as in the Duke himself also and your   60 daughter.

Lear. Ha! sayest thou so?

Knight. I beseech you pardon me, my lord, if I be mistaken, for my duty cannot be silent when I think your Highness wronged.   65

Lear. Thou but rememberest me of mine own conception. I have perceived a most faint neglect of late, which I have rather blamed as mine own jealous curiosity than as a very pretense and purpose of unkindness. I will look further into it. But where's my fool? I have   70 not seen him this two days.

Knight. Since my young lady's going into France, sir, the fool hath much pined away.

Lear. No more of that; I have noted it well. Go you and tell my daughter I would speak with her. (*Exit*   75 *Knight*). Go you, call hither my fool.

Exit an Attendant.

Re-enter Steward.

O, you, sir, you! Come you hither, sir. Who am I, sir?

Oswald. My lady's father.

Lear. "My lady's father"? My lord's knave! You whoreson dog! you slave! you cur!   80

83 **Do you . . . rascal:** Do you dare to look me in the eye (or, exchange looks with me) as an equal?

84 **strucken:** struck.

85 **football player:** Football, an early form of soccer, played by boys in the street in Elizabeth's day, was regarded as a low game and the players were looked on as nuisances. Tripping was perhaps acceptable, as well as tackling, in this rough, un-organized pastime. An anachronism.

88 **differences:** *i.e.*, in rank (between king and servant).

89-90 **If you . . . tarry:** The statement is equivalent to: If you want to be knocked flat again, stay; **Go to:** exclamation of impa-tience; **Have you wisdom:** Have you sense enough to go (before you are flattened again)? **So:** This is said as Oswald retreats. Kent means: You have the sense to go.

92 **earnest:** sum paid in advance to make a bargain binding.

93 **coxcomb:** really *cock's comb*, the peculiar hat affected by pro-fessional jesters, red in colour and designed in the general shape of a cock's comb.

95 **you were best:** It would be best for you to (take my hat).

97 **Why? For . . . favour:** Why? Because you are a fool to sup-port one as much out of favour as Lear.

98-99 **Nay, an . . . shortly:** If you cannot "go along" with prevail-ing opinion, you are sure to be in difficulty soon.

100 **banished:** Lear has made Goneril and Regan independent by dividing his Kingdom and has therefore "banished" them from his former realm; **on's:** of his.

101-2 **a blessing:** Cordelia is Queen of France, though Lear meant to punish her by banishment; **thou must needs:** you absolutely must. "Needs" is emphatic.

105-6 **If I . . . myself:** If I gave my daughter all I owned, I'd be a fool (like you); **mine:** *i.e.*, my coxcomb; **beg:** an intentional thrust at Lear, who is now in the position of a beggar, depen-dent upon his daughters. Indeed, the Fool's comments are cruelly barbed, in keeping with his function as the King's con-science.

108 **the whip:** The Fool has gone far enough.

109-11 **Truth's a . . . stink:** Truth (what the Fool has stated) is disdained, but flattery is allowed full liberty. Literally, the Fool says: Truth is driven away as a disobedient dog is driven to his kennel, but flattery is treated like the favourite hound bitch that may stay in the warmth of the fire even though she smells.

Oswald. I am none of these, my lord! I beseech your pardon.

Lear. Do you bandy looks with me, you rascal?

Strikes him.

Oswald. I'll not be strucken, my lord.

Kent. Nor tripped neither, you base football player? 85

Trips him.

Lear. I thank thee, fellow. Thou servest me, and I'll love thee.

Kent. Come, sir, arise, away! I'll teach you differences. Away, away! If you will measure your lubber's length again, tarry; but away! Go to! Have you wisdom? So. 90

Exit Oswald.

Lear. Now, my friendly knave, I thank thee.

Enter Fool.

There's earnest of thy service. *Gives Kent money.*

Fool. Let me hire him too. Here's my coxcomb.

Offers Kent his cap.

Lear. How now, my pretty knave? How dost thou?

Fool. Sirrah, you were best take my coxcomb. 95

Kent. Why, fool?

Fool. Why? For taking one's part that's out of favour. Nay, an thou canst not smile as the wind sits, thou'lt catch cold shortly. There, take my coxcomb! Why, this fellow has banished two on's daughters, and did the 100 third a blessing against his will. If thou follow him, thou must needs wear my coxcomb.—How now, nuncle? Would I had two coxcombs and two daughters!

Lear. Why, my boy?

Fool. If I gave them all my living, I'd keep my cox- 105 combs myself. There's mine! beg another of thy daughters.

Lear. Take heed, sirrah—the whip.

Fool. Truth's a dog must to kennel; he must be whipped out, when the Lady Brach may stand by the 110 fire and stink.

112 **a pestilent gall:** literally, a plaguing or bothersome sore (caused by rubbing). Lear means: This fellow's taunts make me wince.

115 **nuncle:** a contraction of *mine uncle*, my uncle.

118 **owest:** ownest (own).

116-25 **Have more . . . score:** a string of wise sayings not particularly relevant to Lear, except that they stress the importance of common sense: Don't show all your money. Don't utter all you know. Don't lend your last cent. Don't walk if you can ride. Don't believe all you hear. Don't gamble all you've won in one throw of the dice on the next throw. Don't drink and associate with bad women. Don't gad about. If you follow this advice, your fortune will increase.

127-8 **Then 'tis . . . it:** You get no advice from a lawyer without paying him the proper fee. You got nothing because you gave me nothing.

130-1 **Nothing can . . . nothing:** See I. i. 95. A great deal has come of what Lear thought nothing—his anger and his curses.

132-3 **Prithee tell . . . fool:** a bitter jibe at Lear, who no longer has any land.

141 **for him stand:** stand in his place.

143 **presently:** immediately.

144 **motley:** traditional costume of the jester, made in variegated colours.

138-45 **That lord . . . there:** The Fool suggests that Lear himself is responsible for his own brainless action. With gestures, he indicates that he is the "sweet" fool and Lear the "bitter".

147 **that:** that title (of fool); *i.e.*, you are a born fool.

Lear. A pestilent gall to me!

Fool. Sirrah, I'll teach thee a speech.

Lear. Do.

Fool. Mark it, nuncle.   115
      Have more than thou showest,
      Speak less than thou knowest,
      Lend less than thou owest,
      Ride more than thou goest,
      Learn more than thou trowest,   120
      Set less than thou throwest;
      Leave thy drink and thy whore,
      And keep in-a-door,
      And thou shalt have more
      Than two tens to a score.   125

Kent. This is nothing, fool.

Fool. Then 'tis like the breath of an unfeed lawyer—
you gave me nothing for it. Can you make no use of
nothing, nuncle?

Lear. Why, no, boy. Nothing can be made out of 130
nothing.

Fool (*to Kent*). Prithee tell him, so much the rent of
his land comes to. He will not believe a fool.

Lear. A bitter fool!

Fool. Dost thou know the difference, my boy, between 135
a bitter fool and a sweet one?

Lear. No, lad; teach me.

Fool.   That lord that counselled thee
        To give away thy land,
      Come place him here by me—   140
        Do thou for him stand.
      The sweet and bitter fool
        Will presently appear;
      The one in motley here,
        The other found out there.   145

Lear. Dost thou call me fool, boy?

Fool. All thy other titles thou hast given away; that

149 **fool:** foolish, meaningless.
150 **will not let me:** Add the words: keep all my foolishness for myself.
151 **monopoly:** sole right to deal in foolishness; **they:** the lords and great men; **have part:** share (in).
153 **snatching:** demanding their share.
151-3 Corruption in the Court was a favourite Elizabethan subject for satire, especially in the matter of monopolies granted to favoured persons.
153-4 **Nuncle, give . . . crowns:** a conundrum, or riddle.
158 **clovest:** splitest (split).
159 **thou borest . . . dirt:** You acted as foolishly as a man who carries his donkey instead of riding it.
160 **crown:** top of the head.
166 **apish:** like apes, which imitate.
163-6 Fools are never in more disfavour than now, when even wise men have become foolish (foppish); and fools do not know how to behave, since the wise men have so closely imitated them. Obviously, another stab at Lear by the "all-licensed fool".
167-8 **sirrah:** used when speaking to servants or social inferiors, or as a term of insult to an equal.
169-71 **madest thy . . . mother:** when you put yourself into the charge of your daughters, expecting them to care for you; **when thou . . . breeches:** when you gave them the instrument of punishment and put down your own trousers to be whipped.
174 **play bo-peep:** play hide-and-seek. The implication is that Lear has hidden his eyes as if playing the childhood game, and has put himself among the fools because of his foolish abdication.
177 **fain:** gladly, willingly. The Fool has been bitterly truthful, indeed, to Lear.
178 **an:** if.
182 **holding my peace:** keeping quiet.

thou wast born with.

Kent. This is not altogether fool, my lord.

Fool. No, faith; lords and great men will not let me. 150
If I had a monopoly out, they would have part on't. And
ladies too, they will not let me have all the fool to myself; they'll be snatching. Nuncle, give me an egg, and
I'll give thee two crowns.

Lear. What two crowns shall they be? 155

Fool. Why, after I have cut the egg i' the middle and
eat up the meat, the two crowns of the egg. When thou
clovest thy crown i' the middle and gavest away both
parts, thou borest thine ass on thy back o'er the dirt.
Thou hadst little wit in thy bald crown when thou gavest 160
thy golden one away. If I speak like myself in this, let
him be whipped that first finds it so.

    (*sings*) <u>Fools had ne'er less grace in a year,</u>
        <u>For wise men are grown foppish;</u>
        <u>And know not how their wits to wear,</u> 165
        <u>Their manners are so apish.</u>

Lear. When were you wont to be so full of songs, sirrah?

Fool. I have used it, nuncle, ever since thou madest
thy daughters thy mother; for when thou gavest them the 170
rod, and puttest down thine own breeches,
    (*sings*) Then they for sudden joy did weep,
        And I for sorrow sung,
        That such a king should play bo-peep
        And go the fools among. 175
Prithee, nuncle, keep a schoolmaster that can teach thy
fool to lie. I would fain learn to lie.

Lear. An you lie, sirrah, we'll have you whipped.

Fool. I marvel what kin thou and thy daughters are.
They'll have me whipped for speaking true; thou'lt have 180
me whipped for lying; and sometimes I am whipped for
holding my peace. I had rather be any kind o' thing than
a fool! And yet I would not be thee, nuncle. Thou hast

184   **pared:** cut away, peeled.
185   **parings:** cuttings, peelings. The Fool refers to Goneril as one of
        the "cuttings" of his mind; Regan is the other. Nothing remains
        of his mind according to the Fool. In using this unusual word,
        the Fool suggests that Goneril and Regan are as worthless as
        peelings.
186   **frontlet:** frown. A "frontlet" was a band worn around the head;
        hence, the meaning here.
189-90   **an O . . . figure:** a cipher.
191   **nothing:** a zero with no figure preceding it.
194-5   **nor . . . nor:** neither . . . nor; **crum:** crumb, the inside of a
        loaf. The couplet applies, as usual, to Lear.
196   **a shealed peascod:** a shelled or empty peapod—a quite useless
        thing, emptied of all value.
199   **carp:** complain.
200   **rank:** gross, excessive, brutal; **riots:** fights.
202   **redress:** correction, satisfaction; **grow:** *i.e.,* I become.
204   **protect:** permit; **course:** action; **put it on:** encourage it.
205   **allowance:** permission, overlooking (it).
206   **scape censure:** escape sharp criticism; **nor the redresses sleep:**
        nor would the remedies fail to be applied.
207   **tender:** desire (for); **wholesome weal:** healthy state.
208   **working:** working out, outcome.
209   **else:** otherwise; **were:** would be.
205-10   **which if . . . proceeding:** Goneril is somewhat obscure. What
        she means is: If you permit riotousness among your knights,
        I will place the blame squarely on you, and my measures to
        control your men—owing to my desire for a healthy state—
        may well offend you, and might be considered undaughterly
        behaviour, were it not perfectly clear that my measures are
        necessary.
213   **it . . . it:** its . . . its.
211-13   The cuckoo lays its eggs in other birds' nests. Once hatched,
        the cuckoo outgrows the legitimate young by taking most of the
        food brought by the foster-parents. The cuckoo becomes much
        larger, while still in the nest, than its foster-parents. Hence,
        the Fool's suggestion. How does the couplet apply to Lear?
218   **dispositions:** moods.

pared thy wit o' both sides and left nothing i' the middle.
Here comes one o' the parings.   185
    Enter Goneril.
Lear. How now, daughter? What makes that frontlet
    on? You are too much o' late i' the frown.
Fool. Thou wast a pretty fellow when thou hadst no
    need to care for her frowning. Now thou art an O without
    a figure. I am better than thou art now: I am a fool, thou 190
    art nothing. (*To Goneril*). Yes, forsooth, I will hold my
    tongue. So your face bids me, though you say nothing.
        Mum, mum!
        He that keeps nor crust nor crum,
        Weary of all, shall want some.—   195
    (*Pointing at Lear*). That's a shealed peascod.
Goneril. Not only, sir, this your all-licensed fool,
    But other of your insolent retinue
    Do hourly carp and quarrel, breaking forth
    In rank and not-to-be-endured riots. Sir,   200
    I had thought, by making this well known unto you,
    To have found a safe redress; but now grow fearful,
    By what yourself too late have spoke and done,
    That you protect this course, and put it on
    By your allowance; which if you should, the fault   205
    Would not scape censure, nor the redresses sleep,
    Which, in the tender of a wholesome weal,
    Might in their working do you that offense
    Which else were shame, that then necessity
    Must call discreet proceeding.   210
Fool. For you know, nuncle,
        The hedge-sparrow fed the cuckoo so long
        That it had it head bit off by it young.
    So out went the candle, and we were left darkling.
Lear. Are you our daughter?   215
Goneril. I would you would make use of your good wisdom,
    Whereof I know you are fraught, and put away
    These dispositions which of late transport you

216-19 **I would . . . are:** Goneril suggests that Lear's moods are more violent than usual.

220-1 **May not . . . horse:** Even a fool may see that things are not right when a daughter instructs her father, a king; **Whoop, Jug . . . thee:** no meaning—a mere exclamation of the Fool's to gain attention.

224 **notion:** intellect, understanding; **discernings:** perception.

225 **lethargied:** without life or energy, paralysed; **sleeping or waking:** Am I asleep or awake? This is a Q1 reading. F1 reads *Ha! Waking?*

228-9 **marks of sovereignty:** signs by which I know I am a king.

230 **false:** falsely.

232 **which:** The antecedent seems to be "I" in Lear's speech; read *whom*.

234-5 **admiration:** pretence of wonder or amazement (*i.e.*, pretended ignorance that Goneril, his daughter, stands before him); **the savour of:** the same as.

239 **debauched:** Pope's reading; F1 spelling is *debosh'd*.

241 **shows like:** looks like; **riotous:** immoral; **epicurism:** self-indulgence; **lust:** illicit sexual desire.

242 **tavern:** related to "epicurism"; **brothel:** house of prostitutes, related to "lust" in line 241.

243 **graced:** honourable, gracious, noble.

244 **be then desired:** (imperative mood of verb) be requested.

245 **else will . . . begs:** otherwise will take into her own hands what she is now requesting.

246 **a little . . . train:** to reduce your following of knights somewhat.

247 **remainders:** those that remain; **depend:** stay on as dependents.

248 **besort:** are fitting for, suit.

250 **Darkness and devils:** an explosion of rage.

251 **train:** followers.

252 **Degenerate bastard:** Lear means that Goneril has not only become base, but *cannot* be his lawful daughter.

253 Why is "a daughter" more effective than "another daughter"?

254-5 **strike:** hit; **people:** household servants.

From what you rightly are.

Fool. May not an ass know when the cart draws the 220
horse? Whoop, Jug, I love thee!

Lear. Does any here know me? This is not Lear.
Does Lear walk thus? speak thus? Where are his eyes?
Either his notion weakens, or his discernings
Are lethargied—Sleeping or waking? Ha! Sure 'tis not so! 225
Who is it that can tell me who I am?

Fool. Lear's shadow.

Lear. I would learn that; for, by the marks of sover-
eignty,
Knowledge, and reason, I should be false persuaded 230
I had daughters.

Fool. Which they will make an obedient father.

Lear. Your name, fair gentlewoman?

Goneril. This admiration, sir, is much o' the savour
Of other your new pranks. I do beseech you 235
To understand my purposes aright.
As you are old and reverend, you should be wise.
Here do you keep a hundred knights and squires;
Men so disordered, so debauched, and bold
That this our court, infected with their manners, 240
Shows like a riotous inn. Epicurism and lust
Make it more like a tavern or a brothel
Than a graced palace. The shame itself doth speak
For instant remedy. Be then desired
By her that else will take the thing she begs 245
A little to disquantity your train,
And the remainders that shall still depend
To be such men as may besort your age,
Which know themselves and you.

Lear.   Darkness and devils! 250
Saddle my horses! Call my train together!
Degenerate bastard, I'll not trouble thee;
Yet have I left a daughter.

Goneril. You strike my people, and your disordered

254-5 **your disordered rabble:** your disorderly knights.
256 **betters:** those who are better than they themselves are. The reference is to Goneril's servants.
257 **Woe that . . . repents:** Woe to whoever repents (of his action) too late. Lear refers to himself.
258 **Speak, sir:** What prompts Lear to say this?
259 **marble-hearted:** hard-hearted, cruel.
261 **sea-monster:** probably a reference to the various fearsome monsters that appear in Greek mythology.
263 **kite:** bird of prey of the hawk family (*falconidae*), having long pointed wings and a forked tail. Some species are scavengers; hence, the reference to Goneril.
264 **of choice . . . parts:** of the best and most unusual accomplishments.
265 **particulars:** details.
266-7 **and in . . . name:** and are most conscientious in living up to the reputation that they have established.
267 **most small fault:** What Lear had considered Cordelia's fault now seems petty and unimportant, and he sees the folly of what he did.
269 **an engine:** a crowbar or lever; **wrenched my . . . nature:** twisted my real nature (by the force of the engine).
271 **gall:** bitterness, the bitter heart.
272 **gate:** head or forehead. Lear feels the first indications of madness.
277 **Nature:** goddess of fruitfulness. Compare this with Edmund's prayer I. ii. 1-2.
281 **increase:** birth.
282 **derogate:** debased, corrupt. Accent the second syllable.
283 **teem:** become pregnant.
284 **spleen:** malice.
285 **a thwart disnatured torment:** a stubborn, unnatural ordeal. Lear wants Goneril punished as he is being punished.
287 **cadent:** falling (Lat., *cadere*); **fret channels:** wear marks.
288 **pains and benefits:** cares for her child.

  rabble   255
 Make servants of their betters.
   Enter Albany.
Lear. Woe that too late repents!—O, sir, are you come?
 Is it your will? Speak, sir!—Prepare my horses.
 Ingratitude, thou marble-hearted fiend,
 More hideous when thou showest thee in a child   260
 Than the sea-monster!
Albany.   Pray, sir, be patient.
Lear (to Goneril). Detested kite, thou liest!
 My train are men of choice and rarest parts,
 That all particulars of duty know   265
 And in the most exact regard support
 The worships of their name.—O most small fault,
 How ugly didst thou in Cordelia show!
 Which, like an engine, wrenched my frame of nature
 From the fixed place; drew from my heart all love 270
 And added to the gall. O Lear, Lear, Lear!
 Beat at this gate that let thy folly in
   Beats his forehead with his fist.
 And thy dear judgement out! Go, go, my people.
Albany. My lord, I am guiltless, as I am ignorant
 Of what hath moved you.   275
Lear.   It may be so, my lord.
 Hear, Nature, hear! dear goddess, hear!
 Suspend thy purpose, if thou didst intend
 To make this creature fruitful.
 Into her womb convey sterility;   280
 Dry up in her the organs of increase;
 And from her derogate body never spring
 A babe to honour her! If she must teem,
 Create her child of spleen, that it may live
 And be a thwart disnatured torment to her.   285
 Let it stamp wrinkles in her brow of youth,
 With cadent tears fret channels in her cheeks,
 Turn all her mother's pains and benefits

277-91 **Hear, Nature . . . child:** Lear's invocation, at once a prayer to Nature and a curse on Goneril, is one of the most vehement and terrible in dramatic literature. Compare the invocation of Lady Macbeth, I. v. 39-55.

291 **Away, away:** addressed to all who are near.

293 **afflict:** trouble.

294 **disposition:** mood, humour; **scope:** freedom.

295 **dotage:** senility, second childhood.

296 **at a clap:** all at once, at one blow.

301 **shake my manhood thus:** so disturb my manly dignity that I am reduced to tears.

302 **perforce:** forcibly, whether I will (them) or not.

302-3 Lear is anguished at the thought that Goneril, who has treated him so badly, can make him weep with paternal feeling.

303 **blasts and fogs:** Wind and fog, apart from their discomfort, were thought to carry illness with them; hence, the curse.

304 **th' untented woundings:** raw, open wounds. A surgeon used a *tent*, or probe, to examine and explore wounds and remove foreign matter. If a wound were "untented" and foreign matter were left in the flesh, then the wound would fester. The metaphor, applied here, signifies Lear's desire that his curse will poison every aspect of Goneril's existence.

305 **fond:** foolish.

306 **beweep this cause:** if you (the eyes) should weep again because of Goneril's treatment.

307 **cast:** throw away; **waters that you loose:** F1 reading. The tears that you release.

308 **temper:** moisten for mixing.

310 **comfortable:** willing to give me the comfort I deserve.

312 **flay:** tear away the skin.

309-12 an example of the most intense dramatic irony.

313 **the shape:** the former rank or position of king.

315 **Do you . . . lord:** Goneril refers, not to Lear's insult about her "wolvish visage", but to his threat to resume his royal dignities.

316-17 **I cannot . . . you:** I feel I must protest, even though I am partial to you because of my love for you.

318 **content:** Be quiet.

321-2 **Take the . . . thee:** equivalent, apparently, to: Take the Fool and thy folly.

    To laughter and contempt, that she may feel
    How sharper than a serpent's tooth it is   290
    To have a thankless child! Away, away!   *Exit.*
Albany.   Now, gods that we adore, whereof comes this?
Goneril.   Never afflict yourself to know more of it,
    But let his disposition have that scope
    As dotage gives it.   295
        Re-enter Lear.
Lear.   What, fifty of my followers at a clap?
    Within a fortnight?
Albany.   What's the matter, sir?
Lear.   I'll tell thee. (*To Goneril*). Life and death! I am
    ashamed   300
    That thou hast power to shake my manhood thus;
    That these hot tears, which break from me perforce,
    Should make thee worth them. Blasts and fogs upon thee!
    Th' untented woundings of a father's curse
    Pierce every sense about thee! Old fond eyes,   305
    Beweep this cause again, I'll pluck ye out,
    And cast you, with the waters that you loose,
    To temper clay. Yea, is it come to this?
    Ha! Let it be so. I have another daughter,
    Who I am sure is kind and comfortable.   310
    When she shall hear this of thee, with her nails
    She'll flay thy wolvish visage. Thou shalt find
    That I'll resume the shape which thou dost think
    I have cast off for ever.
        Exeunt Lear, Kent, and Attendants.
Goneril.   Do you mark that, my lord?   315
Albany.   I cannot be so partial, Goneril,
    To the great love I bear you—
Goneril.   Pray you, content.—What, Oswald, ho!
    (*To the Fool*). You, sir, more knave than fool, after your
    master!   320
Fool.   Nuncle Lear, nuncle Lear, tarry! Take the fool
    with thee.

323-7 The Fool's verse makes some sense as: Even a fool would buy a rope to hang a fox, or a daughter like Goneril, if she is caught. Thus the Fool follows the old master and does not remain where such creatures are.

328 **This man . . . counsel:** Lear has been well-advised.

330 **politic:** good policy.

331-2 **at point:** fully armed and ready for action; **buzz:** whisper; **that on . . . dislike:** that on any possible pretext Lear may use their strength to permit him to do as he pleases.

333 **dotage:** senility, second childhood.

330-4 **'Tis politic . . . mercy:** Goneril's ironical words seem to be directed towards what she thinks may be the more tolerant attitude of her husband.

335 Albany protests mildly against Goneril's anger.

337 **still:** always; **harms:** dangers.

340 **sustain:** keep as a guest.

341 **unfitness:** unsuitability (of doing so) or unfitness of Lear as a house guest.

342 **How now:** a common salutation or greeting.

343 **writ:** written.

346 **full:** fully.

348 **compact:** complete or make (it) more convincing.

349 **No, no, my lord:** Goneril stops Albany from making an attempt to speak to Oswald with the intention of tempering his message.

350 **this milky . . . course:** this "mushy" or sentimental approach.

351 **under pardon:** Pardon me for saying so.

352 **more at task for:** Many textual variants for this F1 reading exist. Many editors like the conjecture *attaxed* (Gregory). This phrase from F1 would mean: more likely to be taken to task for; **want:** lack.

353 **than praised . . . mildness:** than you are likely to be praised for dangerous mildness.

354 **How far . . . tell:** What particular insight you may have, I do not know.

355 **Striving to . . . well:** a variant of: Better to leave well enough alone.

357 **event:** outcome.

See also p. 224.

           A fox, when one has caught her,
           And such a daughter,
           Should sure to the slaughter,   325
           If my cap would buy a halter.
           So the fool follows after.   *Exit.*

Goneril.   This man hath had good counsel! A hundred
   knights?
   'Tis politic and safe to let him keep   330
   At point a hundred knights; yes, that on every dream,
   Each buzz, each fancy, each complaint, dislike,
   He may enguard his dotage with their powers
   And hold our lives in mercy.—Oswald, I say!

Albany.   Well, you may fear too far.   335
Goneril.   Safer than trust too far.
   Let me still take away the harms I fear,
   Not fear still to be taken. I know his heart.
   What he hath uttered I have writ my sister.
   If she sustain him and his hundred knights,   340
   When I have showed the unfitness—
      Enter Steward.
                    How now, Oswald?
   What, have you writ that letter to my sister?

Oswald.   Yes, madam.
Goneril.   Take you some company, and away to horse!   345
   Inform her full of my particular fear,
   And thereto add such reasons of your own
   As may compact it more. Get you gone,
   And hasten your return. (*Exit Oswald*). No, no, my lord!
   This milky gentleness and course of yours,   350
   Though I condemn not, yet, under pardon,
   You are much more at task for want of wisdom
   Than praised for harmful mildness.

Albany.   How far your eyes may pierce I cannot tell.
   Striving to better, oft we mar what's well.   355
Goneril.   Nay then—
Albany.   Well, well; the event.
                      Exeunt.

1   **before:** ahead; **Gloucester:** the town; **these letters:** this letter.

2-4   **demand:** asking, rather than the modern sense of a *peremptory request*; **Acquaint my . . . letter:** Tell my daughter no more than she asks as a result of my letter; **If your . . . you:** If you do not hurry, I shall be there before you.

7   **in's:** in his; so written to indicate pronunciation.

8   **kibes:** sores caused by rubbing, or chilblains.

10   **I prithee:** I beg you.

11   **slipshod:** in slippers because of the sores. The humour at which Lear laughs depends on this meaning: Since you have no wits, your brains will have no kibes. The Fool is thinking of Kent's rather lengthy journey, presumably on foot, and also of Lear's, although Lear clearly intends to travel on horseback.

12   **Ha, ha, ha:** one of the few places where Lear shows any sense of humour, and even here his response is mechanical.

13-14   **kindly:** double meaning: *after her kind* and *in an affectionate way*; **she's as . . . apple:** She's as much like her sister as a crabapple (or, very sour wild apple) is like an ordinary apple.

15   **I can . . . tell:** I know a thing or two about what will happen.

17   **She'll taste . . . crab:** She (Regan) will treat you in the same way as Goneril did.

30   **horns:** sign of a cuckolded husband (a husband deceived by his wife)—a favourite Elizabethan butt of humour. Here, the horns are the sign of blind credulity and stupidity.

Scene 5

A COURTYARD OF THE DUKE OF ALBANY'S PALACE.

Enter Lear, Kent, and Fool.

Lear. Go you before to Gloucester with these letters. Acquaint my daughter no further with anything you know than comes from her demand out of the letter. If your diligence be not speedy, I shall be there afore you.

Kent. I will not sleep, my lord, till I have delivered 5 your letter. *Exit.*

Fool. If a man's brains were in's heels, were it not in danger of kibes?

Lear. Ay, boy.

Fool. Then I prithee be merry. Thy wit shall not go 10 slipshod.

Lear. Ha, ha, ha!

Fool. Shalt see thy other daughter will use thee kindly; for though she's as like this as a crab's like an apple, yet I can tell what I can tell. 15

Lear. What canst tell, boy?

Fool. She'll taste as like this as a crab does to a crab. Thou canst tell why one's nose stands i' the middle on's face?

Lear. No. 20

Fool. Why, to keep one's eyes of either side's nose, that what a man cannot smell out, he may spy into.

Lear. I did her wrong.

Fool. Canst tell how an oyster makes his shell?

Lear. No. 25

Fool. Nor I neither; but I can tell why a snail has a house.

Lear. Why?

Fool. Why, to put's head in; not to give it away to his daughters, and leave his horns without a case. 30

34   **mo:** more.

18-34   The Fool's comments, which are critical of Lear's action in dividing his Kingdom, are intended to taunt him for his lack of close examination of the problems he was creating for himself and for his incredible stupidity in giving away his house or castle.

36   **Thou wouldst . . . fool:** The Fool might well have said, if he dared: You are indeed the greatest fool I know.

37   **to take . . . perforce:** an incomplete statement: I intend to re-take my throne by force.

41-42   **Thou shouldst . . . wise:** The sense is as follows: You're certainly old enough to be wise, but you're nonetheless a great fool.

43-44   **in temper:** in a state of sanity, sane; **O, let . . . mad:** Lear feels more strongly than ever the onset of madness. Cf. I. iv. 271-2.

48-50   **She that's . . . shorter:** The Fool, turning to the audience, and perhaps imitating Lear, says in effect: Any young girl who cannot see that the King's departure is a sad one, and merely laughs at his discomfiture, is too stupid to retain her virginity for long, unless men are incapable of seduction. Some editors are of the opinion that this parting shot of the Fool's is spurious. It has a certain relevance, however, in reminding us that insanity may provoke laughter, even though it is in itself a pitiable condition.

See also p. 225.

1   **Save thee:** God save you—a greeting.

Lear. I will forget my nature. So kind a father!—Be
my horses ready?
Fool. Thy asses are gone about 'em. The reason why
the seven stars are no mo than seven is a pretty reason.
Lear. Because they are not eight? 35
Fool. Yes indeed. Thou wouldst make a good fool.
Lear. To take it again perforce! Monster ingratitude!
Fool. If thou wert my fool, nuncle, I'd have thee
beaten for being old before thy time.
Lear. How's that? 40
Fool. Thou shouldst not have been old till thou hadst
been wise.
Lear. O, let me not be mad, not mad, sweet heaven!
Keep me in temper; I would not be mad!
          Enter a Gentleman.
How now? Are the horses ready? 45
Gentleman. Ready, my lord.
Lear. Come, boy.
Fool. She that's a maid now, and laughs at my de-
parture,
Shall not be a maid long, unless things be cut shorter. 50
                                        Exeunt.

ACT II

Scene 1

A COURTYARD INSIDE
GLOUCESTER'S CASTLE.

Enter Edmund the Bastard and Curan, severally.

Edmund. Save thee, Curan.
Curan. And you, sir. I have been with your father, and
given him notice that the Duke of Cornwall and Regan

8 **ear-bussing arguments:** whispered opinions. "Buss" means *kiss*.
10 **toward:** imminent, about to occur; **'twixt:** between. A contraction of *betwixt*.
15 **weaves itself perforce:** unites itself naturally and inevitably; **business:** plot.
17 **of a queasy question:** that needs to be handled delicately. "Queasy" literally means *liable to vomit* and is intended to suggest the delicacy with which the stomach in such a condition must be treated.
18 **act:** accomplish; **work:** verb, imperative mood. The plea is for promptness and good luck.
19 **Brother, a . . . say:** Edmund calls out to his brother.
20 **watches:** keeps watch; **fly:** escape from.
21 **intelligence:** information. The military sense of the term.
26 **upon his party:** on his (Cornwall's) side.
27 **Advise yourself:** Consider, try to recall.
30 **in cunning:** in pretence (to fool Gloucester).
31 **Draw:** the same word as that used in westerns, but the weapons differ; **quit you well:** Do your best.
32 **Yield:** Surrender; **before:** in front of (for an accounting of your actions).
33 **So farewell:** The words are said with satisfaction after a pause. Edmund's plan has worked perfectly.
20-33 **My father . . . farewell:** The whole passage is designed by Edmund to confuse Edgar and force him to leave home in fear for his life.
34 **beget:** produce.

his Duchess will be here with him this night.

Edmund.   How comes that?   5

Curan.   Nay, I know not. You have heard of the news
    abroad—I mean the whispered ones, for they are yet but
    ear-bussing arguments?

Edmund.   Not I. Pray you, what are they?

Curan.   Have you heard of no likely wars toward 'twixt   10
    the Dukes of Cornwall and Albany?

Edmund.   Not a word.

Curan.   You may do, then, in time. Fare you well, sir.

                                                              Exit.

Edmund.   The Duke be here tonight? The better! best!
    This weaves itself perforce into my business.   15
    My father hath set guard to take my brother;
    And I have one thing, of a queasy question,
    Which I must act. Briefness and fortune, work!
    Brother, a word! Descend! Brother, I say!
          Enter Edgar.
    My father watches. O sir, fly this place!   20
    Intelligence is given where you are hid.
    You have now the good advantage of the night.
    Have you not spoken 'gainst the Duke of Cornwall?
    He's coming hither; now, i' the night, i' the haste,
    And Regan with him. Have you nothing said   25
    Upon his party 'gainst the Duke of Albany?
    Advise yourself.

Edgar.   I am sure on't, not a word.

Edmund.   I hear my father coming. Pardon me!
    In cunning I must draw my sword upon you.   30
    Draw, seem to defend yourself; now quit you well.—
    Yield! Come before my father. Light, ho, here!
    Fly, brother.—Torches, torches!—So farewell.

                                                    Exit Edgar.
    Some blood drawn on me would beget opinion
    Of my more fierce endeavour. (*Stabs his arm*). I have seen   35
    drunkards

41-42 **stand:** support or aid; **auspicious:** favouring; **mumbling of . . . mistress:** Edmund excites Gloucester's superstition.

45 **Where is . . . Edmund:** Gloucester is so intent upon finding Edgar that he fails to notice Edmund's self-inflicted wound.

46 **fled this way, sir:** Edmund undoubtedly points in the wrong direction. Why?

50 **that:** when. The expression was often *when that*, "that" being redundant.

51 **parricides:** sons who murder their fathers; **thunder:** wrath; **bend:** direct.

52 **spoke:** The words *when I* are understood before the verb; **manifold and strong:** a double epithet. Both words have the same meaning here.

53 **in fine:** finally.

54 **loathly opposite:** hatefully opposed.

55 **unnatural:** It is not natural for son to murder father; **in fell motion:** with a deadly thrust.

56-57 **prepared:** already drawn; **charges home . . . body:** directed his sword straight at my defenceless body. Edmund implies he had no time to draw his own sword; **lanched:** lanced, pierced.

58 **best alarumed spirits:** my spirit, aroused to its highest pitch.

60 **gasted:** terrified, panic-stricken.

61 **full:** quite.

64 **and found—dispatch:** and when he's found, kill him.

65 **arch and patron:** chief protector (hendiadys).

67 **thanks:** gratitude—and reward.

68 **to the stake:** to the place of his execution or to death.

71 **pight:** determined (past participle of *pitch*—to fix firmly. We still *pitch* a tent); **curst:** strong, angry.

Do more than this in sport.—Father, father!—
Stop, stop! No help?
    Enter Gloucester, and Servants with torches.
Gloucester.   Now, Edmund, where's the villain?
Edmund.   Here stood he in the dark, his sharp sword out,   40
  Mumbling of wicked charms, conjuring the moon
  To stand auspicious mistress.
Gloucester.   But where is he?
Edmund.   Look, sir, I bleed.
Gloucester.   Where is the villain, Edmund?   45
Edmund. Fled this way, sir. When by no means he could—
Gloucester.   Pursue him, ho! Go after. (*Exeunt some Serv-*
  ants). By no means what?
Edmund.   Persuade me to the murder of your lordship;
  But that I told him the revenging gods   50
  'Gainst parricides did all the thunder bend;
  Spoke with how manifold and strong a bond
  The child was bound to the father—sir, in fine,
  Seeing how loathly opposite I stood
  To his unnatural purpose, in fell motion   55
  With his prepared sword he charges home
  My unprovided body, lanched mine arm;
  And when he saw my best alarumed spirits,
  Bold in the quarrel's right, roused to the encounter,
  Or whether gasted by the noise I made,   60
  Full suddenly he fled.
Gloucester.   Let him fly far.
  Not in this land shall he remain uncaught;
  And found—dispatch. The noble Duke my master,
  My worthy arch and patron, comes tonight.   65
  By his authority I will proclaim it,
  That he which finds him shall deserve our thanks,
  Bringing the murderous coward to the stake;
  He that conceals him, death.
Edmund.   When I dissuaded him from his intent   70
  And found him pight to do it, with curst speech

72 **discover:** denounce, reveal his intentions.

73 **unpossessing:** landless, without property.

74-76 **If I . . . faithed:** Do you think if I denied your statements about me that any trust, virtue, or value in your character would cause your words to be believed instead of mine?

78-79 **my very character:** my own handwriting; **turn it all to:** twist matters so that the blame for what happened would rest upon; **suggestion:** evil instigation; **damned practice:** treachery.

80-83 **pregnant and potential:** another double epithet used to give strong emphasis to the sense of *compelling*; **and thou . . . it:** and you must assume that people are stupid indeed if they do not think that gaining something from my death was a very compelling reason for seeking to kill me.

84 **fastened:** confined, beyond redemption.

85 **letter:** No letter, of course, was sent by Edgar, though Edmund had composed one, I.ii; **I never got him:** I never begot him; *i.e.*, I could not be the father of such a son; S.D. **tucket:** sounding by trumpets of a special call identifying a party; here, Cornwall's.

87 **ports:** seaports; **villain:** Edmund.

88 **picture:** drawing, with a description.

90-92 **and of . . . capable:** and I will see that you, my loyal though illegitimate son, may legally inherit my property.

94 **I have . . . news:** *i.e.*, of Edgar's alleged plot. One can imagine that the sensational information that a son was plotting to kill his father would run like wildfire through Gloucester's household.

95 **all vengeance . . . short:** Total revenge is not enough. Regan later reveals herself as an expert in matters of vengeance and cruelty.

98 **godson:** Kittredge interestingly suggests that Regan is making a venomous connection between Lear's character and Edmund's plot.

99 **He whom . . . named:** the son, whom Lear named Edgar.

100 **it:** that Edgar is Lear's godson.

104 **Yes, madam . . . consort:** Edmund loses no opportunity to discredit Edgar.

105 **though he . . . affected:** that he would be made disloyal.

106 **'Tis they . . . death:** It is the association with Lear's riotous knights that has incited him to seek Gloucester's life.

I threatened to discover him. He replied,
"Thou unpossessing bastard, dost thou think,
If I would stand against thee, would the reposal
Of any trust, virtue, or worth in thee   75
Make thy words faithed? No. What I should deny
(As this I would; ay, though thou didst produce
My very character), I'd turn it all
To thy suggestion, plot, and damned practice;
And thou must make a dullard of the world,   80
If they not thought the profits of my death
Were very pregnant and potential spirits
To make thee seek it."
Gloucester.   O strange and fastened villain!
    Would he deny his letter, said he? I never got him.   85
                Tucket within.
    Hark, the Duke's trumpets! I know not why he comes.
    All ports I'll bar; the villain shall not scape;
    The Duke must grant me that. Besides, his picture
    I will send far and near, that all the kingdom
    May have due note of him, and of my land,   90
    Loyal and natural boy, I'll work the means
    To make thee capable.
                Enter Cornwall, Regan, and Attendants.
Cornwall.   How now, my noble friend? Since I came hither
    (Which I can call but now) I have heard strange news.
Regan.   If it be true, all vengeance comes too short   95
    Which can pursue the offender. How dost, my lord?
Gloucester.   O madam, my old heart is cracked, it's cracked!
Regan.   What, did my father's godson seek your life?
    He whom my father named? Your Edgar?
Gloucester.   O lady, lady, shame would have it hid!   100
Regan.   Was he not companion with the riotous knights
    That tended upon my father?
Gloucester.   I know not, madam. 'Tis too bad, too bad!
Edmund.   Yes, madam, he was of that consort.
Regan.   No marvel then though he were ill affected.   105
    'Tis they have put him on the old man's death,

107 **expense and waste:** hendiadys; **revenues:** income. Accent the second syllable.
108 **present:** same.
109 **them:** the "riotous" knights.
110 **sojourn:** stay.
114 **a childlike office:** filial duty, obligation of a son.
116 **bewray his practice:** revealed Edgar's plot.
121-2 **Make your . . . please:** Make whatever arrangements you please in my name, and I'll back you.
123-4 **doth this . . . itself:** is to be so greatly commended or praised; **ours:** under our protection and patronage. The plural *our* is equivalent to the royal *we*. This is the second major advancement in fortune for the illegitimate Edmund within minutes. The first was his father's promise, lines 91-92.
125 The line is an excellent example of dramatic irony.
126 **seize on:** engage in our service.
127-8 **I shall . . . else:** See IV. ii. 28.
129 **for him:** on behalf of my son.
131 **out of season:** at an improper time; **threading dark-eyed night:** making our way through the dark night.
132 **occasions:** situations; **prize:** importance. F1 reading; Q1 reads *poise*.
135 **differences:** strife, dissension, discord.
136 **from our home:** away from home.
137 **from hence:** from here; **attend dispatch:** are waiting to be sent.
138-9 **Lay comforts . . . bosom:** Be comforted; **bestow your . . . businesses:** Give your essential advice to us for our (political) affairs.
140 **which craves . . . use:** which must be put into effect immediately.
142 S.D. **Flourish:** See I. i. 204.
See also p. 226.

To have the expense and waste of his revenues.
I have this present evening from my sister
Been well informed of them, and with such cautions
That, if they come to sojourn at my house,   110
I'll not be there.
Cornwall.   Nor I, assure thee, Regan.
Edmund, I hear that you have shown your father
A childlike office.
Edmund.   'Twas my duty, sir.   115
Gloucester.   He did bewray his practice, and received
This hurt you see, striving to apprehend him.
Cornwall.   Is he pursued?
Gloucester.   Ay, my good lord.
Cornwall.   If he be taken, he shall never more   120
Be feared of doing harm. Make your own purpose,
How in my strength you please. For you, Edmund,
Whose virtue and obedience doth this instant
So much commend itself, you shall be ours.
Natures of such deep trust we shall much need;   125
You we first seize on.
Edmund.   I shall serve you, sir,
Truly, however else.
Gloucester.   For him I thank your Grace.
Cornwall.   You know not why we came to visit you—   130
Regan.   Thus out of season, threading dark-eyed night.
Occasions, noble Gloucester, of some prize,
Wherein we must have use of your advice.
Our father he hath writ, so hath our sister,
Of differences, which I best thought it fit   135
To answer from our home. The several messengers
From hence attend dispatch. Our good old friend,
Lay comforts to your bosom, and bestow
Your needful counsel to our businesses,
Which craves the instant use.   140
Gloucester.   I serve you, madam.
Your Graces are right welcome.
                              Exeunt. Flourish.

S.D. **without:** outside; **severally:** separately.

1 **Good dawning:** equivalent to *Good morning*, but indicative of the fact that it is still dark; **Art of this house:** Are you a member of this household?

2 **Ay:** Yes.

3 **set:** stable.

4 **mire:** mud.

5 **if thou . . . me:** This is facetiously said. Oswald means simply: If you have any courtesy, please tell me.

8 **Lipsbury Pinfold:** an involved pun exhibiting sarcastic humour. "Lipsbury", equivalent to *Liptown*, means *the mouth*. A "pinfold" is *a corral*. The expression therefore means: If I had you in my mouth (or jaws), or, If I had you in my power.

10 **use:** treat.

13 **an eater . . . meats:** an eater of scraps.

14-16 **three-suited:** Three suits per year were allowed a servant by custom; **hundred-pound:** with small property; **worsted-stocking:** cheap stocking scorned by gentlemen, who wore silk; **lily-livered:** cowardly, white-livered; **action-taking:** going to law instead of meeting an enemy in a duel, cowardly; **glass-gazing:** vain, always gazing into the mirror; **super-serviceable:** going beyond the normal limits of a servant's duty in order to gain favour with the master.

17 **finical:** fussy; **one-trunk-inheriting slave:** a servant whose total belongings would fit into one trunk.

18 **bawd:** procurer or pimp. Here, the word seems to mean: one who would perform evil services for his master.

19 **the composition:** the composite of, the combination; **pander:** See "bawd", line 18.

21 **clamorous whining:** noisy wailing, loud crying.

22 **addition:** title (specifically, all the titles Kent has given him).

13-22 **A knave . . . addition:** Kent is much better at gratuitous insult than at sarcastic humour.

23 **monstrous:** grossly discourteous.

24 **rail on:** upbraid, revile, abuse verbally.

25 **brazen-faced:** bold, "nervy"; **varlet:** scoundrel.

29-30 **I'll make . . . you:** I'll put so many holes in you that I'll make you soak up the moonlight as a piece of bread (sop) soaks up liquid. Another meaning, dependent upon a reference to "eggs in moonshine", a dish made of eggs fried in butter, suggests the modern slang expression: I'll settle your hash right now; **cullionly:** rascally, villainous; from the word *cullion*; **barbermonger:** steady customer of the barber. The insulting implication is that Oswald is a fop, dude, or dandy.

Scene 2

WITHOUT THE GATES OF GLOUCESTER'S CASTLE.

Enter Kent and Oswald the Steward, severally.

Oswald.   Good dawning to thee, friend. Art of this house?
Kent.   Ay.
Oswald.   Where may we set our horses?
Kent.   I' the mire.
Oswald.   Prithee, if thou lovest me, tell me.   5
Kent.   I love thee not.
Oswald.   Why then, I care not for thee.
Kent.   If I had thee in Lipsbury Pinfold, I would make
thee care for me.
Oswald.   Why dost thou use me thus? I know thee not.   10
Kent.   Fellow, I know thee.
Oswald.   What dost thou know me for?
Kent.   A knave, a rascal, an eater of broken meats; a
base, proud, shallow, beggarly, three-suited, hundred-
pound, filthy, worsted-stocking knave; a lily-livered, ac-   15
tion-taking, whoreson, glass-gazing, superserviceable,
finical rogue; one-trunk-inheriting slave; one that wouldst
be a bawd in way of good service, and art nothing but
the composition of a knave, beggar, coward, pander, and
the son and heir of a mongrel bitch; one whom I will   20
beat into clamorous whining if thou deny'st the least
syllable of thy addition.
Oswald.   Why, what a monstrous fellow art thou, thus to
rail on one that's neither known of thee nor knows thee!
Kent.   What a brazen-faced varlet art thou, to deny   25
thou knowest me! Is it two days ago since I tripped up
thy heels and beat thee before the King? (*Draws his
sword*). Draw, you rogue! for, though it be night, yet
the moon shines. I'll make a sop o' the moonshine of
you. You whoreson cullionly barbermonger, draw!   30

32-33 **letters against the King:** Kent knows that Oswald is Goneril's servant and guesses what his purpose is in coming to Regan and Cornwall while they are in Gloucester's palace. It is this thought that makes him ungovernably angry; **Vanity the puppet's part:** Goneril's part. Kent means to insult Oswald's mistress as a vain woman and a mere puppet compared to her father. Such a puppet was often a figure in morality plays in which puppets were the "actors".

34-35 **so carbonado:** slash, carve you up. "So" is merely emphatic; **Come your ways:** Come on!

37 **neat:** dandified.

38 S.D. **Beats him:** strikes him (humiliatingly) with the flat side of his sword blade.

1-39 This part of Scene 2 resembles the much exploited situation of man meeting man in television westerns.

40 S.D. **Parts them:** separates Kent and Oswald.

41 **with you:** I'll fight with you (Edmund) then; **goodman:** a mocking expression implying that Edmund the boy is presumptuous to impede Kent the man.

42 **flesh you:** give you your first lesson.

47 **difference:** dispute, quarrel.

48 **scarce in breath:** can scarcely get my breath.

49 **No marvel . . . valour:** No wonder, you have upset your courage so much with the thought that you may have to use it.

50-51 **disclaims in thee:** denies any part of your making; **a tailor made thee:** you're not a man; you're nothing but clothes.

53-55 The implication of Kent's reply to Cornwall is that no artisan—tailor, stone-cutter, or painter—however incompetent, could have produced Oswald, and that he is therefore a freak of some kind.

57 **ancient:** old (Kent is disguised).

58 **At suit . . . beard:** because of his age.

59 **whoreson zed . . . letter:** You nothing! You nonentity! The letter "zed" (z) is not used in Latin and is unnecessary in English since s can usually serve.

60 **unbolted:** unsifted, and therefore useless for its purpose. Unbolted mortar was unsifted and lumpy, and had to be trodden with wooden shoes to remove the lumps.

61 **jakes:** backhouse, privy.

62 **wagtail:** a bird whose characteristic motion is wagging its tail up and down nervously. Oswald is too agitated to remain still.

64 **beastly:** disgusting. The word probably had no more specialized meaning to Shakespeare than it has today; **reverence:** respect for superiors.

Oswald.   Away! I have nothing to do with thee.

Kent.   Draw, you rascal! You come with letters against
the King, and take Vanity the puppet's part against the
royalty of her father. Draw, you rogue, or I'll so carbonado your shanks! Draw, you rascal! Come your ways!   35

Oswald.   Help, ho! murder! help!

Kent.   Strike, you slave! Stand, rogue! Stand, you neat
slave! Strike!   *Beats him.*

Oswald.   Help, ho! murder! murder!
        Enter Edmund, with his rapier drawn.

Edmund.   How now? What's the matter?   *Parts them.*   40

Kent.   With you, goodman boy, if you please! Come,
I'll flesh ye! Come on, young master!
        Enter Gloucester, Cornwall, Regan, Servants.

Gloucester.   Weapons? arms? What's the matter here?

Cornwall.   Keep peace, upon your lives!
He dies that strikes again. What is the matter?   45

Regan.   The messengers from our sister and the King.

Cornwall.   What is your difference? Speak.

Oswald.   I am scarce in breath, my lord.

Kent.   No marvel, you have so bestirred your valour.
You cowardly rascal, nature disclaims in thee; a tailor   50
made thee.

Cornwall.   Thou art a strange fellow. A tailor make a man?

Kent.   A tailor, sir: a stonecutter or a painter could not
have made him so ill, though they had been but two
hours at the trade.   55

Cornwall.   Speak yet, how grew your quarrel?

Oswald.   This ancient ruffian, sir, whose life I have spared
At suit of his grey beard—

Kent.   Thou whoreson zed! thou unnecessary letter!
My lord, if you'll give me leave, I will tread this unbolted   60
villain into mortar and daub the wall of a jakes with him.
"Spare my grey beard," you wagtail?

Cornwall.   Peace, sirrah!
You beastly knave, know you no reverence?

65 **anger hath a privilege:** You must allow something to a man who is in a temper.

67 **sword:** the mark of a man; yet, Oswald is not a man according to Kent.

69-70 **oft bite . . . unloose:** who often destroy the bonds of natural affection (or the bonds of matrimony), which are too closely and intricately tied to be undone by ordinary means; **smooth:** flatter, toady to; **passion:** outburst.

71 **that in . . . rebel:** that break out in their masters.

72 **being oil to fire:** stimulate anger, as oil feeds a fire; **snow to . . . moods:** encourage feelings of indifference, apathy, or disdain.

73-74 **Renege:** Deny; **affirm:** Assert. These things would be done obsequiously to suit the occasion; **and turn . . . masters:** The body of the halcyon (kingfisher) was thought to be an accurate weather-vane, turning its beak into the wind, if hung up near a house. Oswald, and those like him, would obey their masters, just as the kingfisher would obey the wind.

75 **knowing naught . . . following:** understanding nothing, but following their master like obedient dogs.

76 **epileptic:** Oswald's face is twisted into a sort of smile, which fails to hide his fear. He looks to Kent as if he is about to have a fit.

77 **fool:** jester.

78 **goose:** traditionally, but wrongly, a symbol of stupidity; **Sarum Plain:** Salisbury Plain.

79 **Camelot:** site of King Arthur's Court, traditionally associated with a once-fortified hill near Cadbury. The nearby moors provided pasturage for geese. The lines are Kent's alliterative way of saying that he would gladly chase Oswald about, beating him with the flat of his sword, while Oswald utters goose-like shrieks.

81 **How fell you out:** How did you disagree?

82 **contraries:** opponents.

86 **His countenance . . . not:** I just don't like his face!

94-96 **saucy roughness:** rough insolence; **constrains the . . . nature:** forces himself to put on this act or manner of insolence that is contrary to his own nature.

98 **these kind:** a common idiom in Elizabethan English.

99 **harbour:** have within themselves, conceal; **craft:** cunning; **more corrupter ends:** more wicked purposes. The double comparative is common in Shakespeare's writing.

100 **silly-ducking:** constantly bowing; **observants:** fawning, sycophantic servants.

Kent. Yes, sir, but anger hath a privilege.   65
Cornwall. Why art thou angry?
Kent. That such a slave as this should wear a sword,
  Who wears no honesty. Such smiling rogues as these,
  Like rats, oft bite the holy cords atwain
  Which are too intrinse to unloose; smooth every passion   70
  That in the natures of their lords rebel,
  Being oil to fire, snow to the colder moods;
  Renege, affirm, and turn their halcyon beaks
  With every gale and vary of their masters,
  Knowing naught (like dogs) but following.   75
  A plague upon your epileptic visage!
  Smile you my speeches, as I were a fool?
  Goose, if I had you upon Sarum Plain,
  I'd drive ye cackling home to Camelot.
Cornwall. What, art thou mad, old fellow?   80
Gloucester. How fell you out? Say that.
Kent. No contraries hold more antipathy
  Than I and such a knave.
Cornwall. Why dost thou call him knave? What is his
    fault?   85
Kent. His countenance likes me not.
Cornwall. No more perchance does mine, nor his, nor hers.
Kent. Sir, 'tis my occupation to be plain:
  I have seen better faces in my time
  Than stands on any shoulder that I see   90
  Before me at this instant.
Cornwall.   This is some fellow
  Who, having been praised for bluntness, doth affect
  A saucy roughness, and constrains the garb
  Quite from his nature. He cannot flatter, he,   95
  An honest mind and plain, he must speak truth:
  An they will take it, so; if not, he's plain.
  These kind of knaves I know which in this plainness
  Harbour more craft and more corrupter ends
  Than twenty silly-ducking observants   100

101 **that stretch . . . nicely:** that exert themselves with the utmost conscientiousness.

102 **verity:** truth. The phrase "sincere verity" is a deliberately affected one.

103 **under the . . . aspect:** begging the indulgence of your great power. "Aspect", stressed on the second syllable, is an astrological term that refers to the position of heavenly bodies in relation to an observer, and therefore, to the influence of the body exerted upon him.

104 **influence:** another astrological term.

105 **Phœbus' front:** forehead of the sun.

108-11 **He that . . . it:** Kent means: I surmise that someone fooled you in the past with plain words, and therefore made himself a rascal, which I would not be, even if I should make you angry enough by my bluntness to want me to be a flatterer.

114 **late:** recently.

115 **upon his misconstruction:** following his (Lear's) misinterpretation of something I said.

116 **compact:** in compact with, or in agreement with Lear; Q1 reads *conjunct* and has the same meaning; **flattering his displeasure:** encouraging Lear's annoyance.

118-19 **and put . . . him:** and make such a hero of himself in Lear's eyes.

120 **attempting:** attacking, "taking on"; **who:** Oswald; **self-subdued:** self-controlled.

121 **fleshment:** excitement aroused by *fleshing*, or first success.

123-4 **None of . . . fool:** Rascals like this one always declare that compared to them Ajax, the mighty hero, is a fool. This remark enrages Cornwall, who assumes, perhaps rightly, that Kent means him.

125 **stocks:** instrument of punishment for minor offences, consisting of a wooden form with holes for hands and feet, and sometimes the head.

126 **stubborn:** rough, ungovernable; **ancient:** old, reverent, aged.

132 **grace and . . . master:** both the office and person of the King.

That stretch their duties nicely.

Kent. Sir, in good faith, in sincere verity,
Under the allowance of your great aspect,
Whose influence, like the wreath of radiant fire
On flickering Phœbus' front— 105

Cornwall. What meanest by this?

Kent. To go out of my dialect, which you discommend
so much. I know, sir, I am no flatterer. He that beguiled
you in a plain accent was a plain knave, which, for my
part, I will not be, though I should win your displeasure 110
to entreat me to it.

Cornwall. What was the offense you gave him?

Oswald. I never gave him any.
It pleased the King his master very late
To strike at me, upon his misconstruction; 115
When he, compact, and flattering his displeasure,
Tripped me behind; being down, insulted, railed
And put upon him such a deal of man
That worthied him, got praises of the King
For him attempting who was self-subdued; 120
And, in the fleshment of this dread exploit,
Drew on me here again.

Kent. None of these rogues and cowards
But Ajax is their fool.

Cornwall. Fetch forth the stocks! 125
You stubborn ancient knave, you reverend braggart,
We'll teach you—

Kent. Sir, I am too old to learn.
Call not your stocks for me. I serve the King,
On whose employment I was sent to you. 130
You shall do small respect, show too bold malice
Against the grace and person of my master,
Stocking his messenger.

Cornwall. Fetch forth the stocks! As I have life and honour,
There shall he sit till noon. 135

Regan. Till noon? Till night, my lord, and all night too!

139 **being:** since you are.
141 **away:** out, forth.
144 **low:** mean, humiliating, demeaning.
145 **contemnedest:** most despised.
147 **take it ill:** take it as an insult.
148 **so slightly . . . messenger:** given so little respect through the humiliating treatment of his servant.
150 **answer:** be responsible for.
156 **pleasure:** will.
158 **rubbed nor stopped:** thwarted or resisted.
162 **grow out at heels:** become worn out (like the heel of a sock or stocking) or may come to an end.
163 **Give you good morrow:** a salutation: *God* give you, etc. We might say today: See you in the morning.
165-7 **approve the . . . sun:** are fated to prove the truth of the proverb: Out of God's blessing into the warm sun (or, From good to bad). Kent refers to Lear's plight in giving up his Kingdom to his two daughters.
168 **beacon:** sun; **globe:** earth.

Kent.   Why, madam, if I were your father's dog,
  You should not use me so.
Regan.   Sir, being his knave, I will.
Cornwall.   This is a fellow of the selfsame colour   140
  Our sister speaks of. Come, bring away the stocks!
            Stocks brought out.
Gloucester.   Let me beseech your Grace not to do so.
  His fault is much, and the good King his master
  Will check him for it. Your purposed low correction
  Is such as basest and contemnedest wretches   145
  For pilferings and most common trespasses
  Are punished with. The King must take it ill
  That he, so slightly valued in his messenger,
  Should have him thus restrained.
Cornwall.   I'll answer that.   150
Regan.   My sister may receive it much more worse,
  To have her gentleman abused, assaulted,
  For following her affairs. Put in his legs.
            Kent is put in the stocks.
  Come, my good lord, away.
            Exeunt all but Gloucester and Kent.
Gloucester.   I am sorry for thee, friend. 'Tis the Duke's 155
  pleasure,
  Whose disposition, all the world well knows,
  Will not be rubbed nor stopped. I'll entreat for thee.
Kent.   Pray do not, sir. I have watched and travelled
  hard.   160
  Some time I shall sleep out, the rest I'll whistle.
  A good man's fortune may grow out at heels.
  Give you good morrow!
Gloucester.   The Duke's to blame in this; 'twill be ill taken.
            Exit.
Kent.   Good King, that must approve the common saw,   165
  Thou out of heaven's benediction comest
  To the warm sun!
  Approach, thou beacon to this under globe,

169 **comfortable:** comforting.
170-1 **Nothing almost . . . misery:** When we are discouraged, any relief seems a miracle.
173 **obscured:** disguised.
174-5 **this enormous state:** this unnatural condition; **to give . . . remedies:** to make up or repair losses; **o'erwatched:** worn out.
176-7 **Take vantage . . . lodging:** take advantage of sleep in order not to see these disgraceful stocks.
179 **Fortune, good . . . wheel:** According to legend, the goddess Fortune sits by her wheel upon which men are hung, and occasionally turns it. The supremely fortunate are at the top; some, less so, are ascending; and the unlucky remainder are descending or at the very bottom of the wheel. Cf. "The wheel is come full circle", V. iii. 210.
See also p. 227.
1 **proclaimed:** denounced as a renegade.
2 **happy:** lucky, opportune.
3 **port:** seaport. Gloucester alerted all the ports to watch for Edgar. Cf. II. i. 87.
5 **attend:** await; **taking:** capture.
6 **am bethought:** have decided.
8 **penury:** poverty; **in contempt of man:** to show how worthless man is.
10 **elf:** tangle and disarrange into elf-knots; matted locks of hair that resulted from infrequent use of a comb were often said to be the work of elves.
11 **presented:** bold; **outface:** defy.
12 **persecutions of the sky:** distresses caused by the changes in weather.
13 **proof and precedent:** example.
14 **Bedlam beggars:** vagrants of the late sixteenth and early seventeenth centuries who were, or pretended to be, discharged inmates of Bedlam Hospital. They evidently terrorized the countryside. Shakespeare's portrayal of these men through Edgar is thoroughly accurate. The name "Poor Tom", the cry "Poor Tom's a-cold", and the reference to striking objects into the flesh all come from a contemporary source. An anachronism.
15 **numbed and mortified:** double epithet.

That by thy comfortable beams I may
Peruse this letter. Nothing almost sees miracles   170
But misery. I know 'tis from Cordelia,
Who hath most fortunately been informed
Of my obscured course—and (*reads*) "shall find time
From this enormous state, seeking to give
Losses their remedies"—All weary and o'erwatched,   175
Take vantage, heavy eyes, not to behold
This shameful lodging.
Fortune, good night; smile once more, turn thy wheel.
                                        Sleeps.

Scene 3

OPEN COUNTRY IN THE NEIGHBOURHOOD OF GLOUCESTER'S CASTLE.

Enter Edgar.

Edgar.   I heard myself proclaimed,
And by the happy hollow of a tree
Escaped the hunt. No port is free, no place
That guard and most unusual vigilance
Does not attend my taking. Whiles I may scape,   5
I will preserve myself; and am bethought
To take the basest and most poorest shape
That ever penury, in contempt of man,
Brought near to beast. My face I'll grime with filth,
Blanket my loins, elf all my hair in knots,   10
And with presented nakedness outface
The winds and persecutions of the sky.
The country gives me proof and precedent
Of Bedlam beggars, who, with roaring voices,
Strike in their numbed and mortified bare arms   15

17 **object:** sight.
18 **pelting:** paltry.
19 **bans:** curses.
20 **enforce their charity:** extort what they want from others by fear; **Poor Turlygod! poor Tom:** Edgar is practising the beggars' cries.
21 **That's something . . . am:** As "Poor Tom", I may live; as "Edgar", I'm dead.

See also p. 228.
1 **they:** Regan and Cornwall.
6 **remove:** departure.
9 **Makest thou . . . pastime:** Is this shamefulness some sort of game?
11 **cruel:** a pun, *crewel* being a word for *worsted*, a cloth from which garters were made.
14-15 **over-lusty:** too lively; **netherstocks:** stockings.
16 **place:** position, rank.

Pins, wooden pricks, nails, sprigs of rosemary;
And with this horrible object, from low farms,
Poor pelting villages, sheepcotes, and mills,
Sometime with lunatic bans, sometime with prayers,
Enforce their charity. "Poor Turlygod! poor Tom!"   20
That's something yet! Edgar I nothing am.   *Exit.*

Scene 4

WITHOUT THE GATES OF GLOUCESTER'S CASTLE; KENT IN THE STOCKS.

Enter Lear, Fool, and Gentleman.

Lear. 'Tis strange that they should so depart from
    home,
    And not send back my messenger.
Gentleman.   As I learned,
    The night before there was no purpose in them   5
    Of this remove.
Kent.   Hail to thee, noble master!
Lear. Ha!
    Makest thou this shame thy pastime?
Kent.   No, my lord.   10
Fool. Ha, ha! he wears cruel garters.
    Horses are tied by the head, dogs and bears by the neck,
    monkeys by the loins, and men by the legs. When a
    man's over-lusty at legs, then he wears wooden nether-
    stocks.   15
Lear. What's he that hath so much thy place mistook
    To set thee here?
Kent.   It is both he and she—
    Your son and daughter.
Lear. No.   20

28 **durst:** would not dare to.
30 **to do . . . outrage:** to commit such an offence upon one so entitled to respect as a king.
31 **Resolve:** Tell; **modest:** reasonable; **which way:** why.
32 **usage:** treatment.
33 **coming from us:** inasmuch as you come from us (the royal "we"), the King.
35 **commend:** deliver; **letters:** a letter.
37 **duty:** respect; **reeking post:** sweaty messenger.
38 **stewed:** very hot.
40 **spite of intermission:** in spite of the delay in reading (my letter, which should have been read first).
41 **presently:** immediately.
42 **meinie:** retinue, followers, household; **straight:** immediately.
43-44 **attend the . . . answer:** wait until they were good and ready to answer.
46 **poisoned:** nullified, made impossible.
48 **displayed so saucily:** behaved so churlishly or insolently.
49 **more man than wit:** more courage than judgement.
51 **trespass:** the attack on Oswald.
53-54 **Winter's not . . . way:** Your troubles are not over yet.
56 **blind:** *i.e.,* to their duties as sons and daughters.

Kent.   Yes.
Lear.   No, I say.
Kent.   I say yea.
Lear.   No, no, they would not!
Kent.   Yes, they have.   25
Lear.   By Jupiter, I swear no!
Kent.   By Juno, I swear ay!
Lear.   They durst not do it;
   They could not, would not do it. 'Tis worse than murder
   To do upon respect such violent outrage.   30
   Resolve me with all modest haste which way
   Thou mightst deserve or they impose this usage,
   Coming from us.
Kent.   My lord, when at their home
   I did commend your Highness' letters to them,   35
   Ere I was risen from the place that showed
   My duty kneeling, came there a reeking post,
   Stewed in his haste, half breathless, panting forth
   From Goneril his mistress salutations;
   Delivered letters, spite of intermission,   40
   Which presently they read; on whose contents,
   They summoned up their meinie, straight took horse,
   Commanded me to follow and attend
   The leisure of their answer, gave me cold looks,
   And meeting here the other messenger,   45
   Whose welcome I perceived had poisoned mine—
   Being the very fellow which of late
   Displayed so saucily against your Highness—
   Having more man than wit about me, drew.
   He raised the house with loud and coward cries.   50
   Your son and daughter found this trespass worth
   The shame which here it suffers.
Fool.   Winter's not gone yet, if the wild geese fly that
way.
           Fathers that wear rags   55
             Do make their children blind;

57 **bear:** possess; **bags:** bags of money.
58 **kind:** only because of the money.
59 **arrant:** notorious; **whore:** Fortune is referred to in this way because she favours all men, but is constant to none.
60 **turns the key:** opens the door.
61 **dolours:** griefs. The pun is on *dollars*.
62 **tell:** count. Also with the secondary meaning of *relate*.
63-64 **mother swells . . . passio:** hysterical suffering. Lear refers to a growing sense of anguish that begins as a physical sensation below the heart and rises towards it.
65 **thy element's:** thy proper place is.
71 **How chance:** Why?
75-78 **We'll set . . . winter:** The Fool seems to mean that Lear's fortunes have come to an end as do the ant's when winter arrives. The fable of the ant and the cricket was well-known; **follow their noses:** go straight forward; **but:** except; **All that . . . stinking:** All those who possess judgement accept the testimony given by their own eyes, except the blind, who use their sense of smell only, and even a blind man in this way could see the truth of the situation (that Lear's plight is wretched). This wise saw or saying, and those that follow, are meant by the Fool to indicate that he understands not only that Lear is abandoned, but also, that some, like Kent, do not seem to realize how low Lear's fortunes have fallen.
87 **pack:** pack his belongings and desert; **when it . . . rain:** when the situation changes for the worse.
89 **the fool will stay:** The Fool comments ironically on his own loyalty.

But fathers that bear bags
   Shall see their children kind.
Fortune, that arrant whore,
   Ne'er turns the key to the poor.   60
But for all this, thou shalt have as many dolours for thy
daughters as thou canst tell in a year.

Lear. O, how this mother swells up toward my heart!
Hysterica passio! Down, thou climbing sorrow,
Thy element's below! Where is this daughter?   65

Kent. With the Earl, sir, here within.

Lear.   Follow me not;
Stay here.   *Exit.*

Gentleman. Made you no more offense but what you speak of?

Kent. None.   70
How chance the King comes with so small a number?

Fool. An thou hadst been set i' the stocks for that
question, thou'dst well deserved it.

Kent. Why, fool?

Fool. We'll set thee to school to an ant, to teach thee   75
there's no labouring i' the winter. All that follow their
noses are led by their eyes but blind men, and there's not
a nose among twenty but can smell him that's stinking.
Let go thy hold when a great wheel runs down a hill,
lest it break thy neck with following it; but the great   80
one that goes upward, let him draw thee after. When a
wise man gives thee better counsel, give me mine again:
I would have none but knaves follow it, since a fool
gives it.

     That sir which serves and seeks for gain,   85
        And follows but for form,
     Will pack when it begins to rain
        And leave thee in the storm.
     But I will tarry; the fool will stay,
        And let the wise man fly.   90
     The knave turns fool that runs away;

97   **fetches:** pretexts, pretences (from sailing: a *fetch* or a *tack*).

98   **images:** very pictures or clearest indications; **revolt and flying off:** synonyms for *disloyalty*.

101   **quality:** temperament.

102   **unremovable and fixed:** another pair of synonymous words meaning *unyielding, inflexible*.

104   **confusion:** ruination.

105   **What quality:** What has his temperament to do with it?

106   **I'd speak:** I simply wish to speak.

108   **Dost thou . . . man:** Lear simply cannot grasp the idea that he has been deliberately snubbed. (Not in Q1.)

112   **commands, tends service:** Lear commands his daughter's service, and offers his own.

113   **My breath and blood:** a vehement oath.

114   **hot:** hot-tempered.

115   **May be . . . well:** Lear, incredulous, makes excuses for the Duke's snub, since he cannot believe that such a thing could happen to a king.

116   **infirmity:** illness; **neglect all office:** overlook duty.

117   **whereto our . . . bound:** that we are bound to carry out when in good health.

119   **forbear:** be tolerant, be patient.

120   **am fallen out with:** am annoyed with; **more headier:** too head-strong; **will:** impulse.

121   **to take:** because I have mistaken; **indisposed and sickly fit:** an attack of illness (synonymous adjectives).

122   **sound:** healthy; **Death on my state:** A curse on my royal power.

125   **remotion:** avoidance (of me, Lear).

126   **practice:** trickery, deceit.

       The fool no knave, perdy.

Kent.   Where learned you this, fool?

Fool.   Not i' the stocks, fool.

       Enter Lear and Gloucester.

Lear.   Deny to speak with me? They are sick! they are   95
   weary!

   They have travelled all the night! Mere fetches—

   The images of revolt and flying off!

   Fetch me a better answer.

Gloucester.   My dear lord,   100

   You know the fiery quality of the Duke,

   How unremovable and fixed he is

   In his own course.

Lear.   Vengeance! plague! death! confusion!

   Fiery? What quality? Why, Gloucester, Gloucester,   105

   I'd speak with the Duke of Cornwall and his wife.

Gloucester.   Well, my good lord, I have informed them so.

Lear.   Informed them? Dost thou understand me, man?

Gloucester.   Ay, my good lord.

Lear.   The King would speak with Cornwall; the dear   110
   father

   Would with his daughter speak, commands, tends service.

   Are they informed of this? My breath and blood!

   Fiery? the fiery Duke? Tell the hot Duke that—

   No, but not yet! May be he is not well.   115

   Infirmity doth still neglect all office

   Whereto our health is bound. We are not ourselves

   When nature, being oppressed, commands the mind

   To suffer with the body. I'll forbear;

   And am fallen out with my more headier will,   120

   To take the indisposed and sickly fit

   For the sound man. (*Looks at Kent*). Death on my state!
   Wherefore

   Should he sit here? This act persuades me

   That this remotion of the Duke and her   125

   Is practice only. Give me my servant forth.

127 **and's:** and his.

128 **presently:** immediately.

130 **cry sleep to death:** make sleep impossible.

132 **O me . . . down:** The Fool's comment means that Lear is as naive about Regan and Cornwall as a cockney (a city woman) was about making an eel pie. She did not know enough to kill the eels before cooking them, and as they squirmed about, making the pie a mess, she rapped them over the head—when it was too late. Lear's demands are similarly too late because he has caused the situation in which he finds himself.

136-7 **'Twas her . . . hay:** Her brother was evidently no more intelligent or practical, but a born fool like his sister; S.D. **Enter Cornwall,** etc.: Gloucester has evidently made a successful plea.

138 **Good morrow:** Since it is evening, the greeting is ironical.

139 **Grace:** equivalent to *Majesty*.

142-4 **If thou . . . adultress:** If you were not glad to see me, I would renounce any connection with your dead mother, since you could not be my daughter, and your mother must have been false to me. More simply: If you are not glad to see me, you can be no daughter of mine.

145 **Some other . . . that:** We'll deal with that matter of the stocks at some other time.

146 **naught:** wicked (an adjective; cf. *naughty*).

147 **like a vulture:** an illusion to the eternal punishment of Prometheus in the Greek myth.

149 **depraved:** wicked. Lear refers to Goneril's character or "quality".

150 **take patience:** Have patience.

152 **scant:** neglect.

155 **obligation:** *i.e.*, filial obligation, obligation of a son or a daughter to parents.

157 **wholesome:** proper.

Go tell the Duke and's wife I'd speak with them—
Now, presently. Bid them come forth and hear me,
Or at their chamber door I'll beat the drum
Till it cry sleep to death.   130
Gloucester.   I would have all well betwixt you.   *Exit.*
Lear.   O me, my heart, my rising heart! But down!
Fool.   Cry to it, nuncle, as the cockney did to the eels
when she put 'em i' the paste alive. She knapped 'em o'
the coxcombs with a stick and cried "Down, wantons, 135
down!" 'Twas her brother that, in pure kindness to his
horse, buttered his hay.
          Enter Cornwall, Regan, Gloucester, Servants.
Lear.   Good morrow to you both.
Cornwall.   Hail to your Grace!
          Kent here set at liberty.
Regan.   I am glad to see your Highness.   140
Lear.   Regan, I think you are; I know what reason
I have to think so. If thou shouldst not be glad,
I would divorce me from thy mother's tomb,
Sepulchring an adultress. (*To Kent*). O, are you free?
Some other time for that.—Beloved Regan,   145
Thy sister's naught. O Regan, she hath tied
Sharp-toothed unkindness, like a vulture, here!
          Points to his heart.
I can scarce speak to thee. Thou'lt not believe
With how depraved a quality—O Regan!
Regan.   I pray you, sir, take patience. I have hope   150
You less know how to value her desert
Than she to scant her duty.
Lear.   Say, how is that?
Regan.   I cannot think my sister in the least
Would fail her obligation. If, sir, perchance   155
She have restrained the riots of your followers,
'Tis on such ground, and to such wholesome end,
As clears her from all blame.
Lear.   My curses on her!

161-2 **Nature in . . . confine:** You are on the threshold of death.
163 **discretion:** some discreet person; **state:** your mental condition or your dependent condition.
168 **this:** the action Lear immediately performs; **becomes the house:** suits my dignity (as a king).
170 **Age is unnecessary:** A person has no right to become old (ironically spoken).
171 **vouchsafe:** grant; **raiment:** clothing.
172 **unsightly tricks:** undignified actions (of falling to the knees and whining for charity).
175 **abated me . . . train:** reduced my followers to half.
176 **looked black:** glared; **struck me . . . tongue:** abused me with words.
177 **most serpent-like:** like a snake with its flickering tongue (which was thought to be a weapon for stinging).
179 **top:** head; **young bones:** Goneril's white body.
180 **taking:** infectious.
184 **fen-sucked:** sucked up from marshes (by the sun).
185 **fall and blister:** fall upon Goneril and raise blisters on her.
187 **the rash mood:** the mood of compulsive anger.
189 **tender-hefted nature:** disposition governed by tenderness, or gentle disposition.
193 **bandy:** exchange; literally, bat back and forth (like a tennis ball); **scant my sizes:** reduce my allowances.
194 **oppose the bolt:** to close the bolt (or fastener) of the door.

Regan.   <u>O, sir, you are old!</u>   160
  Nature in you stands on the very verge —
  Of her confine. You should be ruled, and led
  By some <u>discretion that discerns your state</u> —
  Better than you yourself. Therefore I pray you
  That to our sister you do make return;   165
  Say you have wronged her.
Lear.   Ask her forgiveness?
  Do you but mark how this becomes the house:
  (*kneeling*) "Dear daughter, I confess that I am old.
  Age is unnecessary. On my knees I beg   170
  That you'll vouchsafe me raiment, bed, and food."
Regan.   Good sir, no more! These are unsightly tricks.
  Return you to my sister.
Lear (*stands up*).   Never, Regan!
  She hath abated me of half my train;   175
  Looked black upon me; struck me with her tongue,
  Most serpent-like, upon the very heart.
  All the stored vengeances of heaven fall
  On her ingrateful top! Strike her young bones,
  You taking airs, with lameness!   180
Cornwall.   Fie, sir, fie!
Lear.   You nimble lightnings, dart your blinding flames
  Into her scornful eyes! Infect her beauty,
  You fen-sucked fogs, drawn by the powerful sun,
  To fall and blister!   185
Regan.   O the blest gods! so will you wish on me
  When the rash mood is on.
Lear.   No, Regan, thou shalt never have my curse.
  Thy tender-hefted nature shall not give
  Thee o'er to harshness. Her eyes are fierce, but thine   190
  Do comfort and not burn. 'Tis not in thee
  To grudge my pleasures, to cut off my train,
  To bandy hasty words, to scant my sizes,
  And, in conclusion, to oppose the bolt
  Against my coming in. Thou better knowest   195

196 **offices of nature:** duties of a daughter. See II. iv. 155; **bond of childhood:** obligation formed in childhood.
197 **effects:** actions; **dues of gratitude:** what gratitude is owing to a father.
200 **to the purpose:** Come to the point, say what you mean.
203 **approves:** confirms.
206-7 **easy, borrowed . . . follows:** confident pride, borrowed from his mistress Goneril because of her protection.
208 **varlet:** scoundrel.
212 **on't:** of it.
214 **sweet sway:** loving authority, gentle rule.
215 **allow:** permit; **obedience:** your obedience to my wish; **if you . . . old:** if you can sympathize with one who is old, if you can understand what it is to be old.
216 **Make it your cause:** Defend its privileges; **Send down:** Send for someone (to explain why Kent was put into the stocks).
213-16 **Who comes . . . part:** These words are addressed to Regan and Cornwall.
220-1 **All's not . . . so:** Not everything is an offence just because your lack of judgement and your senility make you think so.
222-3 **O sides . . . hold:** Because of this extreme distress, Lear again experiences the sensation referred to in II. iv. 64-65.
224 **disorders:** misbehaviour, misconduct.
225 **advancement:** promotion (used ironically).
227 **being weak, seem so:** Since you are powerless, behave as if you are.

The offices of nature, bond of childhood,
Effects of courtesy, dues of gratitude.
Thy half of the kingdom hast thou not forgot,
Wherein I thee endowed.

Regan.   Good sir, to the purpose.   200
Lear. Who put my man in the stocks?   *Tucket within.*
Cornwall.   What trumpet's that?
Regan. I know it—my sister's. This approves her letter
That she would soon be here.

Enter Oswald the Steward.

                    Is your lady come?   205
Lear. This is a slave, whose easy, borrowed pride
Dwells in the fickle grace of her he follows.
Out, varlet, from my sight!

Cornwall.   What means your Grace?
Lear. Who stocked my servant? Regan, I have good 210
hope
Thou didst not know on't.

Enter Goneril.

                    Who comes here? O heavens,
If you do love old men, if your sweet sway
Allow obedience, if you yourselves are old,   215
Make it your cause! Send down, and take my part!
(*To Goneril*). Art not ashamed to look upon this beard?—
O Regan, will you take her by the hand?
Goneril. Why not by the hand, sir? How have I offended?
All's not offense that indiscretion finds   220
And dotage terms so.

Lear.   O sides, you are too tough!
Will you yet hold? How came my man i' the stocks?
Cornwall. I set him there, sir, but his own disorders
Deserved much less advancement.   225
Lear.   You? Did you?
Regan. I pray you, father, being weak, seem so.
If, till the expiration of your month,
You will return and sojourn with my sister,

230 **train:** retinue.

231-2 **I am . . . entertainment:** I am not now at home and unable, therefore, to provide what you require for your comfort.

234 **abjure:** abandon, give up; **roofs:** shelter, to which Lear is entitled.

235 **wage:** struggle, fight.

237 **necessity's sharp pinch:** This is the summary of what Lear has thought and said. It is inevitable that poverty should bring exposure to the cold, the wind, and the rain.

238 **France:** the King of France.

239 **brought:** forced. Since no one has forced Lear to do anything for a long time, he finds the thought of such coercion intolerable.

240 **knee:** bow before; **squire-like:** like a servant.

241 **to keep . . . afoot:** to keep body and soul together, to keep from starvation.

242 **sumpter:** pack-animal, beast of burden.

245 **mad:** insane, not angry.

250 **must needs:** am compelled to; **boil:** sore accompanied by an accumulation of pus.

251 **plague sore:** external sign or mark of bubonic plague; **embossed carbuncle:** particularly large boil forming a distinct lump on the surface of the body.

252 **corrupted:** diseased, infected.

253 **shame:** Goneril's disgrace as a cruel daughter.

254 **Thunder-bearer:** Jupiter.

255 **Jove:** Zeus, judge of all men.

256 **Mend:** Make amends; **be better:** Be a better daughter.

261 **give ear, sir, to:** pay attention to.

262 **those that . . . passion:** who consider reasonably your violent emotion.

263 **and so:** Regan breaks off, implying: You are old, and that explains your irrational actions.

Dismissing half your train, come then to me. 230
I am now from home, and out of that provision
Which shall be needful for your entertainment.
Lear.   Return to her, and fifty men dismissed?
No, rather I abjure all roofs, and choose
To wage against the enmity o' the air, 235
To be a comrade with the wolf and owl—
Necessity's sharp pinch! Return with her?
Why, the hot-blooded France, that dowerless took
Our youngest born, I could as well be brought
To knee his throne, and, squire-like, pension beg 240
To keep base life afoot. Return with her?
Persuade me rather to be slave and sumpter
To this detested groom.   *Pointing at Oswald.*
Goneril.   At your choice, sir.
Lear.   I prithee, daughter, do not make me mad. 245
I will not trouble thee, my child; farewell.
We'll no more meet, no more see one another.
But yet thou art my flesh, my blood, my daughter;
Or rather a disease that's in my flesh,
Which I must needs call mine. Thou art a boil, 250
A plague sore or embossed carbuncle,
In my corrupted blood. But I'll not chide thee.
Let shame come when it will, I do not call it.
I do not bid the Thunder-bearer shoot,
Nor tell tales of thee to high-judging Jove. 255
Mend when thou canst; be better at thy leisure;
I can be patient; I can stay with Regan,
I and my hundred knights.
Regan.   Not altogether so.
I looked not for you yet, nor am provided 260
For your fit welcome. Give ear, sir, to my sister;
For those that mingle reason with your passion
Must be content to think you old, and so—
But she knows what she does.
Lear.   Is this well spoken? 265

266   **avouch:** maintain, stand by, affirm.
268   **sith that:** since; **charge and danger:** expense and risks involved
        in having such large numbers of unruly men about.
271   **hold amity:** keep peace.
274-5   **slack ye:** be neglectful of you.
276   **We could control them:** an insidious, insulting innuendo by
        Regan.
277   **spy:** see, perceive.
278   **but:** only.
279   **notice:** recognition.
280   **I gave you all:** Lear is completely incredulous.
281   **And in . . . it:** You gave up your Kingdom barely in time (be-
        cause you are old and senile).
282   **depositaries:** trustees. Lear thought that his rule was given in
        trust to his daughters, and that all the privileges of his office
        would remain as they had been. They, of course, put no such
        limit on their inheritance.
283-4   **kept a reservation:** reserved the right; **to be . . . number:** to
        be served by my original hundred knights.
287-9   **Those wicked . . . wicked:** Some wicked persons (like Goneril)
        look pleasing by comparison when others (like Regan) are even
        more wicked; **not being . . . praise:** It is in Goneril's favour that
        she is not as bad as Regan.
294   **What need you:** What need have you of . . . ?
295   **twice so many:** fifty (of my servants).
298-9   **O, reason . . . need:** Do not examine the exact need; **Our
        basest . . . superfluous:** Even the poorest beggars have things
        that they do not actually need.
300-301 **Allow not . . . beast's:** If you allow a man only his necessi-
        ties, his life is like that of an animal. See III. iv. 111-13.

Regan.   I dare avouch it, sir. What, fifty followers?
Is it not well? What should you need of more?
Yea, or so many, sith that both charge and danger
Speak 'gainst so great a number? How in one house
Should many people, under two commands,   270
Hold amity? 'Tis hard; almost impossible.
Goneril.   Why might not you, my lord, receive attendance
From those that she calls servants, or from mine?
Regan.   Why not, my lord? If then they chanced to slack
ye,   275
We could control them. If you will come to me
(For now I spy a danger), I entreat you
To bring but five-and-twenty. To no more
Will I give place or notice.
Lear.   I gave you all—   280
Regan.   And in good time you gave it!
Lear.   Made you my guardians, my depositaries;
But kept a reservation to be followed
With such a number. What, must I come to you
With five-and-twenty, Regan? Said you so?   285
Regan.   And speak it again, my lord. No more with me.
Lear.   Those wicked creatures yet do look well-favoured
When others are more wicked; not being the worst
Stands in some rank of praise. (*To Goneril*). I'll go with
thee.   290
Thy fifty yet doth double five-and-twenty,
And thou art twice her love.
Goneril.   Hear me, my lord.
What need you five-and-twenty, ten, or five,
To follow in a house where twice so many   295
Have a command to tend you?
Regan.   What need one?
Lear.   O, reason not the need! Our basest beggars
Are in the poorest thing superfluous.
Allow not nature more than nature needs,   300
Man's life is cheap as beast's. Thou art a lady:

302-4 **If only . . . warm:** If warmth alone were all you require of clothing, then your dazzling dress is obviously unnecessary, since gorgeousness is not naturally essential.

309-10 **fool me . . . tamely:** Do not make such a fool of me that I will take all this meekly.

311 **women's weapons, water drops:** tears.

317 **No, I'll not weep:** Lear approaches closer to the abyss of madness; S.D. The storm and Lear's madness proceed together.

317-20 In this moving passage, observe the number of little words that Shakespeare uses.

323 **bestowed:** lodged, sheltered.

324 **blame:** fault; **hath put . . . rest:** has caused his own discomfiture.

325 **taste his folly:** endure the effects of his foolish actions.

326 **his particular:** himself alone.

334 **will I . . . whither:** I do not know where he intends to go.

335 **give him way:** let him go; **leads himself:** does as he wishes, and will not be hindered.

If only to go warm were gorgeous,
Why, nature needs not what thou gorgeous wearest,
Which scarcely keeps thee warm. But, for true need—
You heavens, give me that patience, patience I need!   305
You see me here, you gods, a poor old man,
As full of grief as age; wretched in both.
If it be you that stirs these daughters' hearts
Against their father, fool me not so much
To bear it tamely; touch me with noble anger,   310
And let not women's weapons, water drops,
Stain my man's cheeks! No, you unnatural hags!
I will have such revenges on you both
That all the world shall—I will do such things—
What they are yet, I know not; but they shall be   315
The terrors of the earth! You think I'll weep.
No, I'll not weep.   *Sounds of an approaching storm.*
I have full cause of weeping, but this heart
Shall break into a hundred thousand flaws
Or ere I'll weep. O fool, I shall go mad!   320
            Exeunt Lear, Gloucester, Kent, and Fool.
Cornwall.   Let us withdraw, 'twill be a storm.
Regan.   This house is little; the old man and's people
Cannot be well bestowed.
Goneril.   'Tis his own blame; hath put himself from rest
And must needs taste his folly.   325
Regan.   For his particular, I'll receive him gladly,
But not one follower.
Goneril.   So am I purposed.
Where is my Lord of Gloucester?
Cornwall.   Followed the old man forth.   330
            Enter Gloucester.
                              He is returned.
Gloucester.   The King is in high rage.
Cornwall.   Whither is he going?
Gloucester.   He calls to horse, but will I know not whither.
Cornwall.   'Tis best to give him way, he leads himself.   335

338 **do sorely ruffle:** are very blustery.
342 **must be their schoolmasters:** must teach them wisdom.
343 **desperate train:** violent group of followers.
344 **incense:** provoke.
345 **to have . . . abused:** to be misled by evil advisers; **wisdom bids fear:** It would be wise to fear (the "desperate train").
See also p. 229.
  2 **minded like . . . unquietly:** with an unquiet (uneasy) mind.
  4 **contending with . . . elements:** struggling with the weather.
  6 **curled waters:** waves; **main:** land.
  7 **things:** Lear's misfortunes.
  8 **blasts:** winds; **eyeless:** unseeing, blind.
  9 **make nothing of:** show no respect for.
 10 **his little . . . man:** man's microcosm, in the sense that man is himself a little world.
 12 **cub-drawn:** hungry. Literally, the expression means: with udders sucked dry by cubs; **couch:** remain in shelter.
 13 **belly-pinched:** gaunt and ravenous.

Goneril. My lord, entreat him by no means to stay.
Gloucester. Alack, the night comes on, and the bleak winds
　Do sorely ruffle. For many miles about
　There's scarce a bush.
Regan.　　　　　　　O, sir, to wilful men　　　　　340
　The injuries that they themselves procure
　Must be their schoolmasters. Shut up your doors.
　He is attended with a desperate train,
　And what they may incense him to, being apt
　To have his ear abused, wisdom bids fear.　　　　345
Cornwall. Shut up your doors, my lord; 'tis a wild night.
　My Regan counsels well. Come out o' the storm.
　　　　　　　　　　　　　　　　　Exeunt.

ACT III

Scene 1

A HEATH.

Storm still. Enter Kent and a Gentleman, severally.

Kent. Who's there, besides foul weather?
Gentleman. One minded like the weather, most unquietly.
Kent. I know you. Where's the King?
Gentleman. Contending with the fretful elements;
　Bids the wind blow the earth into the sea,　　　　5
　Or swell the curled waters 'bove the main,
　That things might change or cease; tears his white hair,
　Which the impetuous blasts, with eyeless rage,
　Catch in their fury and make nothing of;
　Strives in his little world of man to outscorn　　　10
　The to-and-fro-conflicting wind and rain.
　This night, wherein the cub-drawn bear would couch,
　The lion and the belly-pinched wolf

14 **unbonneted:** hatless. *Bonnet* was a general term for headgear.

15 **and bids . . . all:** and invites any destructive force to take his life. The cry "Take all" was a gambler's cry when he was down to his last stake or wager in a game of chance.

17-18 **labours to . . . injuries:** works hard at joking to relieve the pain caused by Lear's heart-breaking plight.

20 **upon the . . . note:** on the strength or guarantee of the fact that I know you.

21 **commend:** entrust; **a dear thing:** an important matter; **division:** discord, disunity.

22-23 **although as . . . cunning:** although the appearance of discord is cunningly concealed.

24-25 **that their . . . high:** that fate has raised to a position of great power; **who seem no less:** who appear nothing more or less (than servants).

26 **speculations:** synonym for *spies.*

27 **intelligent of our state:** having information about our government.

28 **snuffs and packings:** resentments and (consequent) plottings.

29-30 **hard rein . . . King:** arbitrary and cruel way in which they have treated Lear. The metaphor is from the managing of a horse by means of the reins at its mouth—by cruel pressure.

31 **furnishings:** outward evidences (Kent's sentence remains unfinished).

32 **power:** army.

33 **scattered:** divided.

34 **wise in our negligence:** knowing that we are ill-prepared; **have secret feet:** having obtained a secret foothold.

35 **at point:** on the point of, ready to.

37 **if on . . . far:** if you dare to trust me as far as.

38 **make your speed:** hurry.

40 **bemadding:** maddening.

41 **plain:** complain of.

43 **assurance:** reliable information.

44 **office:** assignment, duty.

48 **my out-wall:** my outer wall, exterior, or what I appear to be (Kent is in the disguise of a serving-man).

Keep their fur dry, unbonneted he runs,
And bids what will take all.   15
Kent.   But who is with him?
Gentleman.   None but the fool, who labours to outjest
  His heart-struck injuries.
Kent.   Sir, I do know you,
  And dare upon the warrant of my note   20
  Commend a dear thing to you. There is division
  (Although as yet the face of it is covered
  With mutual cunning) 'twixt Albany and Cornwall;
  Who have (as who have not, that their great stars
  Throned and set high?) servants, who seem no less,   25
  Which are to France the spies and speculations
  Intelligent of our state. What hath been seen,
  Either in snuffs and packings of the Dukes,
  Or the hard rein which both of them have borne
  Against the old kind King, or something deeper,   30
  Whereof, perchance, these are but furnishings—
  But, true it is, from France there comes a power
  Into this scattered kingdom, who already,
  Wise in our negligence, have secret feet
  In some of our best ports and are at point   35
  To show their open banner. Now to you:
  If on my credit you dare build so far
  To make your speed to Dover, you shall find
  Some that will thank you, making just report
  Of how unnatural and bemadding sorrow   40
  The King hath cause to plain.
  I am a gentleman of blood and breeding,
  And from some knowledge and assurance offer
  This office to you.
Gentleman.   I will talk further with you.   45
Kent.   No, do not.
  For confirmation that I am much more
  Than my out-wall, open this purse and take
  What it contains. If you shall see Cordelia

55 **to effect:** in their importance.
56-57 **in which . . . this:** in which your task lies this way (as he has just been instructed by Kent), while mine lies in this direction; **lights on:** discovers.
58 **holla:** shout for, summon.
See also p. 230.
1 **Blow, winds . . . blow:** Old maps were often decorated with faces drawn in the act of furiously blowing air or wind.
3 **cocks:** weather-vanes on the peaks of buildings.
4 **thought-executing:** killing with the speed of thought.
5 **vaunt-couriers:** fore-runners, *avant-coureur* (Fr.); **oak-cleaving:** strong enough to split an oak.
7 **Strike flat . . . world:** Flatten the earth.
8 **Nature's molds:** shapes into which all things are first poured in their creation; *i.e.*, the creative force of Nature, which has cheated Lear through his daughters; **germens:** seeds; **spill:** destroy, kill.
9 **ingrateful:** *Ungrateful* is the modern form, though we still use the noun *ingrate*.
10 **court holy water:** flattering words—a proverbial phrase. Flatter your daughters into giving you shelter for the night.
11-12 **ask thy daughters' blessing:** Apologize and come to terms with your daughters.
15 **nor:** neither.
16 **tax:** accuse; **elements:** forces of the storm.
18 **subscription:** submission, subjection to rule, allegiance.
15-18 Lear feels no bitterness at the storm, which owes him nothing, and implies that what the storm can do to him is nothing compared to what has been done to him by his daughters.

(As fear not but you shall), show her this ring,   50
And she will tell you who that fellow is
That yet you do not know. Fie on this storm!
I will go seek the King.
Gentleman.   Give me your hand. Have you no more to say?
Kent.   Few words, but, to effect, more than all yet: 55
That, when we have found the King (in which your pain
That way, I'll this), he that first lights on him
Holla the other.

Exeunt severally.

Scene 2

ANOTHER PART OF THE HEATH.

Storm still. Enter Lear and Fool.

Lear.   Blow, winds, and crack your cheeks! rage! blow!
You cataracts and hurricanoes, spout
Till you have drenched our steeples, drowned the cocks!
You sulph'rous and thought-executing fires,
Vaunt-couriers of oak-cleaving thunderbolts,   5
Singe my white head! And thou, all-shaking thunder,
Strike flat the thick rotundity o' the world,
Crack Nature's molds, all germens spill at once,
That make ingrateful man!
Fool.   O nuncle, court holy water in a dry house is bet-   10
ter than this rain water out o' door. Good nuncle, in; ask
thy daughters' blessing! Here's a night pities neither wise
men nor fools.
Lear.   Rumble thy bellyful! Spit, fire! Spout, rain!
Nor rain, wind, thunder, fire are my daughters.   15
I tax not you, you elements, with unkindness.
I never gave you kingdom, called you children,
You owe me no subscription. Then let fall

21 **servile ministers:** servants slavishly obeying your masters.

22-23 **pernicious:** evil; **join your . . . battles:** combine your heavenly (and hence, all-powerful) battalions.

26 **headpiece:** hat. The word involves a pun and also means *brain*. Lear should have brains enough to take shelter from the storm.

27 **codpiece:** part of male dress when long tight-fitting hose were worn, providing a *fly*, or opening, in the form of a buttoned flap. Here, it is a symbol of sexual lust.

27-34 The Fool utters three wise sayings in verse: The man who ranks sex higher than shelter will become a verminous beggar. Thus, since man is a great fool, there are many of this kind of beggar who marry eventually. The man who thinks more kindly of his toe than his heart will be kept awake by his hurting corns. Again, the implication of what the Fool says is that Lear has brought on all his troubles by his own incredible folly; *i.e.*, not seeing things in the proper order of importance.

35-36 **fair:** good-looking; **made mouths:** made faces. The Fool means that handsome women like Goneril and Regan are so obviously vain and selfish that Lear should have seen through their vanity and selfishness.

37 **pattern:** example.

40 **grace:** the King's grace or the King himself; **codpiece:** See line 27. The Fool refers to himself. It is said that jesters wore a more elaborate codpiece than others, and tended to flaunt male sexuality satirically. The Fool leaves Kent to decide which is the wise man and which the fool.

44 **gallow:** terrify (still a dialect word).

48 **carry:** bear, endure.

51 **pudder:** turmoil.

Your horrible pleasure. Here I stand your slave,
A poor, infirm, weak, and despised old man.   20
But yet I call you servile ministers,
That will with two pernicious daughters join
Your high-engendered battles 'gainst a head
So old and white as this! O, ho! 'tis foul!

Fool.   He that has a house to put's head in has a good   25
   headpiece.

> The codpiece that will house
>   Before the head has any,
> The head and he shall louse:
>   So beggars marry many.   30
> The man that makes his toe
>   What he his heart should make
> Shall of a corn cry woe,
>   And turn his sleep to wake.

For there was never yet fair woman but she made mouths   35
   in a glass.

    Enter Kent.

Lear.   No, I will be the pattern of all patience;
   I will say nothing.

Kent.   Who's there?

Fool.   Marry, here's grace and a codpiece; that's a wise   40
   man and a fool.

Kent.   Alas, sir, are you here? Things that love night
   Love not such nights as these. The wrathful skies
   Gallow the very wanderers of the dark
   And make them keep their caves. Since I was man,   45
   Such sheets of fire, such bursts of horrid thunder,
   Such groans of roaring wind and rain, I never
   Remember to have heard. Man's nature cannot carry
   The affliction nor the fear.

Lear.   Let the great gods,   50
   That keep this dreadful pudder o'er our heads,
   Find out their enemies now. Tremble, thou wretch,
   That hast within thee undivulged crimes

54 **unwhipped of:** unpunished by; **bloody:** murderous.
55 **simular:** simulator, pretender.
56 **incestuous:** lustful after daughter, sister, or mother—a desire considered abhorrent in all societies, primitive or civilized; **caitiff:** wretch.
57 **covert:** secret; **seeming:** pretence, hypocrisy.
58 **practised:** plotted against.
59-60 **Rive your concealing continents:** Shatter the containers hiding you; **summoners:** church officers who called offenders before the church courts. Here, the summoners are the vengeances against sinful man, represented by the storm; **cry these . . . grace:** beg for mercy from.
65 **hard house:** cruel palace (of Gloucester).
68 **to come in:** entry, welcome.
69 **scanted:** missing, all but omitted.
73 **art:** The reference is to the art of alchemy, which contrived to turn base metals into gold.
74 **vile:** paltry (such as mere straw for bedding).
77-80 The Fool's song is an adaptation of the song in *Twelfth Night* (**V. i. 398-417**). The meaning is that a fool must content himself with what fortune brings him, which will be poor because he is a fool. He may be referring to himself, or to Lear, or to both.
82 **cool a courtesan:** make use of a harlot. The Fool lewdly pretends that the group is entering a brothel.
84 **more in . . . matter:** better in preaching than in conduct.
85 **malt:** part of the ingredients of beer and ale.
86 **their tailors' tutors:** better than their tailors in making clothing.
87 **heretics:** a heretic is one who dissents from accepted religious belief.

Unwhipped of justice. Hide thee, thou bloody hand;
Thou perjured, and thou simular of virtue   55
That are incestuous. Caitiff, to pieces shake
That under covert and convenient seeming
Hast practised on man's life. Close pent-up guilts,
Rive your concealing continents, and cry
These dreadful summoners grace. I am a man   60
More sinned against than sinning.
Kent.   Alack, bareheaded?
Gracious my lord, hard by here is a hovel;
Some friendship will it lend you 'gainst the tempest.
Repose you there, while I to this hard house   65
(More harder than the stones whereof 'tis raised,
Which even but now, demanding àfter you,
Denied me to come in) return, and force
Their scanted courtesy.
Lear.   My wits begin to turn.   70
Come on, my boy. How dost, my boy? Art cold?
I am cold myself. Where is this straw, my fellow?
The art of our necessities is strange,
And can make vile things precious. Come, your hovel.
Poor fool and knave, I have one part in my heart   75
That's sorry yet for thee.
Fool (*sings*).
      He that has and a little tiny wit,
        With hey, ho, the wind and the rain,
      Must make content with his fortunes fit,
        Though the rain it raineth every day.   80
Lear.   True, boy. Come, bring us to this hovel.
                    Exeunt Lear and Kent.
Fool.   This is a brave night to cool a courtesan. I'll
speak a prophecy ere I go:
      When priests are more in word than matter;
      When brewers mar their malt with water;   85
      When nobles are their tailors' tutors,
      No heretics burned, but wenches' suitors;

89 **squire:** boy apprenticed to a knight to learn the art of knighthood.

91 **cutpurses:** thieves (who cut purse strings and make off with the purse).

93 **bawds:** See line 82, a variant of *harlot*.

94 **Albion:** Britain.

95 **confusion:** ruin.

96 **who:** if anyone.

97 **that going . . . feet:** a truism, uttered with great solemnity.

84-97 The Fool speaks a series of prophecies that are based upon common events, and pretends that they will probably never happen.

98 **Merlin:** the magician of King Arthur's Court. The Fool points out the anachronism in his statement. The general setting of *King Lear* is early Britain before the time of King Arthur. See also p. 231.

1-2 **unnatural dealing:** cruel treatment given to Lear.

4 **perpetual displeasure:** permanent hostility.

7 **Go to:** an expression indicating that Kent's remark is an obvious one, roughly equivalent to: That's enough about that matter; **division:** See III. i. 21.

9 **'tis dangerous . . . spoken:** It's dangerous to divulge the contents in speaking.

10 **closet:** private room, or perhaps, cupboard. Cf. *closeted*, which now means: meeting in a private room.

11 **home:** completely, to the utmost.

12 **power:** army; **footed:** landed (from France); **incline to:** support.

13 **look him:** look for him; Q1 reads *seek*; **privily relieve:** secretly aid.

14 **charity:** kind treatment.

When every case in law is right;
No squire in debt nor no poor knight;
When slanders do not live in tongues;   90
Nor cutpurses come not to throngs;
When usurers tell their gold i' the field;
And bawds and whores do churches build:
Then shall the realm of Albion
Come to great confusion.   95
Then comes the time, who lives to see't,
That going shall be used with feet.
This prophecy Merlin shall make, for I live before his
   time.   *Exit.*

Scene 3

INSIDE GLOUCESTER'S CASTLE.

Enter Gloucester and Edmund.

Gloucester. Alack, alack, Edmund, I like not this unnatural
  dealing! When I desired their leave that I might pity
  him, they took from me the use of mine own house;
  charged me on pain of perpetual displeasure neither to
  speak of him, entreat for him, nor any way sustain him.   5
Edmund. Most savage and unnatural!
Gloucester. Go to; say you nothing. There is division between the Dukes, and a worse matter than that. I have
  received a letter this night—'tis dangerous to be spoken—I
  have locked the letter in my closet. These injuries the   10
  King now bears will be revenged home; there is part of a
  power already footed; we must incline to the King. I
  will look him and privily relieve him. Go you and maintain talk with the Duke, that my charity be not of him
  perceived. If he ask for me, I am ill and gone to bed.   15
  If I die for it, as no less is threatened me, the King my

18 **toward:** imminent, about to happen.
19 **courtesy:** service; **forbid:** forbidden, withheld from.
20 **instantly know:** (from Edmund).
21 **a fair deserving:** a service that should bring me the reward I deserve; **draw me:** bring to me.
See also p. 232.
2 **the tyranny . . . night's:** the harshness of the night in the open air.
3 **nature:** man's strength.
9 **'tis much:** that it much matters; **contentious:** contending (in the sense of contending or struggling against man).
11 **invades:** soaks. Observe the greater effectiveness of Shakespeare's word.
12-13 **But where . . . felt:** Where a greater illness is established, the second or lesser is scarcely noticed.
15-17 **i' the mouth:** face to face; **When the . . . delicate:** When the mind is untroubled, the body is sensitive.
19 **save what beats there:** except what troubles my heart—the ungratefulness of Goneril and Regan; **filial ingratitude:** ungratefulness of children. These two words express the theme of the play. Grammatically, they are in apposition to "what beats there".
21 **home:** See III. iii. 11.

old master must be relieved. There are strange things
toward, Edmund. Pray you be careful. *Exit.*
Edmund. This courtesy, forbid thee, shall the Duke
Instantly know, and of that letter too. 20
This seems a fair deserving, and must draw me
That which my father loses—no less than all.
The younger rises when the old doth fall. *Exit.*

Scene 4

BEFORE A HOVEL ON THE HEATH.

Storm still. Enter Lear, Kent, and Fool.

Kent. Here is the place, my lord. Good my lord, enter.
The tyranny of the open night's too rough
For nature to endure. Let me alone.
Lear.
Kent. Good my lord, enter here. 5
Lear. Wilt break my heart?
Kent. I had rather break mine own. Good my lord,
enter.
Lear. Thou thinkest 'tis much that this contentious
storm
Invades us to the skin. So 'tis to thee;
But where the greater malady is fixed,
The lesser is scarce felt. Thou'dst shun a bear;
But if thy flight lay toward the roaring sea,
Thou'dst meet the bear i' the mouth. When the mind's 15
free,
The body's delicate. The tempest in my mind
Doth from my senses take all feeling else
Save what beats there. Filial ingratitude!
Is it not as this mouth should tear this hand 20
For lifting food to it? But I will punish home!

26   **that way:** in thinking of those ills; **shun:** avoid.
31   **on things would:** The relative pronoun *which* is omitted.
32   **houseless poverty:** you poor homeless fellow. Here, the abstract is used for the concrete. Lear then expands the idea in lines 34-42.
33   **pray:** Lear prays to the poor, not to the gods.
35   **bide:** endure; **pelting:** relentless pouring.
37   **looped and windowed raggedness:** ragged clothing full of gaping holes. "Looped" and "windowed" are synonyms. Cf. *loophole*.
39   **this:** this condition of the poor, to which I have been reduced; **Take physic, pomp:** Cure yourselves, you great ones. Lear then gives the remedy.
41-42   **shake the . . . just:** that you may cast away what you do not need and give it to the poor, and show that there is more justice in life than we think.
43   **fathom and half:** Edgar uses the call of the sailor sounding the depth of water in the hold of a sinking ship.
52   **Humh:** Edgar shivers from the cold and damp.
54   **Didst thou . . . daughters:** Lear in his madness thinks that misfortune such as that evident in Poor Tom could only be inflicted by daughters as ungrateful as his own.

    No, I will weep no more. In such a night
    To shut me out! Pour on; I will endure.
    In such a night as this! O Regan, Goneril!
    Your old kind father, whose frank heart gave all!   25
    O, that way madness lies; let me shun that!
    No more of that.
Kent.   Good my lord, enter here.
Lear.   Prithee go in thyself; seek thine own ease.
    This tempest will not give me leave to ponder   30
    On things would hurt me more. But I'll go in.
    (*To the Fool*). In, boy; go first.—You houseless poverty—
    Nay, get thee in. I'll pray, and then I'll sleep.
         The Fool enters the hovel.
    Poor naked wretches, wheresoe'er you are,
    That bide the pelting of this pitiless storm,   35
    How shall your houseless heads and unfed sides,
    Your looped and windowed raggedness, defend you
    From seasons such as these? O, I have ta'en
    Too little care of this! Take physic, pomp;
    Expose thyself to feel what wretches feel,   40
    That thou may'st shake the superflux to them
    And show the heavens more just.
Edgar (*within*).   Fathom and half, fathom and half! Poor
    Tom!
         Re-enter Fool.
Fool.   Come not in here, nuncle, here's a spirit. Help   45
  me, help me!
Kent.   Give me thy hand. Who's there?
Fool.   A spirit, a spirit! He says his name's poor Tom.
Kent.   What art thou that dost grumble there i' the
  straw? Come forth.   50
        Enter Edgar.
Edgar.   Away! the foul fiend follows me! Through the
  sharp hawthorn blow the winds. Humh! go to thy bed,
  and warm thee.
Lear.   Didst thou give all to thy two daughters? And

59 **laid knives . . . pillow:** knives for killing himself; **halters in his pew:** ropes with which to hang himself from a porch.

60 **ratsbane:** rat poison; **porridge:** broth, soup.

61 **bay:** brown; **trotting horse:** horse trained to move gently; **four-inched:** very narrow.

62 **course:** chase; **for:** as; **Bless thy five wits:** May God bless your faculties.

63 **O, do . . . de:** Edgar shudders from the cold; **Bless thee:** May God protect you.

64 **star-blasting:** being struck by a wandering star; **taking:** being struck by disease, infection.

65-66 **There could . . . there:** Edgar pretends to clutch at a spirit or devil that haunts him, suggesting at the same time that he is clutching at vermin on his body.

56-66 Edgar utters a petition that requests charity, but he is not entirely coherent. We must remember that he is playing a part.

67 **Have his . . . pass:** Lear can see in Edgar only the image of his own misfortune.

69 **had been:** would have been.

71 **pendulous air:** air brooding over man.

72 **fated:** fatefully, as agents of fate.

74-75 **Death, traitor:** Lear would condemn Kent to death for expressing the heresy or treason that anything but filial ingratitude could have caused Poor Tom's plight; **subdued nature:** reduced his powers.

79 **judicious:** fitting, appropriate, suitable; **this flesh:** Lear himself; **begot:** fathered.

80 **pelican:** Many references to the legendary character of the pelican are extant. The most appropriate explanation here is that the pelican was thought to feed its young with its own blood. Thus, Lear means that Goneril and Regan have drained their parent of the last drop of blood.

81-82 **Pillicock Hill:** The word "pillicock" is certainly suggested to Edgar by the word "pelican". It was a facetious term of endearment, but had also a lewd sense easily surmised from the context; **Alow, alow, loo, loo:** This is a cry ordinarily used to call a hawk. Edgar's entire cry is primarily intended, whatever its meaning, to convey the impression of profound madness.

86-87 **keep thy word's justice:** Keep your word; **commit not:** do not commit adultery; **man's sworn spouse:** another man's lawful wife.

85-88 Edgar speaks a catechism.

art thou come to this?   55

Edgar. Who gives anything to poor Tom? whom the
foul fiend hath led through fire and through flame,
through ford and whirlpool, o'er bog and quagmire; that
hath laid knives under his pillow and halters in his pew,
set ratsbane by his porridge, made him proud of heart,   60
to ride on a bay trotting horse over four-inched bridges,
to course his own shadow for a traitor. Bless thy five wits!
Tom's acold. O, do de, do de, do de. Bless thee from
whirlwinds, star-blasting, and taking! Do poor Tom
some charity, whom the foul fiend vexes. There could I   65
have him now, and there, and there again, and there!
          Storm still.

Lear. Have his daughters brought him to this pass?
Couldst thou save nothing? Wouldst thou give 'em all?

Fool. Nay, he reserved a blanket, else we had been all
shamed.   70

Lear. Now all the plagues that in the pendulous air
Hang fated o'er men's faults light on thy daughters!

Kent. He hath no daughters, sir.

Lear. Death, traitor! Nothing could have subdued
nature   75
To such a lowness but his unkind daughters.
Is it the fashion that discarded fathers
Should have thus little mercy on their flesh?
Judicious punishment! 'Twas this flesh begot
Those pelican daughters.   80

Edgar. Pillicock sat on Pillicock Hill. Alow, alow, loo,
loo!

Fool. This cold night will turn us all to fools and madmen.

Edgar. Take heed o' the foul fiend; obey thy parents;   85
keep thy word's justice; swear not; commit not with
man's sworn spouse; set not thy sweet heart on proud
array. Tom's acold.

Lear. What hast thou been?

91-92 **wore gloves . . . cap:** wore a favourite girl's glove in his hat as a mark of affection; **served the . . . heart:** satisfied the sexual desires of my mistress.

94-95 **slept in . . . lust:** even in my sleep devised ways and means of satisfying sexual desires.

96 **out-paramoured the Turk:** surpassed the Sultan in the number of mistresses. The comparison is, of course, anachronistic.

97 **light of ear:** ready to listen to any malicious talk; **hog in sloth:** as lazy as a pig. "Sloth" was one of the Seven Deadly Sins.

99-100 **Let not . . . woman:** Do not fall in love with a woman as soon as you hear her shoes creak or her skirts rustle.

101-2 **plackets:** the opening usually in the side-seam of a woman's dress or skirt to make it easier to put the dress or skirt on; **lender's books:** money-lender's record book.

102-4 **Still through . . . wind:** Since Edgar has said these words twice, they are probably the refrain of a song or poem, as are those of line 104; **suum, mun . . . nonny:** an imitation of the sound of the wind; **sessa:** an interjection, perhaps the expression *So, so* used to quiet cattle. The word is an emendation of the editor Malone. F1 and F2 have *sessy* or *sessey*; **Dolphin my . . . by:** The sound of a horse trotting may have been suggested to Edgar by the sound of the storm.

107-10 **cat:** the civet-cat, whose glands function like those of the skunk and provide the base for the best perfume; **Thou owest . . . perfume:** Lear, addressing his words to the Bedlamite (Edgar), says that he has taken nothing from the animals for himself— no silk from the silkworm, no fur from any beast, no wool from the sheep, and no perfume from the civet-cat; **on's:** of us; **sophisticated:** artificial, wearing clothes that are, of course, not a part of themselves.

112 **lendings:** borrowed articles—in this case, Lear's clothing; S.D. **Tearing his garments:** Lear tears at his clothing, trying to re-move it, because he desires himself to be natural rather than "sophisticated". By identifying himself with "unaccommodated man", he escapes from man's vile nature. The tearing off of clothing, a recognized symptom of madness, is also symbolic of Lear's change from pride to humility.

114-16 **Now a . . . cold:** Just as a little fire in a barren field is harmless, so is the lust in a wicked old man's heart, since his body is too weak to do any harm; **a walking fire:** Gloucester, carrying his torch.

117-19 **Flibbertigibbet:** a devil, from Harsnett (see p. xi); **curfew:** 9 p.m.; **first cock:** midnight; **the web . . . pin:** cataract of the eye; **harelip:** congenital defect in the upper lip.

Edgar. A servingman, proud in heart and mind; that 90
curled my hair, wore gloves in my cap; served the lust of
my mistress' heart and did the act of darkness with her;
swore as many oaths as I spake words, and broke them in
the sweet face of heaven; one that slept in the contriving
of lust, and waked to do it. Wine loved I deeply, dice 95
dearly; and in woman out-paramoured the Turk. False of
heart, light of ear, bloody of hand; hog in sloth, fox in
stealth, wolf in greediness, dog in madness, lion in prey.
Let not the creaking of shoes nor the rustling of silks be-
tray thy poor heart to woman. Keep thy foot out of 100
brothels, thy hand out of plackets, thy pen from lender's books, and defy the foul fiend. Still through the hawthorn blows the cold wind; says suum, mun, hey, no,
nonny. Dolphin my boy, my boy, sessa! let him trot by.
        Storm still.

Lear. Thou wert better in thy grave than to answer 105
with thy uncovered body this extremity of the skies. Is
man no more than this? Consider him well. Thou owest
the worm no silk, the beast no hide, the sheep no wool,
the cat no perfume. Ha! Here's three on's are sophisticated! Thou art the thing itself; unaccommodated man 110
is no more but such a poor, bare, forked animal as thou
art. Off, off, you lendings! Come, unbutton here.
        Tearing his garments.

Fool. Prithee, nuncle, be contented! 'Tis a naughty
night to swim in. Now a little fire in a wild field were
like an old lecher's heart—a small spark, all the rest on's 115
body cold. Look, here comes a walking fire.
        Enter Gloucester with a torch.

Edgar. This is the foul Flibbertigibbet. He begins at curfew, and walks till the first cock. He gives the web and
the pin, squints the eye, and makes the harelip; mildews
the white wheat, and hurts the poor creature of earth. 120
        Swithold footed thrice the 'old;
        He met the nightmare, and her nine fold;

121-5 **Swithold footed . . . thee:** The stanza is a charm, having the effect of destroying the power of the demon or nightmare. It means that St. Withold travelled around the world three times, met the demon Nightmare and her nine offspring, ordered her to dismount from the spirits she was riding, promise never to trouble anyone again, and then to depart as rapidly as possible.

131 **todpole:** tadpole; **wall-newt:** wall lizard; **water:** water newt.

133 **sallets:** salads; **old rat . . . ditch-dog:** dead rat and dog carcass found in a ditch.

134 **green mantle:** greenish scum; **standing:** stagnant.

135 **tithing:** parish (or district); **stock-punished:** put into the stocks (like Kent).

136-7 **three suits:** the allowance of a servant. See II. ii. 14; **who hath . . . wear:** The significance of these lines is that Edgar was once a normal human being with the customary belongings of the times.

138-9 **deer:** game; **year:** years (an old plural still occasionally heard in rural speech); **But mice . . . year:** The old couplet recapitulates what Edgar has just stated.

140 **my follower:** my attending friend; **Smulkin:** name of another fiend from Harsnett.

143 **Modo . . . Mahu:** powerful devils mentioned by Harsnett.

144 **our flesh and blood:** our children—Edgar, Goneril, and Regan; **is grown:** has become.

145 **gets:** begets, is father to.

147 **suffer:** permit, allow.

149 **be:** present time—subjunctive mood of the verb in a concessive ("though") clause, expressing an admission or concession, rather than in a clause expressing doubt or uncertainty as in modern English.

153 **philosopher:** scientist. In Elizabethan English, *philosophy* meant science or the accumulation of knowledge.

154 **What is . . . thunder:** a scientific question, frequently discussed before the facts were known.

156 **Theban:** a learned Greek, a scholar, a man of knowledge.

157 **study:** particular field of study or research.

158 **prevent:** avoid, keep ahead of.

     Bid her alight
     And her troth plight,
    And aroint thee, witch, aroint thee!   125
Kent. How fares your Grace?
Lear. What's he?
Kent. Who's there? What is't you seek?
Gloucester. What are you there? Your names?
Edgar. Poor Tom, that eats the swimming frog, the toad, 130
 the todpole, the wall-newt and the water; that in the fury
 of his heart, when the foul fiend rages, eats cow-dung for
 sallets, swallows the old rat and the ditch-dog, drinks the
 green mantle of the standing pool; who is whipped from
 tithing to tithing, and stock-punished and imprisoned; 135
 who hath had three suits to his back, six shirts to his
 body, horse to ride, and weapon to wear;
    But mice and rats, and such small deer,
    Have been Tom's food for seven long year.
 Beware my follower. Peace, Smulkin! peace, thou fiend! 140
Gloucester. What, hath your Grace no better company?
Edgar. The prince of darkness is a gentleman!
 Modo he's called, and Mahu.
Gloucester. Our flesh and blood, my lord, is grown so vile,
 That it doth hate what gets it.   145
Edgar. Poor Tom's acold.
Gloucester. Go in with me. My duty cannot suffer
 T' obey in all your daughters' hard commands.
 Though their injunction be to bar my doors
 And let this tyrannous night take hold upon you, 150
 Yet have I ventured to come seek you out
 And bring you where both fire and food is ready.
Lear. First let me talk with this philosopher.
 What is the cause of thunder?
Kent. Good my lord, take his offer; go into the house. 155
Lear. I'll talk a word with this same learned Theban.
 What is your study?
Edgar. How to prevent the fiend and to kill vermin.

160 **importune:** beg, implore. Pronounced with the stress on *por.*
163 **His daughters . . . death:** See II. iv. 335-6.
167 **outlawed from my blood:** outcast from my family.
169 **no father . . . dearer:** Insert *loved* after "father".
172 **cry you mercy, sir:** I beg your pardon. I did not hear you since I was listening to my philosopher.
181 **soothe him:** Let him have his way.
183 **Take him you on:** You take the Bedlamite to the hovel, and I'll go along with the King.
185 **Athenian:** philosopher, thinker.
187 **child:** a candidate for knighthood; **Rowland:** nephew of Charlemagne and the chief knight of his time, according to the legends surrounding the name of the French King; **Child Rowland . . . came:** a line probably from a lost ballad.
188 **word:** motto; **still:** ever, always.
189-90 **Fie, foh . . . man:** a couplet from *Jack the Giant Killer,* madly unsuitable for a chivalrous knight to use as a motto for his coat of arms.

See also p. 232.

Lear.   Let me ask you one word in private.
Kent.   Importune him once more to go, my lord.   160
   His wits begin to unsettle.
Gloucester.   Canst thou blame him?
         Storm still.
   His daughters seek his death. Ah, that good Kent!
   He said it would be thus—poor banished man!
   Thou sayest the King grows mad: I'll tell thee, friend,   165
   I am almost mad myself. I had a son,
   Now outlawed from my blood. He sought my life
   But lately, very late. I loved him, friend—
   No father his son dearer. True to tell thee,
   The grief hath crazed my wits. What a night's this!   170
   I do beseech your Grace—
Lear.   O, cry you mercy, sir.
   Noble philosopher, your company.
Edgar.   Tom's acold.
Gloucester.   In, fellow, there, into the hovel; keep thee 175
   warm.
Lear.   Come, let's in all.
Kent.   This way, my lord.
Lear.   With him!
   I will keep still with my philosopher.   180
Kent.   Good my lord, soothe him; let him take the
   fellow.
Gloucester.   Take him you on.
Kent.   Sirrah, come on; go along with us.
Lear.   Come, good Athenian.   185
Gloucester.   No words, no words! hush.
Edgar.   Child Rowland to the dark tower came;
   His word was still
            Fie, foh, and fum!
            I smell the blood of a British man.   190
                              Exeunt.

1   **I will . . . revenge:** Edmund has told Cornwall that Gloucester intends to help Lear and to support the army of invasion from France. See III. iii. 10-13.

2   **censured:** judged; **nature:** human nature, the natural bond between father and son.

3   **loyalty:** to Cornwall, not his father; **fears me:** makes me worry.

4-7   **I now . . . himself:** I now understand that it was not only the evil in your brother Edgar that made him want to destroy your father, but also your father's evil. Your brother's wickedness was, however, a necessary motivating factor in bringing about the plot against his father's life. See II. i. 98-107; **a provoking merit:** a deserving that incites action; **a reprovable badness:** a wickedness deserving punishment.

8-9   **repent to be just:** must feel the sting of remorse (at betraying my father) by honouring my loyalty to you, Cornwall; **approves:** proves.

10   **an intelligent party:** a well-informed person; **to the advantages of:** for the assistance of.

11   **were not:** did not exist. "Were" is the subjunctive mood of the verb expressing a condition contrary to fact; **or not I:** or that I were not.

15   **true or false:** The letter itself is evidence enough; the exact facts do not matter.

17   **apprehension:** arrest.

18   **comforting:** aiding.

19   **stuff:** reinforce, strengthen; **his suspicion:** the suspicion that already rests on Gloucester.

See also p. 233.

Scene 5

INSIDE GLOUCESTER'S CASTLE.

Enter Cornwall and Edmund.

Cornwall. I will have my revenge ere I depart his house.

Edmund. How, my lord, I may be censured, that nature thus gives way to loyalty, something fears me to think of.

Cornwall. I now perceive it was not altogether your brother's evil disposition made him seek his death; but a 5 provoking merit, set a-work by a reprovable badness in himself.

Edmund. How malicious is my fortune that I must repent to be just! This is the letter he spoke of, which approves him an intelligent party to the˙advantages of France. O 10 heavens! that this treason were not, or not I the detector!

Cornwall. Go with me to the Duchess.

Edmund. If the matter of this paper be certain, you have mighty business in hand.

Cornwall. True or false, it hath made thee Earl of Glouces- 15 ter. Seek out where thy father is, that he may be ready for our apprehension.

Edmund (*aside*). If I find him comforting the King, it will stuff his suspicion more fully. (*aloud*) I will persevere in my course of loyalty, though the conflict be 20 sore between that and my blood.

Cornwall. I will lay trust upon thee, and thou shalt find a dearer father in my love.

Exeunt.

4 **have:** plural by attraction to "wits"; the subject is "power".
6 **Frateretto:** another devil's name from Harsnett; **Nero:** Nero was condemned to playing the fiddle in hell; it was Trajan, according to Rabelais in *Gargantua*, who was doomed to fishing for frogs in hell. Much work has been done in trying to explain this obscure reference.
7 **innocent:** fool.
10 **yeoman:** a freeholder: that is, one who owned his own land but was somewhat below the rank of gentleman.
12-14 **No, he's . . . him:** This statement has been explained as a reference by Shakespeare to his own efforts to acquire a coat of arms for his father (see p. xxviii). A suggestion is made by the critic Schmidt that there is a pun on "mad" and *made*. To Edgar, the words would convey only nonsense. Lear understands them in the light of his own experience. The passage is not in Q1.
15 **to have a thousand:** Lear exaggerates the number of his off-spring in the vehemence of his desire to torture them either by roasting them on red-hot spits or by beating them; **spits:** iron rods, used to pierce meat in order to turn it over a fire and roast it. Used sometimes as a weapon in an emergency.
16 **hizzing:** hissing (from the heat).
20 **arraign:** bring to trial; **them:** his daughters; **straight:** immediately; **It shall . . . straight:** The references to animals and to the fickleness of human beings prompt Lear again to think of his pelican daughters, and to bring them to *trial* instead of to *torture*, as he first decided. Lear is at the height of his madness here.
21 **justicer:** judge.
22-23 **sapient:** wise; **she-foxes:** symbols of cunning deception and, in folklore, of ingratitude.
24 **he:** a fiend.
25 **eyes:** watchers, spectators; **madam:** Edgar pretends to address Goneril and Regan, turning to the two stools that Lear thinks are his daughters.

Scene 6

AN OUTBUILDING NEAR GLOUCESTER'S CASTLE

Enter Gloucester and Kent.

Gloucester. Here is better than the open air; take it thankfully. I will piece out the comfort with what addition I can. I will not be long from you.

Kent. All the power of his wits have given way to his impatience. The gods reward your kindness! 5

Exit Gloucester.

Enter Lear, Edgar, and Fool.

Edgar. Fraretto calls me, and tells me Nero is an angler in the lake of darkness. Pray, innocent, and beware the foul fiend.

Fool. Prithee, nuncle, tell me whether a madman be a gentleman or a yeoman. 10

Lear. A king, a king!

Fool. No, he's a yeoman that has a gentleman to his son; for he's a mad yeoman that sees his son a gentleman before him.

Lear. To have a thousand with red burning spits 15
Come hizzing in upon 'em—

Edgar. The foul fiend bites my back.

Fool. He's mad that trusts in the tameness of a wolf, a horse's health, a boy's love, or a whore's oath.

Lear. It shall be done; I will arraign them straight. 20
(*To Edgar*). Come, sit thou here, most learned justicer.
(*To the Fool*). Thou, sapient sir, sit here. Now, you she-foxes!

Edgar. Look, where he stands and glares! Wantest thou eyes at trial, madam? 25
Come o'er the bourn, Bessy, to me.

Fool. Her boat hath a leak,
And she must not speak

26-29 **Come o'er . . . thee:** the modified words of an old song, the first line of which is sung correctly by Edgar as he beckons the imagined daughters to come closer to the place of trial. The remaining lines, whimsically modified, are added by the Fool, who may be saying obscurely that the case of Goneril and Regan is not a sound one.

31 **nightingale:** referring to the Fool's singing; **Hoppedance:** another of Harsnett's devils, though the name was spelled *Hobberdidance* or *Haberdidance* in the *Declaration* (see p. xi); **in Tom's belly:** in reference to the digestive rumblings in the stomach, especially those caused by hunger. See also "Croak not", line 32.

32 **white herring:** unsmoked or fresh herring.

34 **How do you, sir:** How do you feel, sir? **amazed:** dumbfounded, stunned.

36 **evidence:** witnesses to testify against Goneril and Regan—an abstract term used for the concrete.

38 **yokefellow of equity:** partner in law.

39 **bench:** a verb—take your place on the bench; **o' the commission:** of those commissioned or legally constituted as justices or law officers.

42-45 **Sleepest or . . . harm:** the words, apparently, of an old song; **in the corn:** in the wheat field; **and for one blast:** and though you take time to play just one tune (on the shepherd's pipe); **minikin:** little, dainty.

46 **Purr:** a cat's cry. Harsnett mentions a devil, Purre. Edgar pretends to refer to a friend in the form of a cat.

47 **arraign:** See line 20.

48 **kicked:** an action conceived in Lear's tortured imagination.

52 **Cry you mercy:** See III. iv. 172; **joint-stool:** literally, a stool made by a joiner or carpenter. The complete phrase was a cliché in Shakespeare's day, signifying: I did not see you. The Fool enjoys the joke of using the phrase here.

53 **another:** Regan; **warped:** twisted by evil thoughts.

55 **store:** sustenance; **on:** of; **Stop her there:** Lear imagines Regan is escaping from the Court.

56 **Corruption in the place:** There is evil in this Court because Regan is being allowed to escape.

57 **scape:** escape.

58 **Bless thy five wits:** See III. iv. 62.

59 **sir:** Lear; **patience:** See I. iv. 262, II. iv. 150, IV. iii. 18.

62 **counterfeiting:** pretending.

63-64 **The little . . . me:** Lear imagines that even his own pets have turned against him.

Why she dares not come over to thee.

Edgar. The foul fiend haunts poor Tom in the voice of a   30
nightingale. Hoppedance cries in Tom's belly for two
white herring. Croak not, black angel; I have no food for
thee.

Kent. How do you, sir? Stand you not so amazed.
Will you lie down and rest upon the cushions?   35

Lear. I'll see their trial first. Bring in their evidence.
(*To Edgar*). Thou, robed man of justice, take thy place.
(*To the Fool*). And thou, his yokefellow of equity,
Bench by his side. (*To Kent*). You are o' the commission,
Sit you too.   40

Edgar. Let us deal justly.
Sleepest or wakest thou, jolly shepherd?
Thy sheep be in the corn;
And for one blast of thy minikin mouth
Thy sheep shall take no harm.   45
Purr! the cat is grey.

Lear. Arraign her first. 'Tis Goneril. I here take my
oath before this honourable assembly, she kicked the poor
King her father.

Fool. Come hither, mistress. Is your name Goneril?   50

Lear. She cannot deny it.

Fool. Cry you mercy, I took you for a joint-stool.

Lear. And here's another, whose warped looks pro-
claim
What store her heart is made on. Stop her there!   55
Arms, arms! sword! fire! Corruption in the place!
False justicer, why hast thou let her scape?

Edgar. Bless thy five wits!

Kent. O pity! Sir, where is the patience now
That you so oft have boasted to retain?   60

Edgar (*aside*). My tears begin to take his part so much
They mar my counterfeiting.

Lear. The little dogs and all,
Tray, Blanch, and Sweetheart, see, they bark at me.

65   **Avaunt:** Away! Out of here!
70   **brach:** bitch; **lym:** bloodhound. A famous conjecture of Sir
     Thomas Hanmer (see p. xxi).
71   **tyke:** dog (still used in Yorkshire speech); **trundle-tail:** dog with
     a long, drooping tail.
74   **hatch:** lower half of a dutch door.
75-76 **Do, de, de, de:** See III. iv. 63; **Sessa:** See III. iv. 104; **Come,
     march . . . towns:** The suggestion has been made that these
     words, taken from an old song, are an invitation from a vaga-
     bond to a companion to go with him on his wanderings; **thy
     horn is dry:** a saying signifying that the speaker is thirsty. It
     also means that Edgar finds it difficult to maintain his pretence.
77-78 **anatomize:** dissect, perform an autopsy upon; **See what
     . . . heart:** Find out whether there is a growth about her heart.
79   **entertain:** engage.
80   **hundred:** his former establishment of knights.
81   **Persian:** Persian clothing was a symbol of gorgeous attire. Lear
     turns Edgar's rags into rich garments.
84   **curtains:** There are none, of course, and no cushions—only
     straw.
85   **So, so:** words spoken as he settles down, as his delirium sub-
     sides; **supper i' the morning:** Lear remembers that he has had no
     meal, and, therefore says: We'll have supper at breakfast time.
86   **And I'll . . . noon:** The Fool, jokingly, takes Lear at his word
     and decides that if breakfast is supper time, bedtime must
     surely be noon.
91   **a plot of death:** See III. iv. 163; also III. vii. 13. Oswald had
     been sent to apprehend Lear.
92   **litter:** device somewhat like a stretcher for carrying a person.
     Some litters had a tent-like covering that would shelter the per-
     son being carried; **in:** The preposition indicates that the litter
     for Lear was equipped with a shelter.
93   **drive:** The verb suggests that the litter was designed to be sus-
     pended between two horses, in tandem, one at each end of the
     litter, and also that great haste was necessary.
97   **stand in assured loss:** are certain to be lost; **Take up:** Lift up the
     litter.

Edgar. Tom will throw his head at them. Avaunt, you   65
  curs!
          Be thy mouth or black or white,
          Tooth that poisons if it bite;
          Mastiff, greyhound, mongrel grim,
          Hound or spaniel, brach or lym,   70
          Bobtail tyke or trundle-tail—
          Tom will make him weep and wail;
          For, with throwing thus my head,
          Dogs leap the hatch, and all are fled.
  Do de, de, de. Sessa! Come, march to wakes and fairs   75
  and market towns. Poor Tom, thy horn is dry.
Lear. Then let them anatomize Regan. See what breeds
  about her heart. Is there any cause in nature that makes
  these hard hearts? (*To Edgar*). You, sir, I entertain for one
  of my hundred; only I do not like the fashion of your gar-   80
  ments. You'll say they are Persian; but let them be
  changed.
Kent. Now, good my lord, lie here and rest awhile.
Lear. Make no noise, make no noise; draw the curtains.
  So, so. We'll go to supper i' the morning.   85
Fool. And I'll go to bed at noon.
        Enter Gloucester.
Gloucester. Come hither, friend. Where is the King my mas-
  ter?
Kent. Here, sir; but trouble him not; his wits are gone.
Gloucester. Good friend, I prithee take him in thy arms.   90
  I have o'erheard a plot of death upon him.
  There is a litter ready; lay him in it
  And drive toward Dover, friend, where thou shalt meet
  Both welcome and protection. Take up thy master.
  If thou shouldst dally half an hour, his life,   95
  With thine, and all that offer to defend him,
  Stand in assured loss. Take up, take up!
  And follow me, that will to some provision
  Give thee quick conduct.

100 **Oppressed nature sleeps:** Lear's mind, overwhelmed by a deep hurt, has caused him to fall into a deep sleep.
101 **balmed:** comforted, helped to cure, healed.
102 **convenience:** circumstances, the present situation.
103 **stand in hard cure:** will be difficult to cure; S.D. **To the Fool:** This stage direction was added to the text by the Shakespearian editor Theobald. The Fool utters his last words in the play a moment before this (line 86) and appears no more; he leaves, following Kent's order and Gloucester's urgent plea to hurry (line 106).
107 **our betters:** those like Lear; **our woes:** the same sort of ills that we ordinary mortals must endure.
108 **We scarcely . . . foes:** We scarcely think our misfortunes are serious.
109 **Who alone . . . mind:** Editors generally agree that "alone" and "most" are the words to be emphasized. The one who suffers alone suffers most deeply.
110 **free:** carefree; **happy shows:** all appearances of happiness.
111 **sufferance:** misery; **o'erskip:** avoid.
112 **mates:** companions, company; **bearing fellowship:** when the endurance of misfortune is made bearable by companionship.
113 **portable:** bearable, endurable.
114 **when that . . . bow:** when what afflicts me also afflicts the King.
115 **He childed . . . fathered:** He had children as cruel as the father I had (and our sorrows are therefore the same).
116-18 **Mark the high noises:** Pay attention to the disagreements among those who are powerful in the country; **and thyself . . . thee:** and reveal yourself when false opinion that deforms you is reversed by your own proof and restores (reconciles) you to your true character.
119 **What will . . . King:** Whatever else may occur tonight, may the King escape safely!
120 **Lurk:** Remain in hiding.
See also p. 234.
1 **Post:** Ride (as a messenger).
2 **France:** the French King; **is landed:** See III. iii. 9-10, 20; III. v. 9-14.

Kent.   Oppressed nature sleeps.   100
This rest might yet have balmed thy broken sinews
Which, if convenience will not allow,
Stand in hard cure. (*To the Fool*). Come, help to bear thy
    master.
Thou must not stay behind.   105
Gloucester.   Come, come, away!
                    Exeunt all but Edgar.
Edgar.   When we our betters see bearing our woes,
We scarcely think our miseries our foes.
Who alone suffers suffers most i' the mind,
Leaving free things and happy shows behind;   110
But then the mind much sufferance doth o'erskip
When grief hath mates, and bearing fellowship.
How light and portable my pain seems now,
When that which makes me bend makes the King bow,
He childed as I fathered! Tom, away!   115
Mark the high noises, and thyself bewray
When false opinion, whose wrong thoughts defile thee,
In thy just proof repeals and reconciles thee.
What will hap more tonight, safe scape the King!
Lurk, lurk.   *Exit.*   120

Scene 7

INSIDE GLOUCESTER'S CASTLE.

Enter Cornwall, Regan, Goneril,
Edmund the Bastard, and Servants.

Cornwall (*to Goneril*).   Post speedily to my lord your hus-
band, show him this letter. The army of France is landed.
—Seek out the traitor Gloucester.
                    Exeunt some of the Servants.
Regan.   Hang him instantly.

7 **sister:** sister-in-law.

9-10 **Advise the . . . preparation:** Tell Albany, to whose palace you are going, to make the swiftest possible preparation for war; **bound to the like:** in the midst of similar preparations; perhaps, *must do the same*; **posts:** couriers, riders (with messages). See line 1.

11 **intelligent:** giving information.

14 **hence:** from here.

16 **hot questrists:** eager, anxious searchers.

17 **lord's:** Gloucester's.

24 **pinion:** tie his arms; **thief:** robber. The word had a stronger sense than it has now.

25-27 **though well . . . justice:** although we may not truly pass judgement on him without some form of trial; **our power . . . wrath:** My power as Duke will enable me to satisfy the anger I feel towards Gloucester (despite the law).

28 **blame:** criticize.

30 **Ingrateful fox:** See III. vi. 22-23.

31 **corky:** stiff, arthritic, withered (by age).

34 **foul play:** not murder, as in the modern sense, but rather injustice—the opposite of *fair play*.

Goneril.   Pluck out his eyes.   5
Cornwall.   Leave him to my displeasure. Edmund, keep
you our sister company. The revenges we are bound to
take upon your traitorous father are not fit for your be-
holding. Advise the Duke where you are going, to a most
festinate preparation. We are bound to the like. Our posts   10
shall be swift and intelligent betwixt us. Farewell, dear
sister; farewell, my Lord of Gloucester.
          Enter Oswald the Steward.
How now? Where's the King?
Oswald.   My Lord of Gloucester hath conveyed him hence.
Some five or six and thirty of his knights,   15
Hot questrists after him, met him at gate;
Who, with some other of the lord's dependants,
Are gone with him toward Dover, where they boast
To have well-armed friends.
Cornwall.   Get horses for your mistress.   20
Goneril.   Farewell, sweet lord, and sister.
Cornwall.   Edmund, farewell.
          Exeunt Goneril, Edmund, and Oswald.
                    Go seek the traitor Gloucester,
Pinion him like a thief, bring him before us.
                    Exeunt other Servants.
Though well we may not pass upon his life   25
Without the form of justice, yet our power
Shall do a court'sy to our wrath, which men
May blame, but not control.
          Enter Gloucester, brought in by two or three.
                    Who's there? the traitor?
Regan.   Ingrateful fox! 'tis he.   30
Cornwall.   Bind fast his corky arms.
Gloucester. What mean your Graces? Good my friends, con-
sider
You are my guests. Do me no foul play, friends.
Cornwall.   Bind him, I say.   35
                    Servants bind him.

36 **hard:** tightly.

37 **none:** no traitor.

38 **S.D.** a consummate insult to an elder. See also line 41.

39 **ignobly:** unworthy of the nobility, mean.

41 **white:** Goneril looks at the hairs of Gloucester's beard that are in her hand and observes, mockingly, that they are white and symbolic of purity.

42 **naughty:** wicked, evil.

43 **ravish:** pluck, tear.

44 **quicken:** come alive; **host:** Gloucester protests against the dishonouring of the age-old rule that courtesy between host and guest is inviolable.

45 **hospitable favours:** my face, which has an expression of hospitality on it.

46 **ruffle:** do violence to. See II. iv. 338. The word was much stronger in Elizabethan English than it is in modern usage.

47 **late:** lately, recently.

48 **simple-answered:** straightforward.

49 **confederacy:** unauthorized alliance or agreement, conspiracy.

50 **footed:** landed.

53 **guessingly set down:** written down without firm knowledge.

54 **of a neutral heart:** taking neither side.

56 **cunning:** Now he is using cunning.

57 **and false:** and he is false as well.

60-61 **charged at peril:** ordered on pain of death.

63-64 **I am . . . course:** I am like a bear chained to a post and must endure as best I can the attacks of the dogs—a reference to the so-called sport of bear-baiting. See *Macbeth*, V. vii. 1-2.

68 **anointed:** blessed with holy oil at his coronation. Therefore, to attack the King is sacrilege; **rash:** slash, as with a tusk, like a boar.

70-71 **hell-black night:** night as black as hell itself. The word suggests the sufferings of hell; **would have . . . fires:** would have risen in one great wave and extinguished the fire of the stars.

Regan.   Hard, hard. O filthy traitor!
Gloucester.   Unmerciful lady as you are, I am none.
Cornwall.   To this chair bind him. Villain, thou shalt find—
        Regan pulls his beard.
Gloucester.   By the kind gods, 'tis most ignobly done
    To pluck me by the beard.   40
Regan.   So white, and such a traitor!
Gloucester.   Naughty lady,
    These hairs which thou dost ravish from my chin
    Will quicken, and accuse thee. I am your host.
    With robber's hands my hospitable favours   45
    You should not ruffle thus. What will you do?
Cornwall.   Come, sir, what letters had you late from France?
Regan.   Be simple-answered, for we know the truth.
Cornwall.   And what confederacy have you with the traitors
    Late footed in the kingdom?   50
Regan.   To whose hands you have sent the lunatic King?
    Speak.
Gloucester.   I have a letter guessingly set down,
    Which came from one that's of a neutral heart,
    And not from one opposed.   55
Cornwall.   Cunning.
Regan.   And false.
Cornwall.   Where hast thou sent the King?
Gloucester.   To Dover.
Regan.   Wherefore to Dover? Wast thou not charged at   60
    peril—
Cornwall.   Wherefore to Dover? Let him answer that.
Gloucester.   I am tied to the stake, and I must stand the
    course.
Regan.   Wherefore to Dover?   65
Gloucester.   Because I would not see thy cruel nails
    Pluck out his poor old eyes; nor thy fierce sister
    In his anointed flesh rash boarish fangs.
    The sea, with such a storm as his bare head
    In hell-black night endured, would have buoyed up   70

72 **holp the . . . rain:** helped the heavens to rain (by his tears).
73 **if:** even if; **dern:** dreadful, Q1 reading; F1 reads *stern*.
74 **turn the key:** open the door (and let them in).
75 **All cruels else subscribe:** Disregard all other cruelties (than that inflicted upon Lear, since all are less diabolical). The passage has stirred much editorial comment.
76 **winged vengeance:** the vengeance of the gods, vengeance like a bird of prey; **children:** the offspring of wickedness and depravity who persecute Lear.
81 **One side . . . another:** An eye remaining would make the eyeless socket look worse. This is the most cynical comment Regan makes, since its pretended solicitude is offered for the greatest possible cruelty, apart from a lingering death; **The other too:** Gouge out the other eye as well.
87 **How now:** What are you up to? What do you think you are doing? A common interrogative expression covering a variety of circumstances.
89 **shake it . . . quarrel:** insult you to provoke an immediate quarrel for this cause—Gloucester's treatment.
91 **villain:** used here in the double sense of *scoundrel* and *serf*.
92-93 **Nay, then:** a denial that he is a serf; **come on:** an invitation to fight; **take the . . . anger:** Take the risk of fighting when angry (and therefore, rash).
94 **peasant:** Regan interprets Cornwall's punning reference to the servant; S.D. **She takes . . . behind:** stabbing him in the back.
96 **mischief:** injury.
97 **lest:** in case that; **vile jelly:** Gloucester's remaining eye.
98 **lustre:** brightness of the living eye.
101 **enkindle:** summon up; **sparks of nature:** feelings of filial affection.
102 **quit:** repay, requite, avenge.
103 **Out:** an interjection, expressing hatred here; abbreviated from *Out upon you!*

And quenched the stelled fires.
Yet, poor old heart, he holp the heavens to rain.
If wolves had at thy gate howled that dern time,
Thou shouldst have said, "Good porter, turn the key."
All cruels else subscribe: but I shall see   75
The winged vengeance overtake such children.
Cornwall.   See it shalt thou never. Fellows, hold the chair.
Upon these eyes of thine I'll set my foot.
Gloucester.   He that will think to live till he be old,
Give me some help!—O cruel! O you gods!   80
          Gloucester's eye is put out.
Regan.   One side will mock another. The other too!
Cornwall.   If you see vengeance—
1. Servant.   Hold your hand, my lord!
I have served you ever since I was a child,
But better service have I never done you   85
Than now to bid you hold.
Regan.   How now, you dog?
1. Servant.   If you did wear a beard upon your chin,
I'd shake it on this quarrel.
Regan.   What do you mean?   90
Cornwall.   My villain!   *They draw and fight.*
1. Servant.   Nay, then, come on, and take the chance of
     anger.
Regan.   Give me thy sword. A peasant stand up thus?
          She takes a sword and runs at him behind.
1. Servant.   O, I am slain! My lord, you have one eye left   95
To see some mischief on him. O!   *He dies.*
Cornwall.   Lest it see more, prevent it. Out, vile jelly!
Where is thy lustre now?
Gloucester.   All dark and comfortless! Where's my son Ed-
     mund?   100
Edmund, enkindle all the sparks of nature
To quit this horrid act.
Regan.   Out, treacherous villain!
Thou callest on him that hates thee. It was he

105-6 "That" and "who" have the same antecedent, "he" (line 104); **overture:** disclosure, revelation.

107 **abused:** deceived, wronged; **O my . . . abused:** Gloucester suddenly realizes that his past is being paid for in (a) his blindness, and (b) his monstrous misjudgement of his sons.

108 **that:** Edgar's wrong; **prosper him:** May he (Edgar) prosper.

109 **smell:** said with strong, malicious emphasis.

113 **slave:** the servant who attempted to defend Gloucester.

114 **apace:** quickly, freely.

115 **untimely:** at the wrong time in my life; **hurt:** wound.

118-20 **If she . . . monsters:** If she lives to a ripe age and dies a normal death, then all women will become wicked (since they will not have to fear punishment for their crimes). See IV. ii. 67-69.

121 **bedlam:** Edgar, evidently known to the servant.

122-3 **His roguish . . . anything:** Since the bedlam beggar is mad, he will not be called to account and can therefore safely lead Gloucester.

124-5 **I'll fetch . . . face:** a treatise on medicine (1616) recommends such treatment for injured eyes.

See also p. 235.

1-2 **thus:** as a bedlam beggar; **known:** aware oneself. This word is stressed; **contemned:** despised; **Yet better . . . flattered:** Yet it is better to be an outcast known only to oneself than to live unaware of one's state in the midst of flattery.

That made the overture of thy treasons to us,   105
Who is too good to pity thee.
Gloucester.   O my follies! Then Edgar was abused.
  Kind gods, forgive me that, and prosper him!
Regan.   Go thrust him out at gates, and let him smell
  His way to Dover.   110

>   *Exit a Servant with Gloucester.*
>   How is't, my lord? How look you?

Cornwall.   I have received a hurt. Follow me, lady.
  Turn out that eyeless villain. Throw this slave
  Upon the dunghill. Regan, I bleed apace.
  Untimely comes this hurt. Give me your arm.   115

>   *Exit Cornwall, led by Regan.*

2. Servant.   I'll never care what wickedness I do,
  If this man come to good.
3. Servant.   If she live long,
  And in the end meet the old course of death,
  Women will all turn monsters.   120
2. Servant.   Let's follow the old Earl, and get the bedlam
  To lead him where he would. His roguish madness
  Allows itself to anything.
3. Servant.   Go thou. I'll fetch some flax and whites of eggs
  To apply to his bleeding face. Now heaven help him!   125

>   *Exeunt.*

ACT IV

Scene 1

THE HEATH.

Enter Edgar.

Edgar.   Yet better thus, and known to be contemned,
  Than still contemned and flattered. To be worst,

2-5   **To be . . . best:** When one's fortunes are at the very worst, there is only hope for the better; thus, the creature whose fortune is at the lowest ebb has everything to hope for and nothing to fear.

6   **The worst . . . laughter:** The worst circumstances can only change to those inspiring laughter.

7   **unsubstantial:** having little substance, not being able to sustain a man's life.

8   **wretch:** Edgar himself.

9   **owes nothing to:** has nothing to fear from.

11-13   **poorly led:** led by a poor old man. These words are accepted by most editors of the text of *King Lear*. The expression has been called the worst crux (or verbal problem) in the play. What Shakespeare actually wrote here is pure conjecture; **World, world . . . age:** O, world, if the strange changes in our fortunes did not make us hate thee, we should not surrender to old age.

16   **fourscore:** eighty, indicating that the man had been a vassal of the family since earliest childhood.

22-24   **I stumbled . . . commodities:** When I was in full possession of my faculties, I was careless (stumbled). Very often, we observe that our own faculties (means) make us feel overconfident (secure us), and our very weaknesses (defects) prove to be beneficial in causing us to take notice of our circumstances.

25   **the food . . . wrath:** the victim of your deceived father's anger.

26-27   **Might I . . . again:** if only I might live to feel as if my sight were restored by the joy of embracing you.

28   **How now:** What's that? See III. vii. 87.

31   **I am . . . was:** Edgar sees his father's pitiful condition and realizes that circumstances are worse than ever.

33-34   **The worst . . . worst:** The worst has not befallen us as long as we can assure ourselves that it is the worst.

The lowest and most dejected thing of fortune,
Stands still in esperance, lives not in fear.
The lamentable change is from the best;   5
The worst returns to laughter. Welcome then,
Thou unsubstantial air that I embrace!
The wretch that thou hast blown unto the worst
Owes nothing to thy blasts.

Enter Gloucester, led by an Old Man.

                            But who comes here?   10
My father, poorly led? World, world, O world!
But that thy strange mutations make us hate thee,
Life would not yield to age.

Old Man.   O my good lord,
    I have been your tenant, and your father's tenant,   15
    These fourscore years.

Gloucester.   Away, get thee away! Good friend, be gone.
    Thy comforts can do me no good at all;
    Thee they may hurt.

Old Man.   You cannot see your way.   20

Gloucester.   I have no way, and therefore want no eyes;
    I stumbled when I saw. Full oft 'tis seen
    Our means secure us, and our mere defects
    Prove our commodities. O dear son Edgar,
    The food of thy abused father's wrath;   25
    Might I but live to see thee in my touch,
    I'd say I had eyes again!

Old Man.   How now? Who's there?

Edgar (aside).   O gods! Who is't can say, "I am at the
    worst"?   30
    I am worse than e'er I was.

Old Man.   'Tis poor mad Tom.

Edgar (aside).   And worse I may be yet. The worst is not
    So long as we can say, "This is the worst."

Old Man.   Fellow, where goest?   35

Gloucester.   Is it a beggarman?

Old Man.   Madman and beggar too.

40   **a worm:** a thing of no consequence. See Job 25:6.
41   **came then . . . mind:** either because he saw something of
     Edgar beneath his disguise or because he thought that Edgar
     must have become a homeless wanderer.
42   **scarce:** scarcely; **friends:** friendly.
44   **wanton:** carelessly playful.
46   **How should this be:** Why should such a plight as my father's
     and mine exist? Edgar answers his own question.
47-48 **Bad is . . . others:** It is bad business that I must disguise my-
     self as a Bedlamite, making myself and others angry, when my
     father is in such sorrow.
53   **i' the way:** on the path or track; **ancient love:** love dating from
     earlier days.
54   **covering:** clothing.
55   **entreat:** humbly request.
57-58 **'Tis the . . . blind:** Gloucester composes an adage on his own
     condition. It is the curse of the times that the leaders of the
     country are mad and that the people whom they lead are blind.
59   **thy pleasure:** what you please.
60   **above the rest:** above all.
61   **'parel:** apparel, clothing.
62   **come on't what will:** no matter what happens to me.
64   **daub it:** pretend. The metaphor is from plastering. See II. ii. 61.

Gloucester. He has some reason, else he could not beg.
  I' the last night's storm I such a fellow saw,
  Which made me think a man a worm. My son   40
  Came then into my mind, and yet my mind
  Was then scarce friends with him. I have heard more
    since.
  As flies to wanton boys are we to the gods.
  They kill us for their sport.   45
Edgar (aside).   How should this be?
  Bad is the trade that must play fool to sorrow,
  Angering itself and others.—Bless thee, master!
Gloucester. Is that the naked fellow?
Old Man.   Ay, my lord.   50
Gloucester. Get thee away. If for my sake
  Thou wilt o'ertake us hence a mile or twain
  I' the way toward Dover, do it for ancient love;
  And bring some covering for this naked soul,
  Which I'll entreat to lead me.   55
Old Man.   Alack, sir, he is mad!
Gloucester. 'Tis the time's plague when madmen lead the
    blind.
  Do as I bid thee, or rather do thy pleasure.
  Above the rest, be gone.   60
Old Man. I'll bring him the best 'parel that I have,
  Come on't what will.   *Exit.*
Gloucester. Sirrah, naked fellow—
Edgar. Poor Tom's acold. (*aside*) I cannot daub it
    further.   65
Gloucester. Come hither, fellow.
Edgar (aside). And yet I must.—Bless thy sweet eyes,
    they bleed.
Gloucester. Knowest thou the way to Dover?
Edgar. Both stile and gate, horseway and footpath. Poor 70
    Tom hath been scared out of his good wits. Bless thee,
    good man's son, from the foul fiend! Five fiends have
    been in poor Tom at once: of lust, as Obidicut; Hobbi-

73-75 **Obidicut,** etc.: another set of Harsnett's fiends, the spelling somewhat modified; **mopping and mowing:** grimacing and making faces.

76 **possesses:** possesses the souls of.

78-81 **plagues:** afflictions, misfortunes; **thou whom . . . still:** you whom the afflictions of the gods have reduced to the lowest kind of misery. The fact that I am wretched makes you appear happier than I. May the gods continue to inflict this kind of punishment—to make my suffering the common experience of the powerful whenever they abuse their power. See Lear's words, III. iv. 34-42.

82-85 **Let the . . . excess:** Let the pampered, fully-satisfied man who treats the commands of the gods as if these commands were his slaves, and who will not see the truth because he is insensitive, feel your power quickly, O ye gods. If this were done, the man with excessive wealth would be willing to distribute it more justly.

88 **bending:** beetling, overhanging.

89 **fearfully:** in such a manner as to inspire terror; **the confined deep:** the channel limited by the comparatively short distance between one shore and the other, the Strait of Dover.

91-92 **and I'll . . . me:** and I will reward you (lessen your misery) by giving you something of value that I have on my person. Gloucester's "leap" over one of the Dover Cliffs has been attacked as a serious dramatic impossibility.

See also p. 236.

1 **our mild husband:** This is the first occasion upon which Goneril has revealed to Edmund her true feeling towards her husband, but see I. iv. 350-3.

2 **not met us:** an inversion—met us not; **on the way:** to Gloucester's castle.

3 **your master:** Albany.

didence, prince of dumbness; Mahu, of stealing; Modo,
of murder; Flibbertigibbet, of mopping and mowing, who   75
since possesses chambermaids and waiting women. So,
bless thee, master!

Gloucester.   Here, take this purse, thou whom the heavens'
plagues
Have humbled to all strokes. That I am wretched   80
Makes thee the happier. Heavens, deal so still!
Let the superfluous and lust-dieted man,
That slaves your ordinance, that will not see
Because he does not feel, feel your power quickly;
So distribution should undo excess,   85
And each man have enough. Dost thou know Dover?

Edgar.   Ay, master.

Gloucester.   There is a cliff, whose high and bending head
Looks fearfully in the confined deep.
Bring me but to the very brim of it,   90
And I'll repair the misery thou dost bear
With something rich about me. From that place
I shall no leading need.

Edgar.   Give me thy arm.
Poor Tom shall lead thee.   95

Exeunt.

Scene 2

OUTSIDE THE DUKE OF
ALBANY'S PALACE.

Enter Goneril and Edmund the Bastard.

Goneril.   Welcome, my lord. I marvel our mild husband
Not met us on the way.
Enter Oswald the Steward.
Now where's your master?

4 **so changed:** The ruthlessness of Goneril and Regan have appalled Albany at last, but he seems incapable of positive action.

8 **loyal service:** denouncing his father to Cornwall; **son:** Edmund.

9 **sot:** blockhead, fool, *not* drunkard.

10 **I had . . . out:** I had seen good as evil, and evil as good; had wrongly accused Gloucester of evil, and given credit wrongly to Edmund for honourable motives.

11-12 **What most . . . offensive:** Oswald asserts that it is Albany, not himself, who has reversed good and evil.

13 **Then shall . . . further:** You will not accompany me at this point towards Gloucester's castle but return to Cornwall. See line 17.

14 **cowish terror:** cowardly fear.

15 **undertake:** transform conviction into action. He will ignore wrongs that demand some responsible action from him.

16-17 **Our wishes . . . effects:** The desire we have for each other may possibly be forfeited; *i.e.*, We may rid ourselves of Albany, and you may take his place as my husband; **brother:** brother-in-law, Cornwall.

19-20 **I must . . . hands:** I must take my husband's sword and present him with a distaff; **this trusty servant:** Oswald.

21 **shall pass between us:** shall be our personal and confidential intermediary or go-between; **like:** likely.

22 **if you . . . behalf:** if you have the initiative to advance yourself.

23 **S.D. favour:** trinket (recognizing Edmund as her lover).

25 **Decline your head:** Bend your head downward (to be kissed).

26 **would stretch . . . air:** would raise your spirits to the skies. Goneril also changes from the formal "your" to the intimate "thy" and "thee".

27 **Conceive:** Please understand what I am suggesting as to our future—without Albany. See I. i. 11.

28 **Yours in . . . death:** Edmund leaves with a prodigiously cynical expression of chivalrous love, falling on his knees and kissing Goneril's hand as a gesture of devotion.

32 **My fool . . . body:** My husband enjoys my body (but Edmund possesses my heart).

34 **I have . . . whistle:** This line is evidently based on an old proverb: It is a poor dog that is not worth the whistling. Goneril means: I was once worth being considered your dog and being given some attention.

37 **I fear your disposition:** I am appalled at your character.

38 **nature:** character; **contemns:** despises; **it:** its; **origin:** source; *i.e.*, Lear (whom Albany admires).

Oswald.   Madam, within, but never man so changed.
  I told him of the army that was landed: 5
  He smiled at it. I told him you were coming:
  His answer was, "The worse." Of Gloucester's treachery
  And of the loyal service of his son
  When I informed him, then he called me sot
  And told me I had turned the wrong side out.   10
  What most he should dislike seems pleasant to him;
  What like, offensive.
Goneril (*to Edmund*).   Then shall you go no further.
  It is the cowish terror of his spirit,
  That dares not undertake. He'll not feel wrongs   15
  Which tie him to an answer. Our wishes on the way
  May prove effects. Back, Edmund, to my brother.
  Hasten his musters and conduct his powers.
  I must change arms at home and give the distaff
  Into my husband's hands. This trusty servant   20
  Shall pass between us. Ere long you are like to hear
  (If you dare venture in your own behalf)
  A mistress's command. Wear this;   *Gives a favour.*
                                Spare speech;
  Decline your head: this kiss, if it durst speak,   25
  Would stretch thy spirits up into the air.
  Conceive, and fare thee well.
Edmund.   Yours in the ranks of death!   *Exit.*
Goneril.   My most dear Gloucester!
  O, the difference of man and man!   30
  To thee a woman's services are due;
  My fool usurps my body.
Oswald.   Madam, here comes my lord. *Exit.*
          Enter Albany.
Goneril.   I have been worth the whistle.
Albany.   O Goneril,   35
  You are not worth the dust which the rude wind
  Blows in your face! I fear your disposition.
  That nature which contemns it origin

39 **cannot be . . . itself:** cannot be kept within set limits.

40 **sliver and disbranch:** synonymous: *be cut off.*

41-42 **material sap:** essential nourishment—in this case, the characteristics Goneril should have received from Lear; **perforce:** of necessity, necessarily; **must wither . . . use:** must be as a dead branch, fit only for burning (or for death).

43 **text:** Goneril must be implying that she recognizes Heb. 6:8 as Albany's text. She means: A sermon from you is not worth hearing, since the text is foolish.

45 **savour:** relish, have a liking for.

48 **whose reverence . . . lick:** who would be (affectionately) licked even by a bear that is being tugged along by a head-harness (or bridle).

50 **brother:** brother-in-law (Cornwall).

51 **him:** Lear.

52 **if that:** if; **visible spirits:** avenging spirits in visible form.

55-56 **Humanity must . . . deep:** Humanity must turn into ferocious animals and devour one another, like the creatures of the ocean. See I. iv. 261.

57 **milk-livered:** cowardly. The expression *white-livered* still exists.

58 **a cheek for blows:** See Matt. 5:39; **a head for wrongs:** a head that would endure injustices against it.

59-60 **who hast . . . suffering:** who has no insight to tell him what should be accepted honourably and what should be considered an offence.

61-62 **Fools do . . . mischief:** Only fools pity the villains (Lear and his supporters) who are punished before they have committed evil acts. Goneril suggests that Lear is a villain because he is in league with France and that Albany is meekly allowing the invasion of the country to take place; **Where's thy drum:** *i.e.,* your war-drum.

64 **with plumed . . . threat:** The subject of the verb "begins" is "France", line 63; **threat:** threaten.

65 **a moral fool:** a fool who moralizes when action is necessary.

67 **See thyself:** See yourself as others see you.

68-69 **Proper deformity . . . woman:** Physical or moral deformity, expected in a fiend, looks much more horrid in woman, where it is not expected. Albany may see the evil passion distorting his wife's face or he may be referring only to moral deformity.

71 **changed:** transformed; **self-covered:** with your real self covered with a woman's body. Muir offers several explanations.

72 **bemonster:** Do not change your appearance into that of a fiend; **were't my fitness:** if it were proper to me.

73 **blood:** impulses.

Cannot be bordered certain in itself.
She that herself will sliver and disbranch   40
From her material sap, perforce must wither
And come to deadly use.
Goneril. No more! The text is foolish.
  Albany. Wisdom and goodness to the vile seem vile;
Filths savour but themselves. What have you done?   45
Tigers, not daughters, what have you performed?
A father, and a gracious aged man,
Whose reverence even the head-lugged bear would lick,
Most barbarous, most degenerate, have you madded.
Could my good brother suffer you to do it?   50
A man, a prince, by him so benefited!
If that the heavens do not their visible spirits
Send quickly down to tame these vile offenses,
It will come,
Humanity must perforce prey on itself,   55
Like monsters of the deep.
Goneril.   Milk-livered man!
That bearest a cheek for blows, a head for wrongs;
Who hast not in thy brows an eye discerning
Thine honour from thy suffering; that not knowest   60
Fools do those villains pity who are punished
Ere they have done their mischief. Where's thy drum?
France spreads his banners in our noiseless land,
With plumed helm thy state begins to threat,
Whiles thou, a moral fool, sittest still, and cries   65
"Alack, why does he so?"
  Albany.   See thyself, devil!
Proper deformity shows not in the fiend
So horrid as in woman.
Goneril.   O vain fool!   70
  Albany. Thou changed and self-covered thing, for shame!
Bemonster not thy feature! Were't my fitness
To let these hands obey my blood,
They are apt enough to dislocate and tear

75 **howe'er:** in whatever ways.

77 **Marry:** By the Virgin Mary; **your manhood—mew:** Confine (or coop up) your feeble manhood until it is strong enough for a man's work; another interpretation is that Goneril is making a scornful sound, imitating a cat's cry. There is evidence that this was a fairly common way of expressing contempt.

83 **bred:** reared, brought up; **thrilled with remorse:** moved or excited by compassion.

84 **opposed against:** tried to prevent; **bending:** turning.

86 **amongst them . . . dead:** Among the lot of them, they killed him.

87 **harmful stroke:** fatal wound.

88 **plucked him after:** drew him along to death after the murdered servant.

90 **justicers:** judges, dispensers of justice, gods; **nether:** on earth, under heaven.

97-99 **But being . . . life:** But since Regan is now a widow, and my lover Edmund is with her, all my dreams of a life with Edmund may be shattered, and escape from my hated life with Albany may be impossible.

100 **tart:** sour, unpleasant.

101 **son:** Edmund.

104 **back:** on his way back. See IV. ii. 17.

Thy flesh and bones. Howe'er thou art a fiend,   75
  A woman's shape doth shield thee.
Goneril.   Marry, your manhood—mew!
        Enter a Gentleman.
Albany.   What news?
Gentleman.   O, my good lord, the Duke of Cornwall's dead,
  Slain by his servant, going to put out   80
  The other eye of Gloucester.
Albany.   Gloucester's eyes?
Gentleman.   A servant that he bred, thrilled with remorse,
  Opposed against the act, bending his sword
  To his great master; who, thereat enraged,   85
  Flew on him, and amongst them felled him dead;
  But not without that harmful stroke which since
  Hath plucked him after.
Albany.   This shows you are above,
  You justicers, that these our nether crimes   90
  So speedily can venge! But O poor Gloucester!
  Lost he his other eye?
Gentleman.   Both, both, my lord.
  This letter, madam, craves a speedy answer.
  'Tis from your sister.   95
Goneril (aside).   One way I like this well;
  But being widow, and my Gloucester with her,
  May all the building in my fancy pluck
  Upon my hateful life. Another way
  The news is not so tart.—I'll read, and answer.   100
                          Exit.
Albany.   Where was his son when they did take his eyes?
Gentleman.   Come with my lady hither.
Albany.   He is not here.
Gentleman.   No, my good lord; I met him back again.
Albany.   Knows he the wickedness?   105
Gentleman.   Ay, my good lord: 'twas he informed against
    him,
  And quit the house on purpose, that their punishment

108-9 **and quit . . . course:** and left deliberately so that those deal-
    ing with Gloucester might have a freer hand in punishment.
See also p. 237.
This scene is omitted from F1 and the plot is clear without it.
Probably, the scene was left out of the players' scripts.

    7 **general:** as general, in charge of his army.

    9 **Queen:** Cordelia, now Queen of France.

 14-16 **It seemed . . . her:** It appeared that she was in control of
    her feelings, which seemed to be trying to control her.

 18-19 **Patience and . . . goodliest:** Her self-control struggled with
    her sorrow as to which would give her the most appropriate
    expression.

   21 **a better way:** *i.e.,* of expressing the ideas; **smilets:** little smiles.

Might have the freer course.
Albany.   Gloucester, I live   110
  To thank thee for the love thou show'dst the King,
  And to revenge thine eyes. Come hither, friend.
  Tell me what more thou knowest.
                             Exeunt.

Scene 3

THE FRENCH CAMP NEAR DOVER.

Enter Kent and a Gentleman.

Kent. Why the King of France is so suddenly gone
back; know you no reason?

Gentleman. Something he left imperfect in the state, which
since his coming forth is thought of, which imports to the
kingdom so much fear and danger that his personal return   5
was most required and necessary.

Kent. Who hath he left behind him general?

Gentleman. The Marshal of France, Monsieur La Far.

Kent. Did your letters pierce the Queen to any demon-
stration of grief?   10

Gentleman. Ay, sir. She took them, read them in my pres-
ence,
  And now and then an ample tear trilled down
  Her delicate cheek. It seemed she was a queen
  Over her passion, who, most rebel-like,   15
  Sought to be king o'er her.

Kent.   O, then it moved her?

Gentleman. Not to a rage. Patience and sorrow strove
  Who should express her goodliest. You have seen
  Sunshine and rain at once: her smiles and tears   20
  Were like. A better way: those happy smilets
  That played on her ripe lip seemed not to know

23 **guests:** tears (visiting her eyes).

24 **as pearls . . . dropped:** a courtly and therefore exaggerated compliment from the messenger, who compares her tears to pearls and her eyes to diamonds.

25-26 **Sorrow would . . . it:** Her sorrow was so becoming to her that those who saw it so expressed would desire to emulate it.

28 **Faith:** In faith; a mild oath.

33 **Let pity . . . believed:** Let it not be believed that pity can exist in a world that sees such deeds, and let it not be believed for the sake of human pity.

35-36 **and clamour moistened:** and moistened clamour; *i.e.,* Cordelia relieved her feelings in sobs and tears; **Then away . . . alone:** Then she simply gave way to her feelings of grief.

37-38 **It is . . . conditions:** The stars themselves control our characters.

39-40 **else one . . . issues:** otherwise the same husband and wife could not produce children so utterly unlike.

45 **in his better tune:** when he is comparatively rational.

47 **yield to see:** submit to the humiliation of seeing.

49 **sovereign:** overwhelming; **elbows:** stands at his side like an associate, jogging his elbow to remind him of what he did to Cordelia.

51 **stripped her . . . benediction:** cut her off from the blessings of his bequest when he abdicated.

52 **foreign casualties:** hazards encountered in foreign countries.

53 **dog-hearted:** cruel.

What guests were in her eyes, which parted thence
As pearls from diamonds dropped. In brief,
Sorrow would be a rarity most beloved,   25
If all could so become it.
Kent.   Made she no verbal question?
Gentleman.   Faith, once or twice she heaved the name of
   father
   Pantingly forth, as if it pressed her heart;   30
   Cried, "Sisters, sisters! Shame of ladies! Sisters!
   Kent! father! sisters! What, i' the storm? i' the night?
   Let pity not be believed!" There she shook
   The holy water from her heavenly eyes,
   And clamour moistened. Then away she started   35
   To deal with grief alone.
Kent.   It is the stars,
   The stars above us, govern our conditions;
   Else one self mate and make could not beget
   Such different issues. You spoke not with her since?   40
Gentleman. No.
Kent. Was this before the King returned?
Gentleman.   No, since.
Kent. Well, sir, the poor distressed Lear's i' the town;
   Who sometime, in his better tune, remembers   45
   What we are come about, and by no means
   Will yield to see his daughter.
Gentleman.   Why, good sir?
Kent. A sovereign shame so elbows him; his own un-
   kindness,   50
   That stripped her from his benediction, turned her
   To foreign casualties, gave her dear rights
   To his dog-hearted daughters—these things sting
   His mind so venomously that burning shame
   Detains him from Cordelia.   55
Gentleman.   Alack, poor gentleman!
Kent. Of Albany's and Cornwall's powers you heard
   not?

61 **some dear cause:** an important matter.
62 **will in . . . awhile:** will occupy my time and conceal my true identity.
63 **aright:** in my true character.
64 **lending:** affording.

See also p. 238.

3 **fumiter:** fumitory, a weed whose leaves and juice are bitter.
4 **hardocks:** perhaps, *burdocks*; **hemlock:** swamp hemlock, a deadly poisonous weed; **nettles:** plural of *nettle*, a weed having fine stinging needles bordering its leaves; **cuckoo-flowers:** probably, the buttercup, which flowers in the spring at the same time as the cuckoo appears.
5 **darnel:** tares (mentioned in Matt. 13:25); **idle:** useless.
6 **sustaining corn:** wheat, which provides us with food; **century:** force of one hundred soldiers.
8-10 **What can . . . sense:** What power has man's accumulated knowledge in restoring his impaired faculties?
11 **outward:** material.
12 **means:** a way.
14 **that to provoke:** to cause that (sleep).
15 **simples operative:** effective medicinal plants (called simples, because they were not compounds).
16 **eye of anguish:** eye of one suffering from some deep sorrow.
17 **secrets:** remedies, once regarded as the special secrets of the physician.
18 **virtues:** here, medicinal plants; **all you . . . earth:** a more impressive way of referring to the secrets.
19 **spring:** grow; **aidant and remediate:** as aids and remedies.

Gentleman. 'Tis so; they are afoot.
Kent. Well, sir, I'll bring you to our master Lear   60
  And leave you to attend him. Some dear cause
  Will in concealment wrap me up awhile.
  When I am known aright, you shall not grieve
  Lending me this acquaintance. I pray you go
  Along with me.   *Exeunt.*   65

Scene 4

SAME.

Enter, with Drum and Colours,
Cordelia, Doctor, and Soldiers.

Cordelia. Alack, 'tis he! Why, he was met even now
  As mad as the vexed sea, singing aloud,
  Crowned with rank fumiter and furrow-weeds,
  With hardocks, hemlock, nettles, cuckoo-flowers,
  Darnel, and all the idle weeds that grow   5
  In our sustaining corn. A century send forth.
  Search every acre in the high-grown field
  And bring him to our eye. (*Exit an Officer*). What can
    man's wisdom
  In the restoring his bereaved sense?   10
  He that helps him take all my outward worth.
Doctor. There is means, madam.
  Our foster nurse of nature is repose,
  The which he lacks. That to provoke in him
  Are many simples operative, whose power   15
  Will close the eye of anguish.
Cordelia.   All blest secrets,
  All you unpublished virtues of the earth,
  Spring with my tears! be aidant and remediate
  In the good man's distress! Seek, seek for him!   20

21 **rage:** insane frenzy.
22 **wants:** lacks; **the means:** here, the reason, the rationality; **lead:** guide, control.
24 **hitherward:** this way, in this direction.
25-26 **Our preparation . . . them:** Our troops are ready to meet them.
28-29 **Therefore great . . . pitied:** For that reason, the King of France (my husband) has taken pity upon my mourning and my importunate tears.
30 **blown:** mighty. It is suggested by Verity that the lines 28-30 were written by Shakespeare to reconcile Elizabethan audiences to the idea of French troops invading their shores.

See also p. 239.

1 **brother's:** brother-in-law's; *i.e.*, Albany's.
4 **ado:** fuss; said sarcastically. Oswald was really Goneril's servant and had little to do with Albany.
5 **Your sister . . . soldier:** because of Albany's reluctance to take arms against Lear. "Soldier" is pronounced as three syllables.
8 **my sister's letter:** Regan suspects that the letter is, in fact, a love letter.
10 **Faith, he . . . matter:** This information Oswald must have given Regan previously.
14 **dispatch:** take.

Lest his ungoverned rage dissolve the life
That wants the means to lead it.
     Enter Messenger.
Messenger.   News, madam.
  The British powers are marching hitherward.
Cordelia. 'Tis known before. Our preparation stands   25
  In expectation of them. O dear father,
  It is thy business that I go about.
  Therefore great France
  My mourning and importuned tears hath pitied.
  No blown ambition doth our arms incite,   30
  But love, dear love, and our aged father's right.
  Soon may I hear and see him!
                         Exeunt.

Scene 5

INSIDE GLOUCESTER'S CASTLE.

Enter Regan and Oswald the Steward.

Regan. But are my brother's powers set forth?
Oswald.   Ay, madam.
Regan. Himself in person there?
Oswald.   Madam, with much ado:
  Your sister is the better soldier.   5
Regan. Lord Edmund spake not with your lord at home?
Oswald. No, madam.
Regan. What might import my sister's letter to him?
Oswald. I know not, lady.
Regan. Faith, he is posted hence on serious matter.   10
  It was great ignorance, Gloucester's eyes being out,
  To let him live. Where he arrives he moves
  All hearts against us. Edmund, I think, is gone,
  In pity of his misery, to dispatch

15 **nighted:** darkened, because of his blindness; **descry:** discover.

21 **charged my duty:** gave me strict instructions.

24 **transport her purposes:** carry her instructions; **belike:** probably.

25 **I'll love thee much:** I'll reward you generously. Observe the broken phrases with which Regan leads up to the request.

27 **Madam, I had rather—:** Oswald does not yield up the letter.

30 **eliads:** *oeillades* (Fr.), loving looks. Cf. *oeil* (Fr.), eye.

34 **take this note:** Take note of this.

35 **talked:** talked about marriage.

37 **You may gather more:** You may assume that we are already lovers.

38 **this:** a love-token, like that Goneril gave Edmund—not a letter, since no such letter was found on his person when searched by Edgar.

39 **thus much:** what I have already told you.

40 **call her . . . her:** have the good sense to accept the situation.

43 **preferment:** promotion.

See also p. 239.

His nighted life; moreover, to descry   15
  The strength o' the enemy.
Oswald.   I must needs after him, madam, with my letter.
Regan.   Our troops set forth tomorrow. Stay with us.
  The ways are dangerous.
Oswald.   I may not, madam.   20
  My lady charged my duty in this business.
Regan.   Why should she write to Edmund? Might not you
  Transport her purposes by word? Belike,
  Some things—I know not what—I'll love thee much—   25
  Let me unseal the letter.
Oswald.   Madam, I had rather—
Regan.   I know your lady does not love her husband;
  I am sure of that; and at her late being here
  She gave strange eliads and most speaking looks   30
  To noble Edmund. I know you are of her bosom.
Oswald.   I, madam?
Regan.   I speak in understanding. Y'are! I know't.
  Therefore I do advise you take this note.
  My lord is dead; Edmund and I have talked,   35
  And more convenient is he for my hand
  Than for your lady's. You may gather more.
  If you do find him, pray you give him this;
  And when your mistress hears thus much from you,
  I pray desire her call her wisdom to her.   40
  So fare you well.
  If you do chance to hear of that blind traitor,
  Preferment falls on him that cuts him off.
Oswald.   Would I could meet him, madam! I should show
  What party I do follow.   45
Regan.   Fare thee well.   *Exeunt.*

2 **labour:** *i.e.*, at going uphill.

3 **methinks:** it seems to me; **the ground is even:** The ground is indeed even. Edgar has only pretended to lead his blind father to where the cliff is "horrible steep".

4 **horrible:** terrifyingly.

5 **Hark:** Listen.

7-8 **Why, then . . . anguish:** Then your other sense must be dulled by physical pain caused by the loss of your eyes.

10-11 **Methinks thy . . . didst:** Edgar uses several different accents during his period of disguise. See **IV.** i. 64-65. Apparently, he has dropped part of his assumed character.

18 **choughs:** jackdaws, a bird that can be taught to talk; pronounced *chuffs.*

19 **gross:** large.

20 **sampire:** samphire or *herbe de Saint Pierre,* a plant used with vinegar to produce a meat relish and gathered from the cliff face at Dover by men suspended on a rope from the top of the cliff; hence, Edgar's comment "Dreadful trade!"

23 **bark:** ship.

24 **diminished to her cock:** reduced in size (by the distance) down to that of her cockboat, the small boat used by the crew to reach shore from the ship; **her cock, a buoy:** the tiny cockboat is similarly reduced in size to that of a buoy.

25 **surge:** surf, breaking waves.

26 **unnumbered:** numberless; **chafes:** rubs.

Scene 6

OPEN COUNTRY NEAR DOVER.

Enter Gloucester, and Edgar.
clothed as a countryman.

Gloucester. When shall I come to the top of that same hill?
Edgar. You do climb up it now. Look how we labour.
Gloucester. Methinks the ground is even.
Edgar.   Horrible steep.
  Hark, do you hear the sea?   5
Gloucester.   No, truly.
Edgar. Why, then, your other senses grow imperfect
  By your eyes' anguish.
Gloucester.   So may it be indeed.
  Methinks thy voice is altered, and thou speakest   10
  In better phrase and matter than thou didst.
Edgar. Y'are much deceived. In nothing am I changed
  But in my garments.
Gloucester.   Methinks y'are better spoken.
Edgar. Come on, sir; here's the place. Stand still. How   15
    fearful
  And dizzy 'tis to cast one's eyes so low!
  The crows and choughs that wing the midway air
  Show scarce so gross as beetles. Halfway down
  Hangs one that gathers sampire—dreadful trade!   20
  Methinks he seems no bigger than his head.
  The fishermen that walk upon the beach
  Appear like mice; and yond tall anchoring bark,
  Diminished to her cock; her cock, a buoy
  Almost too small for sight. The murmuring surge   25
  That on the unnumbered idle pebble chafes
  Cannot be heard so high. I'll look no more,
  Lest my brain turn, and the deficient sight
  Topple down headlong.
Gloucester.   Set me where you stand.   30

32 **extreme:** Accent the first syllable.

41-42 **Why I . . . it:** The reason that I experiment with my father's despair is to cure it—a necessary explanation for the audience, who would otherwise be puzzled by Edgar's behaviour.

46-47 **fall to quarrel with:** rebel against; **opposeless:** not to be opposed, not to be resisted, irresistible.

48 **my snuff . . . nature:** the darkened and hated remainder of my life. The "snuff" is the charred end of a candle wick, which, if not trimmed, dims the light and causes ill-smelling smoke.

52-54 **how conceit . . . theft:** how imagination may be robbing life's treasury of all its strength when life itself surrenders. Edgar is fearful that even though his father's life is saved, Gloucester's imagination may cause him as much anguish as if he were actually on the edge of the cliff, and that, as a result, he may be unable to endure life anyhow.

55 **had:** would have.

56 **Ho you . . . Speak:** Edgar hurries to Gloucester, who has fallen down on the ground from a slight height, but who imagines that he has fallen from a great height. There is, of course, an interval of time between "past" of line 55 and Edgar's next words.

57 **pass:** die.

60 **hadst thou:** if you had; **aught:** anything; **gossamer:** thread of a spider's web.

62 **precipating:** falling.

63 **thou'dst:** you would have; **shivered:** shattered.

64 **hast heavy substance:** are of normal weight, subject to gravity, as opposed to gossamer or feathers, which float on the air indefinitely. Shakespeare did not, of course, have the benefit of Newton's concept.

65 **ten masts at each:** ten masts of a tall ship, one on top of the other.

Edgar.   Give me your hand; you are now within a foot
  Of the extreme verge; for all beneath the moon
  Would I not leap upright.
Gloucester.   Let go my hand.
  Here, friend, 's another purse; in it a jewel   35
  Well worth a poor man's taking. Fairies and gods
  Prosper it with thee! Go thou further off;
  Bid me farewell, and let me hear thee going.
Edgar.   Now fare ye well, good sir.
Gloucester.   With all my heart.   40
Edgar (aside).   Why I do trifle thus with his despair
  Is done to cure it.
Gloucester.   O you mighty gods!   *He kneels.*
  This world I do renounce, and, in your sights,
  Shake patiently my great affliction off.   45
  If I could bear it longer and not fall
  To quarrel with your great opposeless wills,
  My snuff and loathed part of nature should
  Burn itself out. If Edgar live, O, bless him!
  Now, fellow, fare thee well.   50
        He falls forward and faints.
Edgar.   Gone, sir, farewell.—
  And yet I know not how conceit may rob
  The treasury of life when life itself
  Yields to the theft. Had he been where he thought,
  By this had thought been past.—Alive or dead?   55
  Ho you, sir! friend! Hear you, sir? Speak!—
  Thus might he pass indeed. Yet he revives.
  What are you, sir?
Gloucester.   Away, and let me die.
Edgar.   Hadst thou been aught but gossamer, feathers,   60
    air,
  So many fathom down precipitating,
  Thou'dst shivered like an egg; but thou dost breathe;
  Hast heavy substance; bleedest not; speakest; art sound.
  Ten masts at each make not the altitude   65

69 **chalky bourn:** boundary of the sea, composed of chalk.

70 **a-height:** on high, to the height above; **shrill-gorged:** shrill-throated, shrill-voiced.

72 **Alack:** a mild expression of emotion.

73-76 **Is wretchedness . . . death:** Am I in my misfortune to be deprived of the benefit of death? **'Twas yet . . . will:** After all, it was some comfort to know that in my unhappiness I could cheat the tyrant's (Cornwall's) tyranny and foil his aims by means of suicide.

78 **Up—so:** These are the words used by Edgar when he is straining to get Gloucester to his feet again.

80 **above all strangeness:** the strongest (survival) I have ever known.

81-82 **Upon the . . . you:** Edgar now pretends to be a new rescuer of Gloucester—not the Bedlam beggar who led him to the cliff.

84-87 **whelked:** twisted; **As I . . . fiend:** Edgar further confuses Gloucester by convincing him that a fiend led him to the cliff, not Poor Tom, and that the gods pitied him and therefore saved him.

88-89 **Think that . . . thee:** Believe that the most glorious gods, who make themselves honoured by performing miracles impossible to men, have saved you (from the fiend).

91 **affliction:** suffering.

92 **die:** disappear.

93 **'twould:** it would.

94 **the fiend, the fiend:** Edgar's words during his pretended madness. See III. iv. *passim.*

95 **free:** *i.e.,* free from despair; S.D. See IV. iv. 3-6.

97 **The safer . . . thus:** The sane judgement of a man would not permit him to dress in this fashion. Edgar implies that the man he sees must be mad because of his strange dress.

99 **touch:** charge, arrest; **coining:** making counterfeit money. The king in early days coined all the legal money of the realm.

Which thou hast perpendicularly fell.
Thy life's a miracle. Speak yet again.
Gloucester.   But have I fallen, or no?
Edgar.   From the dread summit of this chalky bourn.
  Look up a-height. The shrill-gorged lark so far   70
  Cannot be seen or heard. Do but look up.
Gloucester.   Alack, I have no eyes!
  Is wretchedness deprived that benefit
  To end itself by death? 'Twas yet some comfort
  When misery could beguile the tyrant's rage   75
  And frustrate his proud will.
Edgar.   Give me your arm.
  Up—so. How is't? Feel you your legs? You stand.
Gloucester.   Too well, too well.
Edgar.   This is above all strangeness.   80
  Upon the crown o' the cliff what thing was that
  Which parted from you?
Gloucester.   A poor unfortunate beggar.
Edgar.   As I stood here below, methought his eyes
  Were two full moons; he had a thousand noses,   85
  Horns whelked and waved like the enridged sea:
  It was some fiend; therefore, thou happy father,
  Think that the clearest gods, who make them honours
  Of men's impossibilities, have preserved thee.
Gloucester.   I do remember now. Henceforth I'll bear   90
  Affliction till it do cry out itself,
  "Enough, enough," and die. That thing you speak of,
  I took it for a man. Often 'twould say,
  "The fiend, the fiend"—he led me to that place.
Edgar.   Bear free and patient thoughts.   95
      Enter Lear, mad, garlanded with wild flowers.
                                But who comes here?
  The safer sense will ne'er accommodate
  His master thus.
Lear.   No, they cannot touch me for coining;
  I am the King himself.   100

99-120, 123-47 In his delirium, Lear believes that he is to be arrested for counterfeiting; then, that he has been recruiting soldiers and testing their skill as bowmen. Abruptly, he declares that he sees a mouse and attempts to catch it with toasted cheese. He throws down his gauntlet to all comers, even giants. With the command "Bring up the brown bills", he becomes an army captain again training his men in archery. Seeing Edgar, he demands the password. When Lear overhears Gloucester say "Is't not the King?", he briefly assumes his kingly manner and pardons an imagined adulterer. He has already mistaken Gloucester for Goneril, and now utters bitter words about her superficially virtuous manner. Finally, he pleads with a supposed apothecary for a small amount of perfume with which he may ease his mind.

102 **Nature's above . . . respect:** A born (or natural) king is superior to one dependent upon legal supports.

103-4 **press money:** money paid to conscripted soldiers or sailors; **crow-keeper:** an inexperienced and clumsy boy employed as a chaser of crows; **a clothier's yard:** The accomplished bowman could draw the bow-string back to the full length of the arrow —a clothier's yard—aim it, and let fly.

106 **gauntlet:** leather glove, with metal plates and a flaring wrist extension.

107 **brown bills:** varnished pikes; **bird:** arrow (the feathers of which were from geese); **clout:** the centre of the archer's target.

108 **Hewgh:** onomatopoeic; whistling of a shot arrow; **word:** password.

109 **sweet marjoram:** wild flower; also a remedy for mental illness.

112-16 **Ha! Goneril . . . beard:** Lear mistakes Gloucester for Goneril; **They flattered . . . there:** They flattered me by telling me I had white hair and was therefore wise, although I proved myself by my foolish actions to be a mere boy; **To say . . . said:** Lear's daughters answered as they thought he wished, not what they really believed; **no good divinity:** not good theology. See II Cor. 1:18, James 5:12, and Matt. 5:36-37.

119-20 **men:** women. Lear really means his daughters; **'Tis a . . . ague-proof:** The idea of my invincibility was a myth.

129 **lecher:** copulate. **130** **copulation:** breeding, begetting.

132 **got 'tween . . . sheets:** born legitimately, in wedlock.

133 **To it . . . soldiers:** Go to it wildly, Lust, for in this way more soldiers, which I lack, are bred.

135 **forks:** most often taken to mean *legs*, but probably referring to the pins holding a woman's hair at the temples; **whose face . . . snow:** whose expression suggests virtue.

Edgar. O thou side-piercing sight!

Lear. Nature's above art in that respect. There's your
press money. That fellow handles his bow like a crow-
keeper. Draw me a clothier's yard. Look, look, a mouse!
Peace, peace; this piece of toasted cheese will do it. 105
There's my gauntlet; I'll prove it on a giant. Bring up the
brown bills. O, well flown, bird! i' the clout, i' the clout!
Hewgh! Give the word.

Edgar. Sweet marjoram.

Lear. Pass. 110

Gloucester. I know that voice.

Lear. Ha! Goneril with a white beard? They flattered
me like a dog, and told me I had white hairs in my beard
ere the black ones were there. To say "ay" and "no" to
everything that I said! "Ay" and "no" too was no good 115
divinity. When the rain came to wet me once, and the
wind to make me chatter; when the thunder would not
peace at my bidding; there I found 'em, there I smelt 'em
out. Go to, they are not men o' their words! They told me
I was everything. 'Tis a lie—I am not ague-proof. 120

Gloucester. The trick of that voice I do well remember.
Is't not the King?

Lear.   Ay, every inch a king!
When I do stare, see how the subject quakes.
I pardon that man's life. What was thy cause? 125
Adultery?
Thou shalt not die. Die for adultery? No.
The wren goes to it, and the small gilded fly
Does lecher in my sight.
Let copulation thrive; for Gloucester's bastard son 130
Was kinder to his father than my daughters
Got 'tween the lawful sheets.
To it, luxury, pell-mell! for I lack soldiers.
Behold yond simpering dame,
Whose face between her forks presages snow, 135
That minces virtue, and does shake the head

137 **to hear . . . name:** even to hear the word mentioned.

138 **fitchew:** polecat, a prolific animal, not native to North America, of the weasel family; slang for *prostitute*; **nor:** Modern construction requires *neither* before "fitchew"; **soiled:** fed full with grass in the spring and therefore full of sexual vigour.

139 **riotous:** unrestrained.

140 **Centaurs:** legendary creatures half horse and half man, but slaves to their inherent animal desire.

142-3 **But to . . . fiend's:** Down to the waist, they belong to the gods; below the waist, to devils or to evil.

144-5 **There's hell . . . consumption:** These words serve to emphasize the evil Lear sees in women.

146 **civet:** perfume. The oily substance produced by the musk gland of the African civet cat, still used to blend various scents; **apothecary:** pharmacist.

149 **mortality:** death *or* life; better still: the bitter experience of life.

150-1 **O ruined . . . naught:** What a masterpiece of nature (Lear) is ruined! In such a way will the universe eventually be worn down to nothing.

153 **squint:** the Q3 reading, rather than *squiny*, Q1; look squintingly, like a prostitute; **blind Cupid:** the god of love, used commonly in Shakespeare's day as a sign to designate a brothel.

154 **mark:** observe; **penning:** handwriting; **Read thou . . . it:** Lear's mind suddenly reverts to another subject mentioned in line 106.

156 **I would . . . report:** I would not believe this when it was reported to me; **is:** is so.

159 **case of eyes:** eye-socket.

160 **are you . . . me:** Are you like me in that respect; *i.e.*, having no eyes, or being blind to so much in life?

161-2 **in a heavy case:** in a serious condition. Lear puns on "case"; **light:** in a light case; *i.e.*, empty.

164 **feelingly:** by touch, by pain.

166 **Look with thine ears:** Listen.

167 **justice:** judge; **rails upon:** scolds, lectures.

168 **handy-dandy:** the name of a children's game in which the hands are outstretched, one containing an object so that the chooser can see it. The hands are put behind the back and brought forward closed with some such formula as "Handy-dandy, prickly-pandy!" The other child must then guess which hand holds the prize, and make his choice. The contemporary question is "Which hand will you have?" The point of the line is that it is anyone's guess in this wicked world which is judge and which is thief.

172 **creature:** beggar (above).

To hear of pleasure's name.
The fitchew nor the soiled horse goes to it
With a more riotous appetite.
Down from the waist they are Centaurs,   140
Though women all above.
But to the girdle do the gods inherit,
Beneath is all the fiend's.
There's hell, there's darkness, there is the sulphurous pit;
burning, scalding, stench, consumption. Fie, fie, fie! pah, 145
pah! Give me an ounce of civet; good apothecary,
sweeten my imagination. There's money for thee.
Gloucester.   O, let me kiss that hand!
Lear.   Let me wipe it first; it smells of mortality.
Gloucester.   O ruined piece of nature! This great world   150
Shall so wear out to naught. Dost thou know me?
Lear.   I remember thine eyes well enough. Dost thou
squint at me? No, do thy worst, blind Cupid! I'll not love.
Read thou this challenge; mark but the penning of it.
Gloucester.   Were all thy letters suns, I could not see.   155
Edgar (*aside*).   I would not take this from report. It is,
And my heart breaks at it.
Lear.   Read.
Gloucester.   What, with the case of eyes?
Lear.   O, ho, are you there with me? No eyes in your   160
head, nor no money in your purse? Your eyes are in a
heavy case, your purse in a light. Yet you see how this
world goes.
Gloucester.   I see it feelingly.
Lear.   What, art mad? A man may see how this world   165
goes with no eyes. Look with thine ears. See how yond
justice rails upon yond simple thief. Hark in thine ear.
Change places and, handy-dandy, which is the justice,
which is the thief? Thou hast seen a farmer's dog bark
at a beggar?   170
Gloucester.   Ay, sir.
Lear.   And the creature run from the cur? There thou

169-74 **Thou hast . . . office:** Lear says that anyone in power is obeyed regardless of his character.

175 **beadle:** parish constable; **hold thy bloody hand:** Restrain yourself from giving out punishment.

176-8 **kind:** the sexual act; **Why dost . . . her:** The beadle who publicly beats a prostitute may secretly make use of her services; **usurer:** money-lender, loan-shark.

179 **cozener:** cheat.

180 **small:** Read *even* before "small".

181-3 **Robes and . . . all:** fine dress of those in office, official clothing trimmed with expensive ermine hides all evil; **Plate sin . . . it:** Dress a sinner in expensive clothing and he will be untouched by the law; dress him in rags and the law fails him.

184 **None does . . . 'em:** No person shall be considered guilty. I will authorize all to act as they wish. This is a royal edict, which Lear proposes.

185 **that:** the protection of the edict just issued.

186 **glass eyes:** spectacles—an anachronism.

187 **scurvy politician:** vile trickster.

189 **So:** said as his boots come off—an expression of relief. Lear thinks that he has just completed a journey or tour of inspection.

190 **matter and impertinency:** sense and incoherence.

192-3 **If thou . . . Gloucester:** Lear's mind clears for a moment, and he recognizes his old supporter.

194 **We came crying hither:** Man comes into the world crying.

196 **wawl and cry:** synonyms; **mark:** Listen carefully.

199 **this great stage:** this great world; **This' a good block:** This is a stylish hat. Lear could have been wearing a hat decked with flowers, or he may simply have removed the garland of flowers (See S.D., line 95) from his head and held it in his hand as he began to preach. The reference to "block" suggests "felt" in line 201.

200 **a delicate stratagem:** a very difficult plan.

201 **felt:** material of specially matted fur from which hats are made, and a fanciful means by which a whole troop of horses could be made to move quietly; **put't in proof:** put it to the test.

202 **stolen upon:** with a troop of felt-shod horses; **sons-in-law:** Albany and Cornwall.

203 **kill, kill . . . kill:** a cry used by soldiers, meaning: No Quarter (or, No Mercy). See line 219 as well.

206 **What, a prisoner:** As Lear rushes away, shouting "kill, kill", etc., those about him seize him, so that he feels he is a prisoner.

207 **the natural . . . fortune:** a plaything of fortune.

mightst behold the great image of authority: a dog's
obeyed in office.
Thou rascal beadle, hold thy bloody hand!   175
Why dost thou lash that whore? Strip thine own back.
Thou hotly lusts to use her in that kind
For which thou whippest her. The usurer hangs the
   cozener.
Through tattered clothes small vices do appear;   180
Robes and furred gowns hide all. Plate sin with gold,
And the strong lance of justice hurtless breaks;
Arm it in rags, a pygmy's straw does pierce it.
None does offend, none, I say, none; I'll able 'em:
Take that of me, my friend, who have the power   185
To seal th' accuser's lips. Get thee glass eyes
And, like a scurvy politician, seem
To see the things thou dost not. Now, now, now, now!
Pull off my boots. Harder, harder! So.
Edgar.   O, matter and impertinency mixed!   190
   Reason in madness!
Lear.   If thou wilt weep my fortunes, take my eyes.
   I know thee well enough; thy name is Gloucester.
   Thou must be patient. We came crying hither;
   Thou knowest, the first time that we smell the air   195
   We wawl and cry. I will preach to thee: mark.
Gloucester.   Alack, alack the day!
Lear.   When we are born, we cry that we are come
   To this great stage of fools. This' a good block.
   It were a delicate stratagem to shoe   200
   A troop of horse with felt. I'll put't in proof,
   And when I have stolen upon these sons-in-law,
   Then kill, kill, kill, kill, kill, kill!
       Enter a Gentleman with Attendants.
Gentleman.   O, here he is! Lay hand upon him.—Sir,
   Your most dear daughter—   205
Lear.   No rescue? What, a prisoner? I am even
   The natural fool of fortune. Use me well;

209 **cut:** wounded. Lear imagines that he has suffered a great wound in battle, and that he has been captured by the enemy. This is a particularly poignant phrase.

211 **seconds:** supporters.

212 **Why, this . . . salt:** This would make any man weep.

213-14 **to use . . . dust:** to weep more copiously; **bravely:** in fine dress.

215 **smug:** trim, neat.

216 **masters:** gentlemen.

218 **Then there's life in't:** Then there's still hope; **an:** if.

219 **Sa, sa, sa, sa:** from *ça* (Fr.), a hunting cry to urge on the hounds, also a rallying cry for troops. Lear challenges his followers to chase and catch him.

222 **general:** universal.

223 **twain:** a pair.

225 **speed you:** God bless you; **What's your will:** What do you wish?

226 **toward:** imminent, about to take place, in preparation.

227 **most sure and vulgar:** most certain, and a matter of common knowledge.

228 **which can distinguish sound:** who can hear at all.

231-2 **and on speedy foot:** moving swiftly; **The main . . . thought:** The main body of troops (as distinguished from the reconnoitring troops sent out ahead) are expected to be in view within the hour.

234-5 **Though that . . . on:** Though Cordelia is here for a special reason (to seek her father), her troops have moved ahead.

237 **take my . . . me:** Cause me to die at the appointed time.

238 **worser spirit:** the evil side of my nature.

240 **father:** This word would not reveal Edgar's identity to Gloucester, since it was used as a term of respect by younger to older men.

You shall have ransom. Let me have surgeons;
I am cut to the brains.
Gentleman.   You shall have anything.   210
Lear.   No seconds? All myself?
   Why, this would make a man a man of salt,
   To use his eyes for garden waterpots,
   Ay, and laying autumn's dust. I will die bravely,
   Like a smug bridegroom. What! I will be jovial.   215
   Come, come, I am a king; masters, know you that?
Gentleman.   You are a royal one, and we obey you.
Lear.   Then there's life in't. Come, an you get it, you
   shall get it by running. Sa, sa, sa, sa!
            Exit running followed by Attendants.
Gentleman.   A sight most pitiful in the meanest wretch,   220
   Past speaking of in a king! Thou hast one daughter
   Who redeems nature from the general curse
   Which twain have brought her to.
Edgar.   Hail, gentle sir.
Gentleman.   Sir, speed you. What's your will?   225
Edgar.   Do you hear aught, sir, of a battle toward?
Gentleman.   Most sure and vulgar. Every one hears that
   Which can distinguish sound.
Edgar.   But, by your favour,
   How near's the other army?   230
Gentleman.   Near and on speedy foot. The main descry
   Stands on the hourly thought.
Edgar.   I thank you, sir. That's all.
Gentleman.   Though that the Queen on special cause is here,
   Her army is moved on.   235
Edgar.   I thank you, sir.
                  Exit Gentleman.
Gloucester.   You ever-gentle gods, take my breath from me;
   Let not my worser spirit tempt me again
   To die before you please!
Edgar.   Well pray you, father.   240
Gloucester.   Now, good sir, what are you?

242 **made tame:** rendered submissive, resigned.

243-4 **who, by . . . pity:** literally: who, through the instruction provided by the experience of heartfelt sorrow, am easily moved to pity. More simply, Edgar says: Since I have experienced deep sorrow, I can readily feel pity for the sorrow of others.

245 **biding:** shelter, lodging.

247 **bounty and the benison:** reward and the blessing.

248 **to boot, and boot:** in the highest degree.

249 **a proclaimed prize:** a criminal with a reward on his head. "Proclaimed" is accented on the first syllable; **most happy:** This is a happy opportunity for me!

250 **framed:** created.

252 **thyself remember:** Pray for your sins; **the sword is out:** Oswald draws his sword as he speaks.

257 **published:** See "proclaimed", line 249.

258-9 **Lest that . . . thee:** Lest his ill-luck become yours.

260 **chill:** I'll. This and many of the words to follow are in conventional stage rustic dialect, much like that of rural Somerset; **zir:** sir; **'casion:** occasion, reason.

262 **go your gait:** Go your way.

263-4 **volk:** folk, people; **An chud . . . vortnight:** If I could have been swaggered out of my life, it would not have been as long as it is by at least a fortnight. (Edgar accuses Oswald of mere swagger, not real courage.)

265-7 **Keep out . . . you:** Stand back, I warn you, or I shall try to find out whether your head or my club is the harder. I'll be plain with you.

269-70 **Chill pick . . . foins:** I'll knock your teeth out, sir. Come at me. I don't care about your sword thrusts.

271 **villain:** serf (but see "villain", line 276).

273 **letters:** letter. (See also line 281.)

Edgar.   A most poor man, made tame to fortune's blows,
  Who, by the art of known and feeling sorrows,
  Am pregnant to good pity. Give me your hand;
  I'll lead you to some biding.   245
Gloucester.   Hearty thanks.
  The bounty and the benison of heaven
  To boot, and boot!
          Enter Oswald the Steward.
Oswald.   A proclaimed prize! Most happy!
  That eyeless head of thine was first framed flesh   250
  To raise my fortunes. Thou old unhappy traitor,
  Briefly thyself remember: the sword is out
  That must destroy thee.
Gloucester.   Now let thy friendly hand
  Put strength enough to't.   255
          Edgar interposes.
Oswald.   Wherefore, bold peasant,
  Darest thou support a published traitor? Hence!
  Lest that th' infection of his fortune take
  Like hold on thee. Let go his arm.
Edgar.   Chill not let go, zir, without vurther 'casion.   260
Oswald.   Let go, slave, or thou diest!
Edgar.   Good gentleman, go your gait, and let poor
  volk pass. An chud ha' bin zwagger'd out of my life,
  'twould not ha' bin zo long as 'tis by a vortnight.
  Nay, come not near the old man. Keep out, che vor' 265
  ye, or Ise try whither your costard or my ballow be
  the harder. Chill be plain with you.
Oswald.   Out, dunghill!
Edgar.   Chill pick your teeth, zir. Come! No matter vor
  your foins.   270
          They fight and Oswald falls.
Oswald.   Slave, thou hast slain me. Villain, take my purse.
  If ever thou wilt thrive, bury my body,
  And give the letters which thou find'st about me
  To Edmund Earl of Gloucester. Seek him out

275 **upon the English party:** on the side of the English.

276 **serviceable villain:** evil fellow ready to be used.

277 **duteous:** obedient.

282 **may be my friends:** may be able to help me.

283 **deathsman:** executioner.

284 **wax:** with which the letter was sealed; **manners, blame us not:** The ordinary respect with which we view the letters of others should not count here.

285-6 **to know . . . lawful:** To know what our enemies are thinking, we would tear their hearts from their bodies; to rip open their letters is more justifiable.

287 **reciprocal vows:** See IV. ii. 24-28.

288 **to cut him off:** to murder Albany; **if your . . . not:** if you are not lacking in desire.

289 **time and place:** *i.e.*, for his murder.

293 **would:** would like to; **servant:** lover.

294 **O indistinguished . . . will:** O, the limitless scope of a woman's lust.

297 **rake up:** cover up, bury; **post unsanctified:** unholy messenger.

298 **murderous lechers:** lustful and murderous persons (Goneril and Edmund); **in the mature time:** when the proper moment arrives. The first syllable of "mature" is stressed.

299-300 **ungracious paper:** evil letter; **strike the . . . Duke:** show to the Duke of Albany, whose death is plotted.

302-7 **How stiff . . . themselves:** How stubborn is my hated capacity for feeling my overwhelming sorrows. It would be better if I were mad (like Lear); then, my thoughts and griefs would be separated, and my sorrows would be lost amid mad imaginings.

Upon the English party. O, untimely death! Death! 275
      He dies.
Edgar. I know thee well. A serviceable villain,
  As duteous to the vices of thy mistress
  As badness would desire.
Gloucester.   What, is he dead?
Edgar. Sit you down, father; rest you. 280
  Let's see these pockets; the letters that he speaks of
  May be my friends. He's dead; I am only sorry
  He had no other deathsman. Let us see.
  Leave, gentle wax; and manners, blame us not:
  To know our enemies' minds, we rip their hearts; 285
  Their papers is more lawful.   *Reads the letter.*
    "Let our reciprocal vows be remembered. You have
  many opportunities to cut him off. If your will want not,
  time and place will be fruitfully offered. There is nothing
  done if he return the conqueror. Then am I the prisoner, 290
  and his bed my jail; from the loathed warmth whereof
  deliver me, and supply the place for your labour.
    Your (wife, so I would say) affectionate servant,"
                             GONERIL.

  O indistinguished space of woman's will!
  A plot upon her virtuous husband's life, 295
  And the exchange my brother! Here in the sands
  Thee I'll rake up, the post unsanctified
  Of murderous lechers; and in the mature time
  With this ungracious paper strike the sight
  Of the death-practised Duke. For him 'tis well 300
  That of thy death and business I can tell.
Gloucester. The King is mad. How stiff is my vile sense,
  That I stand up, and have ingenious feeling
  Of my huge sorrows! Better I were distract.
  So should my thoughts be severed from my griefs, 305
  And woes by wrong imaginations lose
  The knowledge of themselves.
      A drum afar off.

310   **bestow you with:** leave you in the care of.
See also p. 240.

3   **measure:** attempt.

4   **to be acknowledged:** to be recognized (for one's work).

5   **All my . . . truth:** Everything I have reported (about Lear) conforms to the simple truth.

6   **nor more nor clipped:** no more, no less; **so:** as I say (used for emphasis).

7   **suited:** dressed.

8   **weeds:** clothes; **memories:** reminders; **worser:** archaic comparative degree of the adjective.

9   **I prithee:** I beg you.

11   **Yet to . . . intent:** If I am to reveal myself now, I shall not be able to carry out my intentions.

12   **boon:** request; **make it:** ask, request.

13   **meet:** suitable.

18   **breach in . . . nature:** damage in his disturbed mind.

19-20   **Th' untuned . . . father:** Tune the untuned and discordant senses of this father who has been made mad (also made into a child) by the savagery of his children. The image is based upon the tuning of a stringed musical instrument.

22   **that we may:** may we.

23   **be governed by:** proved according to.

24   **i' the sway of:** according to.

Edgar.   Give me your hand.
   Far off methinks I hear the beaten drum.
   Come, father, I'll bestow you with a friend.   *Exeunt.*   310

Scene 7

A TENT IN THE FRENCH CAMP.

Enter Cordelia, Kent, Doctor, and Gentleman.

Cordelia.   O thou good Kent, how shall I live and work
   To match thy goodness? My life will be too short
   And every measure fail me.
Kent.   To be acknowledged, madam, is o'erpaid.
   All my reports go with the modest truth;   5
   Nor more nor clipped, but so.
Cordelia.   Be better suited:
   These weeds are memories of those worser hours:
   I prithee put them off.
Kent.   Pardon, dear madam.   10
   Yet to be known shortens my made intent.
   My boon I make it that you know me not
   Till time and I think meet.
Cordelia.   Then be it so, my good lord. (*To the Doctor*). How
   does the King?   15
Doctor.   Madam, sleeps still.
Cordelia.   O you kind gods,
   Cure this great breach in his abused nature!
   Th' untuned and jarring senses, O, wind up
   Of this child-changed father!   20
Doctor.   So please your Majesty
   That we may wake the King? He hath slept long.
Cordelia.   Be governed by your knowledge, and proceed
   I' the sway of your own will. Is he arrayed?
          Enter Lear in a chair carried by Servants.

27 **Be by:** Be nearby, remain close at hand.

28 **I doubt . . . temperance:** I have no doubt that his sanity will have returned.

31-32 **restoration hang . . . lips:** May my love become the medicine to restore you to your former state.

34 **in thy reverence:** to thee, to whom all showed reverence.

36 **had you not been:** even if you had not been; **these white flakes:** these strands of white hair.

37 **had challenged:** would have called for; **of:** from.

39 **dread-bolted:** with its dreadful thunderbolts.

41 **perdu:** a lost one (Fr.); used also of a sentinel sent to a dangerous and lonely post.

42 **this thin helm:** this head, with scanty hair.

44 **fain:** glad.

45 **to hovel thee:** to take shelter; **rogues:** vagabonds, tramps.

46 **short and musty straw:** old straw much used and therefore broken into short lengths and spoiled by dampness.

47 **at once:** at a single moment.

48 **concluded all:** come to an end.

49 **fittest:** most fitting, most suitable, best.

53 **that:** so that.

57 **far wide:** far wide of the mark, far away from sanity.

58 **scarce:** scarcely.

Gentleman.   Ay, madam. In the heaviness of sleep.   25
  We put fresh garments on him.
Doctor.   Be by, good madam, when we do awake him.
  I doubt not of his temperance.
Cordelia.   Very well.
     Music.
Doctor.   Please you draw near. Louder the music there!   30
Cordelia.   O my dear father, restoration hang
  Thy medicine on my lips, and let this kiss
  Repair those violent harms that my two sisters
  Have in thy reverence made!
Kent.   Kind and dear princess!   35
Cordelia.   Had you not been their father, these white flakes
  Had challenged pity of them. Was this a face
  To be opposed against the warring winds?
  To stand against the deep dread-bolted thunder?
  In the most terrible and nimble stroke   40
  Of quick, cross lightning? to watch—poor perdu!—
  With this thin helm? Mine enemy's dog,
  Though he had bit me, should have stood that night
  Against my fire; and wast thou fain, poor father,
  To hovel thee with swine and rogues forlorn,   45
  In short and musty straw? Alack, alack!
  'Tis wonder that thy life and wits at once
  Had not concluded all.—He wakes; speak to him.
Doctor.   Madam, do you; 'tis fittest.
Cordelia. How does my royal lord? How fares your Majesty?   50
Lear.   You do me wrong to take me out o' the grave.
  Thou art a soul in bliss; but I am bound
  Upon a wheel of fire, that mine own tears
  Do scald like molten lead.
Cordelia.   Sir, do you know me?   55
Lear.   You are a spirit, I know. Where did you die?
Cordelia.   Still, still, far wide!
Doctor.   He's scarce awake. Let him alone awhile.
Lear.   Where have I been? Where am I? Fair daylight?

60   **mightily abused:** greatly deceived, greatly deluded.
61   **thus:** in my present state.
66   **benediction:** blessing.
69   **fond:** in dotage, senility, second childhood.
70   **fourscore:** eighty years.
74   **mainly:** entirely.
75   **skill:** sense.
89   **abuse:** deceive.
90   **rage:** frenzy, madness.
91-92   **and yet . . . lost:** and yet it is dangerous to make him try to fill in the gap in the time that he does not recollect.
93   **desire him:** ask him.
94   **till further settling:** till his mind settles still further.

I am mightily abused. I should e'en die with pity,   60
To see another thus. I know not what to say.
I will not swear these are my hands. Let's see:
I feel this pin prick. Would I were assured
Of my condition!
Cordelia.   O, look upon me, sir,   65
And hold your hands in benediction o'er me.
No, sir, you must not kneel.
Lear.   Pray, do not mock me.
I am a very foolish fond old man,
Fourscore and upward, not an hour more nor less;   70
And, to deal plainly,
I fear I am not in my perfect mind.
Methinks I should know you, and know this man;
Yet I am doubtful; for I am mainly ignorant
What place this is; and all the skill I have   75
Remembers not these garments; nor I know not
Where I did lodge last night. Do not laugh at me;
For (as I am a man) I think this lady
To be my child Cordelia.
Cordelia.   And so I am, I am.   80
Lear.   Be your tears wet? Yes, faith. I pray weep not.
If you have poison for me, I will drink it.
I know you do not love me, for your sisters
Have, as I do remember, done me wrong:
You have some cause, they have not.   85
Cordelia.   No cause, no cause.
Lear.   Am I in France?
Kent.   In your own kingdom, sir.
Lear.   Do not abuse me.
Doctor.   Be comforted, good madam. The great rage   90
You see is killed in him; and yet it is danger
To make him even o'er the time he has lost.
Desire him to go in. Trouble him no more
Till further settling.
Cordelia.   Will't please your Highness walk?   95

96 **bear with:** be sympathetic towards, be understanding towards.
98-99 **Holds it . . . slain:** Is it confirmed as truth?
101 **conductor:** leader.
102 **the bastard . . . Gloucester:** We can scarcely expect Kent to address Edmund in other terms—certainly not by his recent title.
105 **changeable:** unreliable.
106 **powers:** military forces; **apace:** speedily.
107 **The arbitrement . . . bloody:** The decision reached in this encounter is likely to be a bloody one.
109 **my point and period:** the end of my life. "Point" and "period" are synonyms; **wrought:** worked out.
110 **or . . . or:** either . . . or.

See also p. 241.

Lear.   You must bear with me.
　　Pray you now, forget and forgive. I am old and foolish.
　　　　Exeunt Lear, Cordelia, Doctor, and Attendants.
Gentleman. Holds it true, sir, that the Duke of Cornwall was
　　so slain?
Kent. Most certain, sir.   100
Gentleman. Who is conductor of his people?
Kent. As 'tis said, the bastard son of Gloucester.
Gentleman. They say Edgar, his banished son, is with the
　　Earl of Kent in Germany.
Kent. Report is changeable. 'Tis time to look about; 105
　　the powers of the kingdom approach apace.
Gentleman. The arbitrement is like to be bloody.
　　Fare you well, sir.   *Exit.*
Kent. My point and period will be throughly wrought,
　　Or well or ill, as this day's battle's fought.   *Exit.* 110

ACT V

Scene 1

THE BRITISH CAMP NEAR DOVER.

Enter, with Drum and Colours,
Edmund, Regan, Gentlemen, and Soldiers.

Edmund. Know of the Duke if his last purpose hold,
　　Or whether since he is advised by aught
　　To change the course. He's full of alteration
　　And self-reproving. Bring his constant pleasure.
　　　　　　　　　　　　Exit an Officer.
Regan. Our sister's man is certainly miscarried.   5
Edmund. 'Tis to be doubted, madam.
Regan.   Now, sweet lord,

8   **intend upon:** intend to confer upon.
11 **honoured:** honourable.
12 **brother's:** brother-in-law's.
13 **forfended place:** forbidden place—Albany's bed, forbidden to Edmund by the commandment against adultery.
14 **abuses:** compound meaning: *deceives* and also, *is unworthy of.*
15-16 **doubtful:** fearful; **conjunct and bosomed:** joined in the most intimate way; **as far . . . hers:** so that you may be regarded as belonging to her.
20 **fear:** distrust.
24 **loosen him:** separate him from.
25 **well bemet:** a greeting signifying: We are fortunate in meeting you.
27 **rigour of our state:** oppression of our rule.
28 **cry out:** protest; **honest:** honourable.
29-32 **For this . . . oppose:** This business (of Cordelia's returning to her father) concerns us, not because it assists Lear and some others who are against us, but because the King of France is invading our territory.
34 **Why is this reasoned:** How do you arrive at that conclusion?
36 **these domestic . . . broils:** these family and personal quarrels.
39 **ancient:** those with experience.
40 **presently:** immediately.

You know the goodness I intend upon you.
Tell me, but truly, but then speak the truth,
Do you not love my sister?   10
Edmund.   In honoured love.
Regan.   But have you never found my brother's way
   To the forfended place?
Edmund.   That thought abuses you.
Regan.   I am doubtful that you have been conjunct   15
   And bosomed with her, as far as we call hers.
Edmund.   No, by mine honour, madam.
Regan.   I never shall endure her. Dear my lord,
   Be not familiar with her.
Edmund.   Fear me not.   20
   She and the Duke her husband!
            Enter, with Drum and Colours, Albany, Goneril,
            Soldiers.
Goneril (aside).   I had rather lose the battle than that
      sister
   Should loosen him and me.
Albany.   Our very loving sister, well bemet.   25
   Sir, this I hear: the King is come to his daughter,
   With others whom the rigour of our state
   Forced to cry out. Where I could not be honest,
   I never yet was valiant. For this business,
   It touches us as France invades our land,   30
   Not bolds the King, with others, whom, I fear,
   Most just and heavy causes make oppose.
Edmund.   Sir, you speak nobly.
Regan.   Why is this reasoned?
Goneril.   Combine together 'gainst the enemy;   35
   For these domestic and particular broils
   Are not the question here.
Albany.   Let's then determine
   With th' ancient of war on our proceeding.
Edmund.   I shall attend you presently at your tent.   40
Regan.   Sister, you'll go with us?

43 **convenient:** fitting.
44 **riddle:** hidden meaning.
47 **overtake:** catch up to (spoken to Goneril, Regan, and Edmund).
49 **ope:** open.
52 **champion:** a knight who is willing to undergo trial of combat with another knight in place of a pitched battle between two armies; **prove:** reach a military decision by single combat.
53 **avouched:** claimed, asserted, maintained; **if you miscarry:** if you should have an accident (*i.e.*, are defeated and killed).
55 **machination:** plotting to take your life; **Fortune love you:** Good luck!
58 **herald:** official appointed to conduct a knightly combat.
60 **o'erlook:** look over.
61 **draw up your powers:** Deploy your forces.
62 **here:** Edmund holds up a paper; **guess:** estimate.
63 **by diligent discovery:** by careful observation.
65 **We will . . . time:** We will face the crisis promptly.
67-68 **jealous:** suspicious; **as the . . . adder:** just as those who are bitten by a snake are suspicious of it; *i.e.*, both know only too well what has happened to them.
72 **carry out my side:** successfully complete my plans.

Goneril. No.

Regan. 'Tis most convenient; pray go with us.

Goneril (aside). O, ho, I know the riddle.—I will go.

> *As they are going out, enter Edgar disguised.*

Edgar. If e'er your Grace had speech with man so poor, 45
Hear me one word.

Albany.   I'll overtake you.

> *Exeunt all but Albany and Edgar.*

Speak.

Edgar. Before you fight the battle, ope this letter.
If you have victory, let the trumpet sound   50
For him that brought it. Wretched though I seem,
I can produce a champion that will prove
What is avouched there. If you miscarry,
Your business of the world hath so an end,
And machination ceases. Fortune love you!   55

Albany. Stay till I have read the letter.

Edgar.   I was forbid it.
When time shall serve, let but the herald cry,
And I'll appear again.

Albany. Why, fare thee well. I will o'erlook thy paper.   60

> *Exit Edgar.*

> *Enter Edmund.*

Edmund. The enemy's in view; draw up your powers.
Here is the guess of their true strength and forces
By diligent discovery; but your haste
Is now urged on you.

Albany.   We will greet the time.   *Exit.*   65

Edmund. To both these sisters have I sworn my love;
Each jealous of the other, as the stung
Are of the adder. Which of them shall I take?
Both? one? or neither? Neither can be enjoyed
If both remain alive. To take the widow   70
Exasperates, makes mad her sister Goneril;
And hardly shall I carry out my side,
Her husband being alive. Now then, we'll use

74 **countenance:** authority.

79-80 **my state . . . debate:** My future demands that I act rather than argue.

See also p. 242.

S.D. **alarum:** alarm, a call on trumpets accompanied by drums, signifying that troops must press forward to the attack.

2 **host:** shelter.

6 **Away:** Leave this place.

7 **ta'en:** taken prisoner, captured.

9 **rot:** die.

10 **in ill thoughts:** in a despairing mood.

12 **ripeness:** readiness (for death); Hamlet expresses this view also in V. ii. 209-14.

See also p. 243.

His countenance for the battle, which being done,
Let her who would be rid of him devise   75
His speedy taking off. As for the mercy
Which he intends to Lear and to Cordelia,
The battle done, and they within our power,
Shall never see his pardon; for my state
Stands on me to defend, not to debate.   *Exit.*   80

Scene 2

A FIELD BETWEEN THE TWO CAMPS.

*Alarum within. Enter, with Drum and Colours,
Lear, Cordelia, and the Powers of France over
the stage, and exeunt.
Enter Edgar and Gloucester.*

Edgar.   Here, father, take the shadow of this tree
For your good host. Pray that the right may thrive.
If ever I return to you again,
I'll bring you comfort.
Gloucester.   Grace go with you, sir!   5
                              Exit Edgar.
Alarum and retreat within. Enter Edgar.
Edgar.   Away, old man! give me thy hand! away!
King Lear hath lost, he and his daughter ta'en.
Give me thy hand! come on!
Gloucester.   No further, sir. A man may rot even here.
Edgar.   What, in ill thoughts again? Men must endure   10
Their going hence, even as their coming hither;
Ripeness is all. Come on.
Gloucester.   And that's true too.   *Exeunt.*

1-3 **Good guard . . . them:** Keep them under strict guard until the desires of those in command, who may pass judgement upon them, are known.

5 **meaning:** intention; **incurred:** suffered; **worst:** worst outcome.

6 **cast down:** very sad, dejected.

7 **else outfrown . . . frown:** otherwise overlook misfortune.

13 **tell old tales:** talk over old times.

14 **gilded butterflies:** courtiers; **rogues:** vagabonds (the opposite of courtiers).

16 **in . . . out:** in favour . . . out of favour.

17-18 **and take . . . spies:** and pretend that we can solve all the mysteries of nature as if God had given us special powers of observation; **wear out:** outlast.

19 **packs and sects:** synonymous terms for *parties, "sets"*.

20 **that ebb . . . moon:** that change as often as the moon (the symbol of changeability).

22 **sacrifices:** the renunciation of the world by Lear and Cordelia.

23 **throw incense:** bestow their blessing; **Have I caught thee:** Are you to be with me always? This seems to be a rhetorical question.

24 **brand:** flame.

25 **fire us . . . foxes:** and part us as hunters part (or drive) foxes from their burrows with fire.

26 **goodyears:** a strange word, which has inspired much ingenious research and speculation. Lear means that some misfortune—probably disease or pestilence—will overtake those who try to hurt him and Cordelia again; **fell:** skin.

29 **hark:** Listen, pay attention.

30 **note:** death warrant.

Scene 3

THE BRITISH CAMP, NEAR DOVER.

Enter, in conquest, with Drum and Colours, Edmund;
Lear and Cordelia as prisoners; Soldiers, Captain.

Edmund.   Some officers take them away. Good guard
  Until their greater pleasures first be known
  That are to censure them.
Cordelia.   We are not the first
  Who with best meaning have incurred the worst.   5
  For thee, oppressed king, I am cast down;
  Myself could else outfrown false Fortune's frown.
  Shall we not see these daughters and these sisters?
Lear.   No, no, no, no! Come, let's away to prison.
  We two alone will sing like birds i' the cage.   10
  When thou dost ask me blessing, I'll kneel down
  And ask of thee forgiveness. So we'll live,
  And pray, and sing, and tell old tales, and laugh
  At gilded butterflies, and hear poor rogues
  Talk of court news; and we'll talk with them too,   15
  Who loses and who wins; who's in, who's out;
  And take upon's the mystery of things,
  As if we were God's spies; and we'll wear out,
  In a walled prison, packs and sects of great ones
  That ebb and flow by the moon.   20
Edmund.   Take them away.
Lear.   Upon such sacrifices, my Cordelia,
  The gods themselves throw incense. Have I caught thee?
  He that parts us shall bring a brand from heaven
  And fire us hence like foxes. Wipe thine eyes.   25
  The goodyears shall devour 'em, flesh and fell,
  Ere they shall make us weep! We'll see 'em starved first.
  Come.   *Exeunt Lear and Cordelia, guarded.*
Edmund.   Come hither, Captain; hark.
  Take thou this note (*Gives a paper*). Go follow them to   30

34-35 **that men . . . is:** that men must act as the circumstances dictate; *i.e.*, that they must act cruelly in time of war.
36 **sword:** soldier active in war; **employment:** assignment.
37 **bear question:** permit discussion.
40 **About it:** equivalent to: Go to it, then! **write happy:** regar l yourself as happy; **th':** thou.
41 **Mark:** Note, observe.
42 **set it down:** planned it (in the warrant given, line 30).
43 **I cannot . . . oats:** I'm not a horse—a beast of burden—but a man.
45 **valiant strain:** courageous lineage or descent.
47 **opposites:** enemies.
48 **I do . . . you:** I ask you to turn them over to me.
49 **merits:** deserts.
53 **retention:** detention, imprisonment.
54-57 **whose age . . . them:** whose age and whose royal rank even more attract the sympathy of the people and turn the conscripted forces, which we command, against us.
58 **my reason . . . same:** for the same reason.
59 **at further space:** at a later time.
60 **session:** trial.
62-63 **and the . . . sharpness:** Even the worthiest objectives are cursed by those who feel the pain when events are at their most painful stage.

    prison.
One step I have advanced thee; if thou dost
As this instructs thee, thou dost make thy way
To noble fortunes. Know thou this, that men
Are as the time is; to be tender-minded   35
Does not become a sword. Thy great employment
Will not bear question; either say thou'lt do't,
Or thrive by other means.
Captain.   I'll do't, my lord.
Edmund. About it! and write happy when th' hast done.   40
    Mark—I say, instantly; and carry it so
    As I have set it down.
Captain. I cannot draw a cart, nor eat dried oats;
    If it be man's work, I'll do't.   *Exit.*
         Flourish. Enter Albany, Goneril, Regan, Soldiers.
Albany. Sir, you have showed today your valiant strain,   45
    And fortune led you well. You have the captives
    Who were the opposites of this day's strife;
    I do require them of you, so to use them
    As we shall find their merits and our safety
    May equally determine.   50
Edmund.   Sir, I thought it fit
    To send the old and miserable King
    To some retention and appointed guard;
    Whose age had charms in it, whose title more,
    To pluck the common bosom on his side   55
    And turn our impressed lances in our eyes
    Which do command them. With him I sent the Queen,
    My reason all the same; and they are ready
    Tomorrow, or at further space, t' appear
    Where you shall hold your session. At this time   60
    We sweat and bleed: the friend hath lost his friend,
    And the best quarrels, in the heat, are cursed
    By those that feel their sharpness.
    The question of Cordelia and her father
    Requires a fitter place.   65

66 **by your patience:** I beg your pardon—you do not understand my meaning.

67 **subject:** subordinate.

68 **brother:** equal.

69 **That's as . . . him:** That is the manner in which we wish to regard him; *i.e.*, as an equal.

70 **pleasure:** wishes.

72-74 **bore the . . . brother:** was fully accredited by me as my deputy, and his present rank (immediacy) justifies him in being considered your equal.

75 **hot:** fast.

76 **grace:** merit; **exalt himself:** become more powerful.

77 **in your addition:** in your granting of powers to him.

79 **invested:** granted; **compeers:** equals.

80 **were:** would be; **the most:** fully accomplished; **husband:** a verb, *marry*.

81 **Jesters do . . . prophets:** Those who make jokes often hit upon the truth (or, Many a true word is spoken in jest).

82 **Holla, holla:** Hello, hello! Equivalent to an expression of feigned surprise: Well, well!

83 **That eye . . . asquint:** Whoever told you that could not see well.

85 **from a full-flowing stomach:** with a flood of anger; **General:** *i.e.*, Edmund.

86 **patrimony:** inheritance from my father.

87 **the walls are thine:** a common military metaphor based on the idea of an attack upon a castle or walled town. It means: You have gained the victory by storm.

90 **enjoy:** possess. Goneril's sarcasm, considering what she has done, has no parallel. See line 115.

91 **The let-alone . . . will:** The prevention is not within your power (or, You have no right to forbid her to take him as her husband).

93 **half-blooded fellow:** bastard.

94 **prove:** by trial of combat, if necessary.

97 **on capital treason:** on the charge of treason punishable by death or of high treason; **attaint:** infection. Albany means that Edmund's high treason has infected or tainted Goneril as well.

98 **this gilded serpent:** Goneril, whose appearance is beautiful but whose nature is like a venomous snake's.

99 **sister:** sister-in-law—Regan.

100 **bar:** forbid.

101 **sub-contracted:** bound by a contract—engagement to Edmund—whose terms include the breaking of another contract, the marriage contract between her and me.

Albany.   Sir, by your patience,
   I hold you but a subject of this war,
     Not as a brother.
Regan.   That's as we list to grace him.
   Methinks our pleasure might have been demanded   70
   Ere you had spoke so far. He led our powers,
   Bore the commission of my place and person,
   The which immediacy may well stand up
   And call itself your brother.
Goneril.   Not so hot!   75
   In his own grace he doth exalt himself
   More than in your addition.
Regan.   In my rights
   By me invested, he compeers the best.
Goneril.   That were the most if he should husband you.   80
Regan.   Jesters do oft prove prophets.
Goneril.   Holla, holla!
   That eye that told you so looked but asquint.
Regan.   Lady, I am not well; else I should answer
   From a full-flowing stomach. General,   85
   Take thou my soldiers, prisoners, patrimony;
   Dispose of them, of me; the walls are thine.
   Witness the world that I create thee here
   My lord and master.
Goneril.   Mean you to enjoy him?   90
Albany.   The let-alone lies not in your good will.
Edmund.   Nor in thine, lord.
Albany.   Half-blooded fellow, yes.
Regan (*to Edmund*).   Let the drum strike, and prove my
     title thine.   95
Albany.   Stay yet; hear reason. Edmund, I arrest thee
   On capital treason; and, in thine attaint,
   This gilded serpent (*Points to Goneril*). For your claim,
     fair sister,
   I bar it in the interest of my wife.   100
   'Tis she is sub-contracted to this lord,

102 **contradict your banes:** stand up and protest against the announcement of your marriage to him; **banes:** banns. The proclamation in church made on three Sundays, announcing a forthcoming marriage. In each announcement, an opportunity is provided for anyone to give valid reasons against performing the marriage within the church.

104 **bespoke:** promised, engaged.

105 **interlude:** little play, comedy.

106-7 **armed:** in full armour. Edmund has just come from battle; **Let the trumpet sound:** See V. i. 50.

108 **prove:** See line 94.

109 **heinous:** villainous, monstrous; **manifest, and many:** synonymous terms.

110-11 **pledge:** Throwing down the gauntlet meant pledging oneself to do battle; **make it . . . heart:** I'll prove the truth of my allegation (see line 109) by trying to take your life.

112 **ere I taste bread:** before I eat again; **thou art:** *that* thou art.

114 **Sick, O sick:** I am very sick.

115 **medicine:** poison. Goneril has poisoned her sister.

116 **exchange:** the glove thrown down with Albany's, signifying that Edmund has accepted the challenge.

118 **he lies:** the *lie-direct*—a duel to the death.

120 **on him . . . not:** on anybody at all.

124 **thy single virtue:** your unaided courage.

125 **levied:** recruited.

126 **took:** taken.

132 **of quality or degree:** of rank and social standing.

133 **lists:** nominal rolls, list of names.

And I, her husband, contradict your banes.
If you will marry, make your loves to me;
My lady is bespoke.
Goneril.   An interlude!   105
Albany.   Thou art armed, Gloucester. Let the trumpet
    sound.
    If none appear to prove upon thy person
    Thy heinous, manifest, and many treasons,
    There is my pledge (*Throws down a glove*)! I'll make it on 110
    thy heart,
    Ere I taste bread, thou art in nothing less
    Than I have here proclaimed thee.
Regan.   Sick, O, sick!
Goneril (*aside*).   If not, I'll ne'er trust medicine.   115
Edmund.   There's my exchange (*Throws down a glove*).
    What in the world he is
    That names me traitor, villain-like he lies.
    Call by thy trumpet. He that dares approach,
    On him, on you, who not? I will maintain   120
    My truth and honour firmly.
Albany.   A herald, ho!
Edmund.   A herald, ho, a herald!
Albany.   Trust to thy single virtue; for thy soldiers,
    All levied in my name, have in my name   125
    Took their discharge.
Regan.   My sickness grows upon me.
Albany.   She is not well. Convey her to my tent.
                            Exit Regan, led.
       Enter a Herald.
    Come hither, herald. Let the trumpet sound,
    And read out this.   130
Captain.   Sound, trumpet!   *A trumpet sounds.*
Herald (*reads*).   "If any man of quality or degree within
    the lists of the army will maintain upon Edmund, sup-
    posed Earl of Gloucester, that he is a manifold traitor, let
    him appear by the third sound of the trumpet. He is bold 135

138 S.D. **a Trumpet before him:** a trumpeter ahead of him.
139 **purposes:** intentions.
142 **quality:** See line 132.
145 **by treason's . . . canker-bit:** partly eaten away by the cater-pillar, treason. Edgar means: My name has been smeared and stained by some person's treason.
147 **cope:** meet.
148 **that:** so that.
154 **mine:** Edgar stretches out his right hand, having drawn his sword.
155-6 **Behold, it . . . profession:** Note well that my arms and sword enjoy the privileges of knighthood with all its honours and its oath of loyalty.
157 **maugre:** in spite of. Cf. *malgré* (Fr.); **place:** high command; **eminence:** position as newly appointed Earl of Gloucester.
158 **victor sword:** victory in the recent battle; **fire-new fortune:** completely new (recently forged) wealth and power.
159 **valour and thy heart:** "Heart" is synonymous with "valour".
161 **conspirant:** conspirator; **prince:** Albany.
162 **extremest upward:** topmost part.
163 **descent and dust:** lowest part of the body.
164 **toad-spotted:** covered with the poisonous marks of treason as a toad is covered with venomous warts. The toad's spots are not venomous, but exude an unpleasantly bitter fluid; **say:** if you say.
165 **spirits:** courage; **bent:** directed.
167 **liest:** See line 118.
168 **name:** Edmund would not be obliged under the rules of combat to accept the challenge of one who was not a gentleman.

in his defense."   *First trumpet.*
Herald.   Again!   *Second trumpet.*
Herald.   Again!   *Third trumpet.*
                              Trumpet answers within.
            Enter Edgar, armed, a Trumpet before him.
Albany.   Ask him his purposes, why he appears
    Upon this call o' the trumpet.   140
Herald.   What are you?
    Your name, your quality? and why you answer
    This present summons?
Edgar.   Know my name is lost;
    By treason's tooth bare-gnawn and canker-bit.   145
    Yet am I noble as the adversary
    I come to cope.
Albany.   Which is that adversary?
Edgar.   What's he that speaks for Edmund Earl of
        Gloucester?   150
Edmund.   Himself. What sayest thou to him?
Edgar.   Draw thy sword,
    That, if my speech offend a noble heart,
    Thy arm may do thee justice. Here is mine.
    Behold, it is the privilege of mine honours,   155
    My oath, and my profession. I protest,
    Maugre thy strength, place, youth, and eminence,
    Despite thy victor sword and fire-new fortune,
    Thy valour and thy heart, thou art a traitor,
    False to thy gods, thy brother, and thy father;   160
    Conspirant 'gainst this high illustrious prince;
    And from th' extremest upward of thy head
    To the descent and dust beneath thy foot,
    A most toad-spotted traitor. Say thou "no,"
    This sword, this arm, and my best spirits are bent   165
    To prove upon thy heart, whereto I speak,
    Thou liest.
Edmund.   In wisdom I should ask thy name;
    But since thy outside looks so fair and warlike,

170 **say:** sign, indication. This would signify Edgar's accent.
171 **safe and nicely:** cautiously, with precise, legal justification; **delay:** postpone.
172 **spurn:** cast aside, ignore.
174 **the hell-hated lie:** the lie (of high treason), hated even in hell.
175 **which:** antecedent is "treasons"; **for they . . . bruise:** since as yet they do not harm you.
176-7 **This sword . . . ever:** This sword of mine will return (them) with more force upon your head, where they will remain forever.
178 **save:** spare, do not kill.
179 **practice:** trickery.
180-1 **By the . . . opposite:** See line 168; **opposite:** opponent.
182 **cozened and beguiled:** synonymous terms—*deceived, fooled.*
184-5 S.D. See IV. vi. 287-93; **Hold, sir:** Just a moment please.
189-90 **Say if I do:** *You* say, if you like, whether I know the letter or not; **the laws . . . for't:** The laws are mine to make, not yours (since I am the ruling sovereign). Who can bring me to trial? As sovereign, I am above the law.
192 **this paper:** the letter referred to in S.D., line 184.
194 **desperate:** distraught, not in her right mind; **govern:** control.
199 **that hast . . . me:** that hast won this victory over me.
201 **charity:** forgiveness.
202 **blood:** lineage.
203 **more:** more noble in blood, since Edmund is only half-noble because of his illegitimacy.

And that thy tongue some say of breeding breathes, 170
What safe and nicely I might well delay
By rule of knighthood, I disdain and spurn;
Back do I toss those treasons to thy head,
With the hell-hated lie o'erwhelm thy heart,
Which, for they yet glance by and scarcely bruise, 175
This sword of mine shall give them instant way
Where they shall rest for ever. Trumpets, speak!
     Alarums. Fight. Edmund falls.
Albany. Save him, save him!
Goneril.   This is mere practice, Gloucester.
By the law of arms thou wast not bound to answer 180
An unknown opposite. Thou art not vanquished,
But cozened and beguiled.
Albany.   Shut your mouth, dame,
Or with this paper shall I stop it. (*Shows her her letter to
    Edmund*).—(*To Edmund*). Hold, sir. 185
    (*To Goneril*). Thou worse than any name, read thine own
    evil.
No tearing, lady! I perceive you know it.
Goneril. Say if I do—the laws are mine, not thine.
Who can arraign me for't? 190
Albany.   Most monstrous! O!
Knowest thou this paper?
Goneril.   Ask me not what I know. *Exit.*
Albany. Go after her. She's desperate; govern her.
                      Exit an Officer.
Edmund. What you have charged me with, that have I 195
    done,
And more, much more. The time will bring it out.
'Tis past, and so am I. But what art thou
That hast this fortune on me? If thou'rt noble,
I do forgive thee. 200
Edgar.   Let's exchange charity.
I am no less in blood than thou art, Edmund;
If more, the more th' hast wronged me.

205 **pleasant:** pleasure-giving.

207 **the dark . . . got:** the secret and sinful place where Edmund was conceived. Cf. Gloucester's joking about this incident in I. i. 20-22.

208 **cost him his eyes:** Edgar regards Gloucester's blindness as the price of his sin in fathering Edmund.

210 **The wheel . . . circle:** The Wheel of Fortune has made a complete revolution. Edmund began at the bottom, rose to the top, and now finds himself at the bottom again, as the goddess Fortune sat by and turned the wheel to which all mortals were said to cling. See II. ii. 178.

211 **gait:** manner, demeanour, carriage; **prophesy:** suggest.

214 **thee:** Edgar.

218 **by nursing them:** by caring for them—as Edgar did when he led his father; **list:** listen to.

220-4 **The bloody . . . rags:** The necessity of escaping the death warrant that was issued for me and that came near to claiming me taught me to dress in a madman's rags; **O, our . . . once:** How sweet life is that we choose to suffer death every hour rather than die at once and have it over! **semblance:** dress, appearance.

225 **habit:** clothing.

226 **rings:** eye-sockets.

227 **precious stones:** eyes.

230 **past:** ago.

231 **success:** victory over Edmund.

233 **pilgrimage:** the flight Edgar took after being declared an outlaw by his father; **flawed:** broken.

234 **conflict:** direct object of "to support"—the conflicting ideas of sadness at the suffering he had inflicted upon Edgar and the joy of knowing him to be a loving, faithful son, who performed his filial duty fully aware of what his father had done to him.

236 **burst smilingly:** The words indicate that Gloucester died happy.

My name is Edgar and thy father's son.
The gods are just, and of our pleasant vices   205
Make instruments to plague us.
The dark and vicious place where thee he got
Cost him his eyes.
Edmund.   Th' hast spoken right; 'tis true.
The wheel is come full circle; I am here.   210
Albany.   Methought thy very gait did prophesy
A royal nobleness. I must embrace thee.
Let sorrow split my heart if ever I
Did hate thee, or thy father!
Edgar.   Worthy prince, I know't.   215
Albany.   Where have you hid yourself?
How have you known the miseries of your father?
Edgar.   By nursing them, my lord. List a brief tale;
And when 'tis told, O that my heart would burst!
The bloody proclamation to escape   220
That followed me so near (O, our lives' sweetness!
That we the pain of death would hourly die
Rather than die at once!) taught me to shift
Into a madman's rags, t' assume a semblance
That very dogs disdained; and in this habit   225
Met I my father with his bleeding rings,
Their precious stones new lost; became his guide,
Let him, begged for him, saved him from despair;
Never (O fault!) revealed myself unto him
Until some half hour past, when I was armed;   230
Not sure, though hoping of this good success,
I asked his blessing, and from first to last
Told him my pilgrimage. But his flawed heart
(Alack, too weak the conflict to support!)
'Twixt two extremes of passion, joy and grief,   235
Burst smilingly.
Edmund.   This speech of yours hath moved me,
And shall perchance do good; but speak you on;
You look as you had something more to say.

241 **dissolve:** let tears flow.
243-6 **This would . . . extremity:** After this story (lines 232-3), it would have seemed to those who do not bear sadness well that sorrow was at an end; but one more sorrow, too freely described, would take us beyond the extreme limit.
247 **big in clamour:** loud in my grief.
248 **estate:** condition.
252 **as:** as if; **him:** himself.
254 **recounting:** telling.
255-6 **puissant:** overwhelming; **strings of . . . crack:** threads of life, which kept him alive, began to break; **Twice then . . . sounded:** signalling the battle.
257 **tranced:** insensible.
260-1 **enemy:** hostile; **service improper . . . slave:** lowest and most menial duties, those necessary to care for an old and helpless man; S.D. **Gentleman:** member of the court circle, not of the highest aristocracy, but of a known and respected family.
271 **contracted:** engaged to be married.
272 **marry:** unite, or *are united.*

Albany.   If there be more, more woeful, hold it in;   240
   For I am almost ready to dissolve,
   Hearing of this.
Edgar.   This would have seemed a period
   To such as love not sorrow; but another,
   To amplify too much, would make much more,   245
   And top extremity.
   Whilst I was big in clamour, came there a man,
   Who, having seen me in my worst estate,
   Shunned my abhorred society; but then, finding
   Who 'twas that so endured, with his strong arms   250
   He fastened on my neck, and bellowed out
   As he'd burst heaven; threw him on my father;
   Told the most piteous tale of Lear and him
   That ever ear received; which in recounting
   His grief grew puissant, and the strings of life   255
   Began to crack. Twice then the trumpets sounded,
   And there I left him tranced.
Albany.   But who was this?
Edgar.   Kent, sir, the banished Kent; who in disguise
   Followed his enemy king and did him service   260
   Improper for a slave.
      Enter a Gentleman with a bloody knife.
Gentleman.   Help, help! O, help!
Edgar.   What kind of help?
Albany.   Speak, man.
Edgar.   What means this bloody knife?   265
Gentleman.   'Tis hot, it smokes.
   It came even from the heart of—O, she's dead!
Albany.   Who dead? Speak, man.
Gentleman.   Your lady, sir, your lady! and her sister
   By her is poisoned; she hath confessed it.   270
Edmund.   I was contracted to them both. All three
   Now marry in an instant.
Edgar.   Here comes Kent.
      Enter Kent.

274 **be they . . . dead:** whether they are alive or dead.
276 **touches us . . . pity:** does not cause us to feel pity; **is this he:** Is it you, Kent?
277 **compliment:** ceremony.
278 **very manners:** ordinary politeness. "Manners" is singular.
280 **aye:** forever.
290 **mean:** intend.
292 **writ:** written order.
293 **on the life of:** to take the life of.
296 **office:** duty, assignment.
297 **token of reprieve:** sign of pardon.
300 **for thy life:** as if *your* life depended on it.
304 **fordid:** destroyed, killed.

Albany.   Produce the bodies, be they alive or dead.
                                   Exit Gentleman.
  This judgement of the heavens, that makes us tremble,   275
  Touches us not with pity. (*To Kent*). O, is this he?
  The time will not allow the compliment
  Which very manners urges.
Kent.   I am come
  To bid my king and master aye good night.   280
  Is he not here?
Albany.   Great thing of us forgot!
  Speak, Edmund, where's the King? and where's Cordelia?
          The bodies of Goneril and Regan are brought in.
  Seest thou this object, Kent?
Kent.   Alack, why thus?   285
Edmund.   Yet Edmund was beloved.
  The one the other poisoned for my sake,
  And after slew herself.
Albany.   Even so. Cover their faces.
Edmund.   I pant for life. Some good I mean to do,   290
  Despite of mine own nature. Quickly send
  (Be brief in't) to the castle; for my writ
  Is on the life of Lear and on Cordelia.
  Nay, send in time.
Albany.   Run, run, O, run!   295
Edgar.   To who, my lord? Who has the office? Send
  Thy token of reprieve.
Edmund.   Well thought on. Take my sword;
  Give it the Captain.
Edgar.   Haste thee for thy life. *Exit an Officer.*   300
Edmund.   He hath commission from thy wife and me
  To hang Cordelia in the prison and
  To lay the blame upon her own despair
  That she fordid herself.
Albany.   The gods defend her! Bear him hence awhile.   305
                         Edmund is borne off.
          Enter Lear, with Cordelia in his arms,

308 **vault:** wide arch of heaven, sky.
310 **a looking glass:** a mirror.
311 **stone:** crystal or polished stone.
313 **the promised end:** the Day of Doom, the Last Judgement.
314 **or image . . . horror:** or the exact likeness of that fatal day.
315 **Fall and cease:** Let the heavens fall, and let there be an end to everything.
320 **Prithee away:** Lear does not at first recognize Kent.
330 **biting falchion:** sharp sword.
332 **crosses:** troubles; **spoil me:** weaken me as a swordsman.
333 **I'll tell you straight:** I'll recognize you in a moment.
334-5 **If fortune . . . behold:** If destiny ever had two men whom she raised to the heights of favour and dashed to the depths of misery, Lear is certainly one of them.
336 **This is . . . sight:** My sight is poor.
340 **strike:** *i.e.*, a blow.

       Captain and others following.
Lear.   Howl, howl, howl! O, you are men of stones.
   Had I your tongues and eyes, I'd use them so
   That heaven's vault should crack. She's gone for ever!
   I know when one is dead, and when one lives.
   She's dead as earth. Lend me a looking glass.   310
   If that her breath will mist or stain the stone,
   Why, then she lives.
Kent.   Is this the promised end?
Edgar.   Or image of that horror?
Albany.   Fall and cease!   315
Lear.   This feather stirs; she lives! If it be so,
   It is a chance which does redeem all sorrows
   That ever I have felt.
Kent.   O my good master!
Lear.   Prithee away!   320
Edgar.   'Tis noble Kent, your friend.
Lear.   A plague upon you, murderers, traitors all!
   I might have saved her; now she's gone for ever!
   Cordelia, Cordelia! stay a little. Ha!
   What is't thou sayest? Her voice was ever soft,   325
   Gentle, and low—an excellent thing in woman.
   I killed the slave that was a-hanging thee.
Captain.   'Tis true, my lords, he did.
Lear.   Did I not, fellow?
   I have seen the day, with my good biting falchion   330
   I would have made 'em skip. I am old now,
   And these same crosses spoil me. Who are you?
   Mine eyes are not o' the best, I'll tell you straight.
Kent.   If fortune brag of two she loved and hated,
   One of them we behold.   335
Lear.   This is a dull sight. Are you not Kent?
Kent.   The same;
   Your servant Kent. Where is your servant Caius?
Lear.   He's a good fellow, I can tell you that.
   He'll strike, and quickly too. He's dead and rotten.   340

342 **I'll see that straight:** I'll attend to that in a moment.

343 **from your . . . decay:** from the beginning of your change in fortunes and their decline.

348 **have fordone:** See line 304.

349 **desperately:** in despair.

355 **trifle:** occurrence of no importance here where the dying Lear and the dead Cordelia are.

357 **decay:** the tragic decline of Lear.

358-60 **applied:** used, employed; **For us . . . power:** Albany, the present ruler because Cornwall, Goneril, Regan, and Edmund are dead, uses the royal "we" in resigning his office for the short time that Lear has to live so that Lear may die as King; **you to your rights:** The words *We will restore* are understood before "you".

362 **with boot . . . addition:** with such additional titles and rights; **honours:** brave deeds.

366 **fool:** Cordelia. "Fool" was a term of endearment. Some scholars express the opinion that since the Fool made Lear face absolute truthfulness, and since Cordelia also stood for utter truthfulness, the two have become as one in Lear's mind.

369 **Never, never . . . never:** The utter simplicity of this line and the sense of finality conveyed by it attest fully to the poetic genius of Shakespeare.

370 **Pray you . . . sir:** Lear feels the suffocation preceding his death, but thinks that his clothing restricts his breathing. It has been argued that he refers to a button at the neck of Cordelia's dress. See III. iv. 112.

371 **Do you . . . lips:** Upon the understanding of these words stands the interpretation of the tragedy. Bradley says that Lear, like Gloucester, dies of joy, believing Cordelia to be alive. Lear's happiness at death is based not on any truth, however, but at best upon the illusion that Cordelia is alive. He is trying to believe that the terrible finality of Cordelia's death is impossible.

374 **Break, heart . . . break:** Kent may be speaking of his own heart, as Bradley suggests, but more probably he is expressing a prayer, which is continued in his next speech, for mercy on Lear.

ACT V/SCENE 3 • *217*

Kent.   No, my good lord; I am the very man—
Lear.   I'll see that straight.
Kent.   That from your first of difference and decay
  Have followed your sad steps.
Lear.   You are welcome hither.   345
Kent.   Nor no man else! All's cheerless, dark, and
    deadly.
  Your eldest daughters have fordone themselves,
  And desperately are dead.
Lear.   Ay, so I think.   350
Albany.   He knows not what he says; and vain is it
  That we present us to him.
Edgar.   Very bootless.
    Enter a Captain.
Captain.   Edmund is dead, my lord.
Albany.   That's but a trifle here.   355
  You lords and noble friends, know our intent.
  What comfort to this great decay may come
  Shall be applied. For us, we will resign,
  During the life of this old Majesty,
  To him our absolute power; (*To Edgar and Kent*). you to   360
    your rights;
  With boot, and such addition as your honours
  Have more than merited. All friends shall taste
  The wages of their virtue, and all foes
  The cup of their deservings.—O, see, see!   365
Lear.   And my poor fool is hanged! No, no, no life!
  Why should a dog, a horse, a rat, have life,
  And thou no breath at all? Thou'lt come no more,
  Never, never, never, never, never!
  Pray you undo this button. Thank you, sir.   370
  Do you see this? Look on her! look! her lips!
  Look there, look there!   *He dies.*
Edgar.   He faints! My lord, my lord!
Kent.   Break, heart; I prithee break!
Edgar.   Look up, my lord.   375

376   **ghost:** departing spirit.

377   **rack:** instrument of torture that stretched a victim's joints until dislocation took place.

381   **usurped:** lived beyond his rightful span of life.

382   **business:** The three syllables are pronounced.

385   **gored:** wounded, war-ravaged; **sustain:** maintain support.

386-7   **I have . . . no:** Kent evidently feels that after Lear's death little is left in life, and that he therefore must prepare for his own death.

388-91   **weight:** sorrow; **oldest:** Lear and Gloucester; **The weight . . . long:** This speech is given to Albany in Q1 and to Edgar in F1. Kittredge feels that Q1 is right in giving this epilogue to Albany, the older man. If this is accepted, it is difficult to explain the phrase "We that are young. . . ."

See also p. 243.

Kent.   Vex not his ghost. O, let him pass! He hates him
   That would upon the rack of this tough world
   Stretch him out longer.
Edgar.   He is gone indeed.
Kent.   The wonder is, he hath endured so long.   380
   He but usurped his life.
Albany.   Bear them from hence. Our present business
   Is general woe. (*To Kent and Edgar*). Friends of my soul,
      you twain
   Rule in this realm, and the gored state sustain.   385
Kent.   I have a journey, sir, shortly to go.
   My master calls me; I must not say no.
Edgar.   The weight of this sad time we must obey,
   Speak what we feel, not what we ought to say.
   The oldest hath borne most; we that are young   390
   Shall never see so much, nor live so long.
                                    Exeunt with a dead march.

ACT I, SCENE 1

Dramatic Importance

The first scene of *King Lear* is like no other in Shakespeare. It begins serenely enough, but ends in catastrophe—the King's favourite daughter and his most faithful subject are banished. The remainder of the play, it has been stated, with a measure of accuracy, is dénouement. This one scene begins a train of events that leads to chaos and death in the Kingdom. At the beginning, we witness Gloucester joking with Kent about Edmund's illegitimate birth.

In contrast to this casual conversation, spoken in prose, is Lear's formal, dignified entrance to the accompaniment of martial music, to initiate the ceremonial disposition of his territories to his three daughters. His voice is firm and his manner truly regal as he expresses his "darker purpose". Alfred Harbage points out that this scene is, to Lear, merely symbolic, the speeches being in formal parallel sequence: Lear—Goneril—Cordelia—Lear, and Lear—Regan—Cordelia—Lear. Because of his firmness and decision, we are amazed when Lear, as the smoothness of the ritual is thwarted by Cordelia's completely honest answer, becomes at first nettled and finally enraged by her candour, but remains blind to the glaring hypocrisy of his other two daughters. Then follows the reckless and headlong banishment of Cordelia and Kent.

The scene thus falls into three contrasting parts—the casual opening, the formal court ritual, and the enraged banishment of Cordelia and Kent.

Questions

1. (a) Describe the atmosphere created in each of the three parts of this first scene, and compare and contrast

221

your findings with the atmosphere created by the opening of another play of Shakespeare's.

(b) Explain how Shakespeare has created the atmosphere of each of the three parts of the scene.

2. What is the first impression of (a) Gloucester? (b) Kent? (c) Lear? (d) Goneril? (e) Regan? (f) Cordelia?

3. What information indicates that Lear's intentions have been made clear before this meeting of the court and that the formal division of his lands is ceremony only?

4. What warning is given in this scene that the old King's activities are going to be curbed as soon as he abdicates?

ACT I, SCENE 2

Dramatic Importance

Edmund is one of Shakespeare's consummate villains. Richard III is an unscrupulous, greedy, ambitious schemer; Iago in *Othello* is the ambitious officer who has been overlooked; Edmund is the machiavellian votary of the goddess Nature, obsessed with his own bastardy and intent on destroying or consuming everything that stands in his way to possession of his father's earldom. Like all Shakespearian villains, he fascinates us with his intrepid wickedness, his cunning, and his wit, all of which are sharply contrasted with the bumbling honesty of his father and the innocent credulity of his half-brother. Edmund at once shocks and beguiles by thriving on the honesty and decency of others and by successfully deceiving even the most designing, unscrupulous, and ambitious of women, Goneril and Regan.

The scene falls into three parts: Edmund's invocation, the gulling of his father, and the deception of Edgar, who observes "Some villain hath done me wrong".

Questions

1. What dramatic purposes are served by Edmund's soliloquy "Thou, Nature, art my goddess"?
2. Gloucester completely accepts Edmund's accusation of Edgar. Explain why Edmund succeeds so easily.
3. Contrast the ideas expressed by Gloucester in lines 102-15 with those expressed by Edmund in lines 116-30.
4. Why does the second stage of Edmund's plot succeed as easily with Edgar as with Gloucester?

ACT I, SCENE 3

Dramatic Importance

We may momentarily find ourselves in a sympathetic state towards Goneril at the beginning of this scene, since we surmise that Lear will be a difficult guest to handle and that no visit of his to any house could be without incident. We are alienated, however, by Goneril's use of the obsequious, time-serving Oswald—the kind of creature we might expect a woman like Goneril to employ—in an effort to provoke Lear to undesirable actions and "breed from hence occasions", so that she may create pretexts to bar her household to him. We begin to see how Lear has himself blindly set in motion a plot that will exclude him from all the prerogatives of rank and age.

Questions

1. How does Goneril intend to provoke Lear into blame-worthy action?
2. (a) Though Oswald makes only three short replies to Goneril, what is the impression of him as a servant?
   (b) What do Goneril's words indicate about the status of Oswald in her household?

ACT I, SCENE 4

Dramatic Importance

Kent has not left England as he was ordered by Lear, but has decided to remain near the old King in order to perform whatever service he may offer, even though he is in disguise. Lear shows himself as peremptory and demanding as ever: he wants everything instantly—his dinner, his daughter, and his Fool. Suddenly, as in the first scene, we find Lear in a high rage, this time at Oswald, and Kent is by no means loath to assist him in word and deed. Our image of the monarch is dimmed until we remember that this is a carefully planned provocation that Goneril knows will make Lear lose his regal dignity and provide the opportunity for alienation that she desires. He is a man more sinned against than sinning. In the face of this subtle plot, the bitter thrusts of the Fool, and the demand from Goneril that he reduce his retinue, Lear is driven to mighty anger in which he curses Goneril and consigns her to a fate far worse than the exile of Cordelia. The irony of Lear's words, "I have another daughter", pervades the last moments of the scene.

The scene is in four parts: the meeting with the disguised

Kent, the quarrel with Oswald, the gibes of the Fool, and the cursing of Goneril.

Questions

1. What motive prompts Kent to assume a disguise?
2. Lear in this scene creates an impression that arouses sympathy for Goneril's annoyance. Discuss.
3. What is the dramatic purpose of the Fool's speeches in this scene?
4. (a) Why is Lear incredulous when he hears Goneril's complaint, lines 197-210?
   (b) What action of Goneril drives him to fury and causes him to turn to Regan?
5. When Lear curses Goneril, he calls upon Nature to work the curse; when Edmund (in Scene 2) decides to destroy both his father and his half-brother, he recognizes Nature as his particular duty. What does the word "nature" mean to each?
6. (a) What is Albany's role in this scene?
   (b) Explain the irony created by his words, "Striving to better, oft we mar what's well" (line 355).

ACT I, SCENE 5

Dramatic Importance

Lear by this time is shaken. Already his retinue has been reduced to all but the most loyal of his gentlemen. Two daughters have failed him and the Fool insists that the third is as much like the second "as a crab's like an apple". The preoccupied observations of Lear as the Fool chatters away poignantly reveal his state, as the cruel realization of what has happened to him stands grinning in his mind as the Fool does at his side. Lear begins to feel the approach of madness as the scene ends—a scene insignificant in length, but of remarkable dramatic skill.

Questions

1. What is the dramatic effect of the Fool's words in this scene?
2. Although Lear scarcely hears what the Fool is saying, his replies teem with meaning for the audience. Explain.
3. What words of Lear indicate the terrible impact of Goneril's treatment?
4. Write a short paragraph on the dramatic skill shown by Shakespeare in this scene.

ACT II, SCENE 1

Dramatic Importance

In this scene, we return to Edmund's plot against his father and his half-brother (I. ii). He manipulates his father's mind and emotions with ease, and contrives to make Edgar fear for his life.

Discord arises as Albany and Cornwall dispute their rights to the Kingdom, while Regan and Cornwall, powerful as they are, resort to the pettiness of being out when Lear arrives.

The meanness and duplicity of Edmund, Regan, and Cornwall are strongly contrasted with the honesty (and obtuseness) of Gloucester and the credulity of Edgar.

Questions

1. What important rumour is given to Edmund by Curan?
2. Give the details of Edmund's actions that advance the plot against both his father and Edgar.
3. What important promise does Gloucester make to Edmund?
4. Deduce the contents of Goneril's letter to Regan from Regan's words.
5. Why do Regan and Cornwall visit Gloucester at this time?

ACT II, SCENE 2

Dramatic Importance

This is a scene of considerable physical action. After the initial excitement of the first scene, there is, of course, a lull, and we are ready for the strenuous activity and the comic relief it affords in Oswald's yelps of pain and fear. The relief is short-lived, however, since the noise made by Oswald and Kent brings Cornwall and Edmund on the run, Edmund with his sword already drawn. For his insolence, Kent is set in the stocks—a bold act on the part of Cornwall, since Kent is one of the King's men, and thereby protected by a kind of diplomatic immunity. (It seems a monstrous and incomprehensible act to Lear when he learns about it later in Scene 4.) In this scene, we are left in no doubt about Kent's loyalty to Lear, Oswald's repellent cowardice and effeminacy, and the unscrupulous audacity of Cornwall.

The scene is in three parts: Kent's quarrel with Oswald, his detention in the stocks, and his resignation to fate and the quiet work of aiding Cordelia in rescuing her father.

Questions

1. Explain Kent's rashness in this scene.
2. For what reason, other than punishment for his attack on Oswald, is Kent placed in the stocks?
3. What is the effect of Cordelia's letter on Kent?

ACT II, SCENE 3

Dramatic Importance

Edgar has not been far away since having to flee for his life. He, too, like Lear, has been reduced in fortune and has nothing. Therefore, he makes an easy transition into the protective disguise of Poor Tom—one of the many unfortunate mental cases whose wanderings about the countryside were commonplace in Shakespeare's day, but anachronistic in Lear's. Unlike Lear, Edgar is never plagued by despair, but contrives always to "outface the winds and persecutions of the sky".

Question

1. Why is the disguise of a Bedlam beggar the safest one for Edgar?

ACT II, SCENE 4

Dramatic Importance

In this scene, we become aware of the evil that now surrounds Lear. His human failings—pride, anger, haste—we forgive in the face of the harsh decisions of Goneril, Regan, and Cornwall. They will stop at nothing, and the stocking of Kent, as incredible as it may be to Lear, is a visual mockery of his royalty and the cause of his outbursts of anger, to which the Fool adds a background of gleeful thrusts. When Regan appears, he pleads:

> O Regan, she hath tied
> Sharp-toothed unkindness, like a vulture, here!

Still incredulous at the coldness of his daughter, he kneels in ironical supplication before her, asking her if this is what he should do before Goneril—beg for "raiment, bed, and food". Even these, they deny him. The hard-heartedness and cruelty of Goneril and Regan, so evident even in their rational arguments, wring from Lear the anguished cry, "O, reason not the need!" Even though we may agree that Lear no longer needs his retinue of a hundred knights, we feel his sense of desolation at being stripped of the last vestiges of his pride and place. Where there should be love and forbearance, there is stony-hearted indifference, impatience—and the evil of ultimate rapacity. To this evil, Gloucester raises a feebly protesting hand. Albany, the mild honest man, is not present, and therefore is preserved from defilement by his amoral colleagues. Lear is no longer a king: he is merely a troublesome old man, always in the way, upon whom the doors should be shut.

The scene is in five parts: the arrival of Lear, the mediation of Gloucester, the appearance of Cornwall and Regan, the arrival of Goneril, and the climactic denial of Lear's slightest claims.

Questions

1. What two incredible circumstances puzzle Lear at the beginning of this scene?

2. What definite indication is there that Lear's retinue has already been reduced?

3. What is the third shock to which Lear is subject in this scene?

4. When Goneril rejected him, Lear cursed her. How does Lear try to persuade Regan to accept him in her household?

5. Many references to clothing appear in the play. Show what use is made of such references in this scene.

6. Point out the use of foreshadowing in this scene.

7. Explain Lear's expressions "Age is unnecessary" and "O, reason not the need."

ACT III, SCENE 1

Dramatic Importance

Lear now distracted by the total rejection of his daughters wanders about the barren country surrounding Gloucester's castle. Before we see Lear, we learn of his wanderings from Kent, who speaks with a gentleman, one of Lear's men. The movement to Dover begins here with Kent's sending the gentleman there with the intelligence that trouble is imminent between Albany and Cornwall.

The scene is low-keyed to provide relief after the strain of the previous one, and to prepare for the volcanic rage of Lear as he defies the storm.

Questions

1. Why are Lear's wanderings on the heath related to the audience before he is actually seen?
2. (a) What reasons does Kent give for the dissension between the Dukes?
   (b) What implication does he leave in the mind of the gentleman?

ACT III, SCENE 2

Dramatic Importance

The storm scene is admittedly difficult to produce. Realistic effects of thunder, lightning, and rain can detract from the passionate protests of Lear as the champion of blind, struggling, aspiring humanity, tormented by corruption and evil. Even though he declares:

> Here I stand your slave,
> A poor, infirm, weak, and despised old man.

he grows larger than life, larger than the regal figure that was so impressive for a few moments in the first scene. As Alfred Harbage says, "He is both titan and old man in distress, both grand and pathetic; and his admissions of weakness, 'My wits began to turn', and unexpected display of tenderness, 'How dost, my boy? Art cold?' are very moving."

Questions

1. Explain the symbolism of the storm that forms the background of this scene.
2. How might the storm scene be dramatically handled?

3. The Fool's utterances, though disjointed, are nonetheless biting comments on Lear's present state. Discuss Shakespeare's use of the Fool in this role.

ACT III, SCENE 3

Dramatic Importance

Gloucester, the decent but obtuse father, trusts Edmund so implicitly that he reveals to him the contents of the letter that gives details of the quarrel between Albany and Cornwall. With this letter and with his declaration that he is going to help Lear despite the orders of Cornwall, Gloucester enables Edmund to denounce him to Cornwall as a traitor. Gloucester is not aware that he lives in the same world as Cornwall—a world of evil and treachery.

Questions

1. "Gloucester is fatally betrayed by his own trustfulness." Explain.
2. Explain the part that letters have played in the course of events up to this point in the play.

ACT III, SCENE 4

Dramatic Importance

In this scene, Kent does little speaking: his only care is the safety and shelter of his master. After dwelling for a moment on his own troubles, Lear addresses the "poor naked wretches" of the world, having acquired a new awareness of human misery and a consciousness that he has ignored too long the bitter facts of human life. At the sight of Poor Tom, madness comes upon him, and he thinks that the Bedlamite has been brought to his fate by ungrateful daughters; in Poor Tom, Lear sees himself, brought to the lowest level of human existence. In the midst of all this madness, there is a clarification and revelation of values as Lear looks at Poor Tom and asks the question, "Is man no more than this?" Edgar's imitation of the demented talk, full of nightmarish images, of a Bedlam beggar affects Lear's tortured consciousness and produces feelings of guilt. Lear begins tossing away his clothing, ready to commence a new life of humility, justice, and love.

Questions

1. In this scene Edgar, as Poor Tom, displaces the Fool, whose comments here become more comic than relevant. G. Wilson Knight says that "where the humour of the Fool made no contact with Lear's mind, the fantastic appearance and incoherent words of Edgar are immediately assimilated. . . ." Write an explanation of the relationship between the thoughts expressed by Edgar and their effect on Lear's state of mind.
2. What is the dramatic significance of Lear's cry (line 112) "Off, off, you lendings! Come, unbutton here"?

ACT III, SCENE 5

Dramatic Importance

Edmund's success continues. He is granted the earldom of Gloucester by Cornwall. At the same time as we observe the madness of Lear, brought on by the harsh ingratitude of his daughters, we also see the shaping of Gloucester's fate at the hands of his bastard son. The results of the two plots against the fathers interact with great dramatic force. Thus, the underplot supplements and reinforces the main plot.

Questions

1. Cornwall assumes that Gloucester is in league with the French against him. (a) What is Gloucester's purpose in this conspiracy? (b) What is Edmund's purpose in informing Cornwall of Gloucester's implication?
2. Why is the betrayal of Gloucester by Edmund more sinister and heartless than that of Lear by Goneril and Regan?

ACT III, SCENE 6

Dramatic Importance

While Lear shelters in the house prepared by Gloucester, after the first stage of his madness is over, he is overcome with a desire for revenge. He begins a trial of two stools, which he sees and addresses as his daughters. He accuses the Fool, in the role of the judge, of being a "false justicer" for allowing Regan to escape. In this scene, we find a grim kind of comedy as Lear solemnly arraigns his daughters, as Edgar sings irrelevant snatches of song, and as the Fool happily clowns through his part in the trial. And we may wish to laugh, as only we can when pity is too great for tears, when Lear plaintively observes that even his dogs Tray, Blanch, and Sweetheart have turned against him. At last, Kent persuades him to lie down and rest; but even as Lear is settling down the dire news comes that his life is in danger and he must "drive toward Dover". Edgar's sententious couplets at the end of the scene seem superfluous.

At this point in the play, the Fool disappears and is not seen again. There is no place for laughter in the succeeding events of the tragedy.

Questions

1. What is the dramatic purpose of Lear's acting out his delusion that he is trying his daughters in court?
2. For what dramatic reason does the Fool disappear after this scene?

ACT III, SCENE 7

Dramatic Importance

This is a scene of the most bestial cruelty. Gloucester's eyes are gouged out by Cornwall urged on by Regan, Cornwall is fatally stabbed by a servant, and the servant is killed by Regan. Gloucester learns from Regan, as he cries for Edmund's help, that Edmund is his betrayer. At the moment of his physical blinding, he sees Edmund and Edgar in their true roles and prays for forgiveness. Edmund is the real cause of the horrible mutilation of his father, for flesh and blood have turned against themselves, and ironically, a humble servant is the instrument of vengeance on the Duke of Cornwall. It is Gloucester's finest hour. No plea for mercy is forced from his lips, only a searing

denunciation of Regan and a cry for help from those around
him and for the false Edmund.

Critics who have condemned this scene as too cruel for the
stage have misunderstood its symbolism: the child tearing the
parental flesh is the physical expression of the evil in the total
abandonment of Lear by his daughters. Repellent though it may
be, it represents the totality of evil that Shakespeare saw in the
destruction of the bond of love, and forces us to look evil
straight in the face, as we must again, at the end of the play,
when we witness the unutterable agony of Lear's final separation
from Cordelia.

Questions

1. What is Gloucester's defence against the charge that he
   is a traitor?
2. Just as Cornwall is the instrument of retributive justice in
   the life of Gloucester, so a humble servant is the instrument of retributive justice in the life of Cornwall. Sketch
   the careers of Gloucester and Cornwall, and show why
   they are victims of fate.
3. Why is the death of the servant not regarded as an in-
   stance of retributive justice?

ACT IV, SCENE 1

Dramatic Importance

In deep despair, Gloucester has reached the same point in life
as Lear had when he uttered his plea for the "poor naked
wretches" of the world. How different is this blind, despairing

Gloucester to the joking, confident Gloucester in the first scene of the play! His only thought is that he may reach the cliffs of Dover, where he may put an end to his misery. Edgar's fidelity is amply demonstrated in this scene.

Questions

1. What dramatic purpose is served by the meeting of Gloucester and his son Edgar?
2. Since Edgar no longer needs his disguise as protection from his father's pursuit, why does he retain it?
3. Compare the comment that Gloucester makes in lines 78-85 with that of Lear in lines 34-42 of Act III, Scene 4.

ACT IV, SCENE 2

Dramatic Importance

Albany, who was not present at Gloucester's blinding, and who has become disenchanted by Goneril's behaviour towards her father, is reluctant to fight against the French army, even though it is invading the territory over which he shares the rule with Cornwall. When he learns of Cornwall's death and Gloucester's blindness, he pledges vengeance, and assumes the position of ruler of the kingdom. Goneril has other ideas, and weighs the chances that she and Edmund have to take control themselves, from Albany on the one hand, and Regan on the other. The evil begun by Goneril and Regan is now involving them in a fatal power-struggle. Albany emerges as the just ruler, even though he is bound to resist the French invasion under Cordelia and her husband.

Questions

1. In his judgement of human motives and character, Albany has been as blind as Gloucester and Lear. Explain.
2. Contrast the responses of Albany and Goneril to the news of Gloucester's blinding.
3. What does Albany determine to do after he has received the news of Gloucester's betrayal by Edmund?

ACT IV, SCENE 3

Dramatic Importance

This scene is relatively unimportant and was not included in the First Folio. The King of France has been recalled to his country, leaving a marshal in command of his army. A gentleman tells us of Cordelia's sorrow at Lear's suffering, and Kent tells us that Lear cannot, because of his sense of shame, bear to meet Cordelia. Though still in disguise, Kent plans to reveal himself soon.

Questions

1. Though the account of Lear's madness (III. i. 4-15) is dramatically necessary, the narration of Cordelia's sorrow is unnecessary here. Discuss.
2. Comment on the style of expression used by the gentleman in this scene.
3. Why does Lear not wish to see Cordelia?

ACT IV, SCENE 4

Dramatic Importance

Cordelia, with the help of her soldiers, searches for her father, who, according to report, is wandering in the countryside, dressed "in fantastic garlands" of weeds and wild flowers. A doctor comforts her with the thought that Lear can be cured. Cordelia's loving, selfless concern for her father is irreconcilably opposed to the animalistic cruelty of her sisters. She is shown here by Shakespeare, with considerable dramatic effect, at the head of an army that is invading the territories that, except for a perverse whim of her father's, might have belonged in part to her, and that were her father's before his fatal abdication.

Question

1. Why is it dramatically necessary to have this scene, in which Cordelia is assured that her father can be cured, precede Lear's next stage of madness (IV. vi. 96-203)?

ACT IV, SCENE 5

Dramatic Importance

Immediately following the scene in which we see Cordelia in the midst of her sad but loving task of finding her father, we witness the jealous attempt of Regan to read a letter that Oswald is carrying to Edmund from Goneril. Sister intrigues against sister, and Edmund has gone to kill Gloucester. Oswald, who was so fearful of violence when attacked earlier by Kent, now eagerly undertakes to hunt down and kill the blind Gloucester. These matters—invasion, intrigue, and treachery—are treated briefly in order to keep the attention of the audience on the event of primary importance, the reconciliation of Lear and Cordelia.

Questions

1. What dramatic contrast is provided by this scene and the previous one?
2. Regan and Goneril are deadly rivals at this point in the course of events. Explain.

ACT IV, SCENE 6

Dramatic Importance

This scene, which is difficult to produce on the stage whether the effect sought is symbolic or realistic, has been the cause of much critical comment. Can a blind man be deceived into thinking he has been miraculously saved after a plunge over a high cliff? Here more than anywhere else, we are required to indulge in "a willing suspension of disbelief"—to use Coleridge's phrase —and accept the change in Gloucester from pessimism to patience, which Shakespeare shows in this scene, as a symbolic representation of a spiritual transformation.

The two plots of the play are joined here as we see the two victims of their own crimes brought together again, Gloucester, blind, penitent, and resigned, and Lear, at the point in his madness where his words become revelation. It is worth noting that some of his speeches are in prose, while others are in verse.

Questions

1. The two wronged fathers are brought together in this scene. Show that Lear's comments, which contain "matter and impertinency mixed", apply both to himself and Gloucester.
2. What memories prompt Lear to comment bitterly upon (a) flattery? (b) adultery? (c) authority?
3. Of what importance is the letter taken from Oswald by Edgar?
4. What is the reason for the fact that some of Lear's speeches are in prose, while others are in verse?

ACT IV, SCENE 7

Dramatic Importance

If the scene in which Gloucester is blinded is the cruelest in dramatic literature, surely this is one of the tenderest. Cordelia has not seen her father since the first scene of the play. Her utter forgiveness,

O my dear father, restoration hang
Thy medicine on my lips, and let this kiss
Repair those violent harms that my two sisters
Have in thy reverence made!

and Lear's total humility,

> Pray, do not mock me.
> I am a very foolish, fond old man.

are most moving. The reconcilation is complete; but later in the play, when Lear enters with the dead Cordelia in his arms, the pathos of his grief is greatly intensified by our memory of this scene.

Question

1. By what means does Shakespeare heighten the pathos of this scene?

ACT V, SCENE 1

Dramatic Importance

This scene advances the two plots to a critical point. Edmund and Regan are at the head of an army rushing to repel the French; Albany, who is in a difficult position, states that his purpose is to drive the French out of Britain, not to assist Lear. His position is therefore "correct". At the same time that this military and political manoeuvring is taking place, Regan is trying desperately to keep Goneril and Edmund apart. Edgar, disguised still, but in knightly dress, gives Albany the letter that was taken from Oswald, which indicated that if Albany were out of the way Edmund could enjoy Goneril's favours and Albany's power. Edgar proposes to challenge Edmund to a mortal duel, according to the rules of knightly combat. At the end, Edmund tells us in a soliloquy that no matter which sister he marries, he will destroy Albany, Cordelia, and Lear, leaving himself in undisputed power. This is a scene of many threads, which Shakespeare manages to weave neatly in less than a hundred lines.

Questions

1. What is Albany's stated role in the military conflict?
2. What sort of conflict do Edgar's words foreshadow as he hands the letter (line 49) to Albany?
3. By what means does Edmund intend to secure complete power for himself?

ACT V, SCENE 2

Dramatic Importance

Shakespeare does no more here than suggest the conflict that is taking place. The French are routed. Our anxiety for the fate of Lear and Cordelia is heightened by the news that Edgar brings to his father that Lear and Cordelia have been taken prisoner—and we have already heard Edmund's plans for them.

Question

1. How does Shakespeare heighten suspense in this short scene?

ACT V, SCENE 3

Dramatic Importance

Lear and Cordelia are prisoners of the exultant Edmund. The

reconciliation of father and daughter has made Lear completely joyful and oblivious to everything else. There is intense irony in the contrast between his joyous, defiant words and the sinister plan that Edmund arranges with an ambitious captain.

Albany, now forced by events to be more decisive, demands the prisoners, since he is the legal ruler of the country, and he declares Edmund a traitor. Regan, already doomed by Goneril's poison, claims power for Edmund, asserting that he is the successor to Cornwall. Goneril and Regan quarrel over Edmund, as Albany issues a challenge to Edmund if no other champion appears. At the herald's summons, however, Edgar, still disguised, but wearing full armour, challenges Edmund and mortally wounds him. Albany shows Goneril her letter to Edmund, and she leaves distraught.

For the first time, we become aware of some good in Edmund, for he is changed on the point of death by his half-brother's story of Gloucester's joyful death, Kent's loyalty to Lear, and the retribution following on a ruthless bid for power. By this time, the desperate Goneril has stabbed herself and confesses to the poisoning of Regan. As the bodies of the sisters are brought in, Kent arrives, and Albany is reminded of the prisoners Lear and Cordelia. Edmund confesses his plot against them and great haste is made to save them. Before a messenger can reach the place where Lear and Cordelia are in custody, Lear arrives with the body of the dead Cordelia in his arms. What follows is the greatest example of pathos and agony in English dramatic literature.

Questions

1. (a) Account for Lear's joyful mood in the first part of the scene.
   (b) What dramatic purpose does the presentation of Lear's joy serve in this final scene?
2. (a) What is Edmund's stated reason for retaining Lear and Cordelia in custody?

(b) What serious discrepancy exists between his orders to the captain (lines 30-38) and his explanation to Albany (lines 51-60)?

3. What are the details of Albany's charge that Edmund is guilty of "capital treason" (line 97)?

4. On what grounds could Edmund have avoided the duel with Edgar?

5. When Edmund falls, there is nothing left in life for Goneril. What was her fatal error?

6. We find some good in Edmund at the last. How does he show it?

7. The concluding scene of *King Lear*, when Lear enters with the dead Cordelia in his arms, is the most moving of all the concluding scenes that Shakespeare wrote. In the view of some critics, Lear dies in a state of joy believing that Cordelia lives; in the view of others, there is no mitigation of pain in the scene, and Lear dies in the utmost mental agony. Using the speeches of Lear, Kent, and Edgar, write a concise account of your interpretation of this final scene.

GENERAL QUESTIONS ON THE WHOLE PLAY

PART A   The elements of tragedy, based on Bradley's *Shakespearean Tragedy*.[1]

1. "A Shakespearean tragedy is a story of human actions producing exceptional calamity and ending in the death

[1] A. C. Bradley, *Shakespearean Tragedy* (London, Macmillan & Co., Ltd., 1904), *passim*.

of a man in high estate."[1] To what extent does Bradley's definition apply to *King Lear*?

2. Conflict is indispensable to drama. Show that *King Lear* presents both an outward and an inward conflict.

3. The central feeling in a great tragedy is, according to Bradley, one of waste. How is this illustrated in *King Lear*?

4. "The ultimate power in the tragic world is a moral order."[2] How does the outcome of *King Lear* exemplify this idea?

5. "Character is destiny." To what extent does this statement explain Lear's fate?

PART B   The elements of Greek tragedy according to Aristotle.

6. After studying Aristotle's conception of tragedy and the tragic hero, show how *King Lear* and Lear conform to or differ from Aristotle's observations.

7. Compare Bradley's view of tragedy with that of Aristotle.

PART C   General

Structure

8. D. A. Traversi[3] sees the development of *King Lear* in three stages: the entry of uncontrolled passion as a disruptive force into Lear's mind; the tempest as a symbol of this disruptive force, corresponding to the conflict within Lear; and the rebirth of Lear through self-revelation, although it does not affect Lear's external fortunes. By specific reference to the plot of the play, show that the foregoing statement is valid.

[1] *Ibid.*
[2] *Ibid.*
[3] D. A. Traversi, *An Approach to Shakespeare* (London, Sands & Company Ltd., 1956), p. 182.

9. Apply the following terms to the play: exposition, complication, crisis, falling action (sometimes called resolution), catastrophe (climax), and outcome.

10. Select the crisis or turning point of the play and give reasons for your choice.

11. What part do letters play in *King Lear*?

12. Is the tragedy of Lear lessened by the inclusion of the Gloucester plot? Discuss.

13. What is the purpose of the Fool's role in the play?

Time

14. In what historical period is the play supposedly set?

15. What evidence is there that Shakespeare thought of the action as taking place in the England of his own day?

16. How much time appears to elapse between the beginning and the end of the play? Refer to incidents that suggest the passage of time.

Atmosphere

17. Act I, Scene 1 of *Hamlet* sets the atmosphere of the play. In which act and scene of *King Lear* is the atmosphere set? (Describe the effects used by Shakespeare to create this atmosphere.)

18. What use has Shakespeare made of humour in the play?

19. Sir Laurence Olivier's production of *Hamlet* was filmed in black and white. Would the use of colour contribute to the effectiveness of a film version of *King Lear*? Discuss.

20. How is the principle of nemesis illustrated in the play?

21. Illustrate the following dramatic devices: surprise, contrast, effective timing, foreshadowing of events, coincidence.

22. Find examples of the following: pathos, satire, irony (as distinct from dramatic irony), parallelism.

Theme

23. "The centre of attention within the play lies in the hero's efforts to do his duty."[1] Illustrate this statement.

24. The chaos that follows the division of Lear's Kingdom is due to the breaking of the essential bonds of human society. Outline the various bonds that are broken in the course of the play.

25. "Lear's initial crime against his paternity is fittingly balanced by his elder daughters' disregard of all natural feeling, and this double reversal of the order of 'nature' demands, once set afoot, a complete working out in terms of tragic disunity."[2] Discuss.

26. "Lear's wilful impulses liberate forces of anarchy which nothing less than utter exhaustion can ultimately contain."[3]

27. The theme of *King Lear* is treachery. Discuss.

Setting

28. (a) Of what importance is the general setting of the play?

(b) How should the reader interpret such stage directions as: Inside Lear's palace, Inside Gloucester's castle, A Heath?

(c) In what ways is the setting, as suggested in the stage directions, anachronistic?

Characters and Characterization

29. Using the three main methods of characterization; that is, what a character says, what a character does, what others say about him, show that Lear is authoritarian, arrogant, and self-willed.

[1]Bradley, *op. cit.*, p. 82.
[2]Traversi, *op. cit.*, p. 185.
[3]*Ibid.*, p. 182.

30. Lear is a lineal descendant of Job. What qualities have they in common?
31. "The whole story turns upon the peculiar character of the hero."[1] Justify this comment.
32. What do the following suggest when applied to characters or situations in *King Lear*—devotion, villainy, bestiality, cowardice, cunning, indecision, passion, retributive justice?
33. Write an account of the use of disguise in *King Lear*.
34. Compare and contrast the various stages of Lear's madness.
35. "Every person important to the action is thrust into an unnatural way of life."[2] Discuss.
36. Lear "is a horribly strong man who is powerless. He is so strong that he cannot die."[3] Discuss.
37. In *King Lear*, the characters are static rather than developing and their actions are predictable. Discuss.
38. Compare and contrast the following: Cornwall and Albany, Kent and Oswald, Cordelia and Goneril, Edmund and Edgar.
39. Select one important person in the play and show how his character affects the outcome of events.

Style

40. Find examples of as many of the following as possible in the play and explain the function of each in its context:
    (a) onomatopoeia, assonance, cacophony, euphony, hendiadys, double epithet.
    (b) simile, metaphor, personification, synecdoche, metonymy.

[1]Bradley, *op. cit.*, p. 89.
[2]John Masefield, "Introduction to *King Lear*" from *Five Great Tragedies*, William Aldis Wright, ed. (New York, Pocket Books Inc., 1942), p. 328.
[3]*Ibid.*, p. 328.

(c) ambiguity (an expression capable of more than one meaning), irony, tension (the production of maximum effect with a minimum of words).

41. Select a passage from the play and indicate its qualities as great poetry.

42. Choose three images from the play and show the effectiveness of each.

43. Write an explanation of the use of prose in the play.

Sir Donald Wolfit 1902-

Robert Bruce Mantell 1854-19

906 · 962 · 7451

Sir Henry Irving 1838-1905

Edwin Forrest 1806-1872